New Photography 2023

Kelani Abass, Akinbode Akinbiyi, Yagazie Emezi, Amanda Iheme, Abraham Oghobase, Karl Ohiri, Logo Oluwamuyiwa

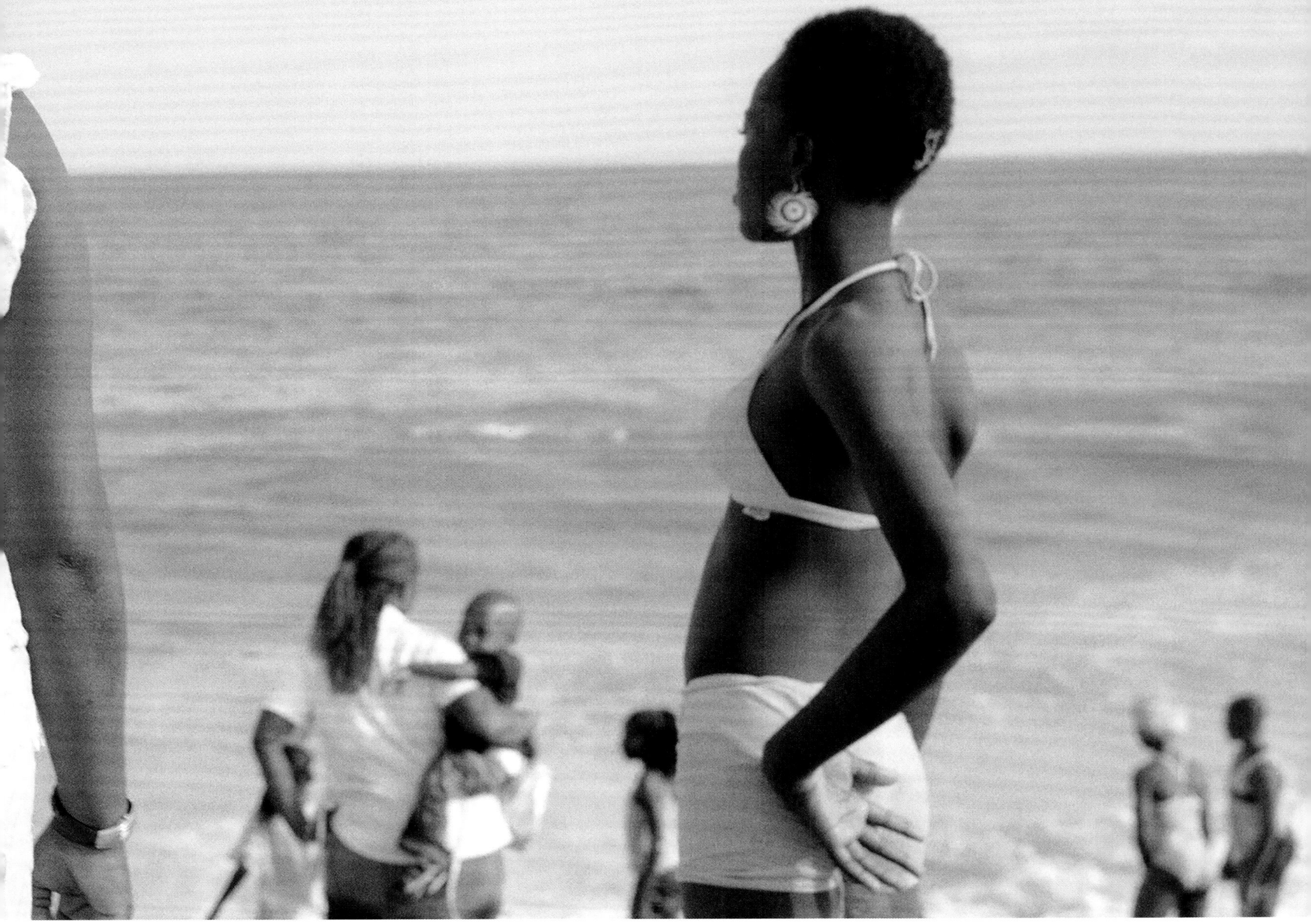

MoMA

**Through Sep 16
Book tickets online**

Summer 2023
Being & Becoming:
Asian in America

Words & Pictures

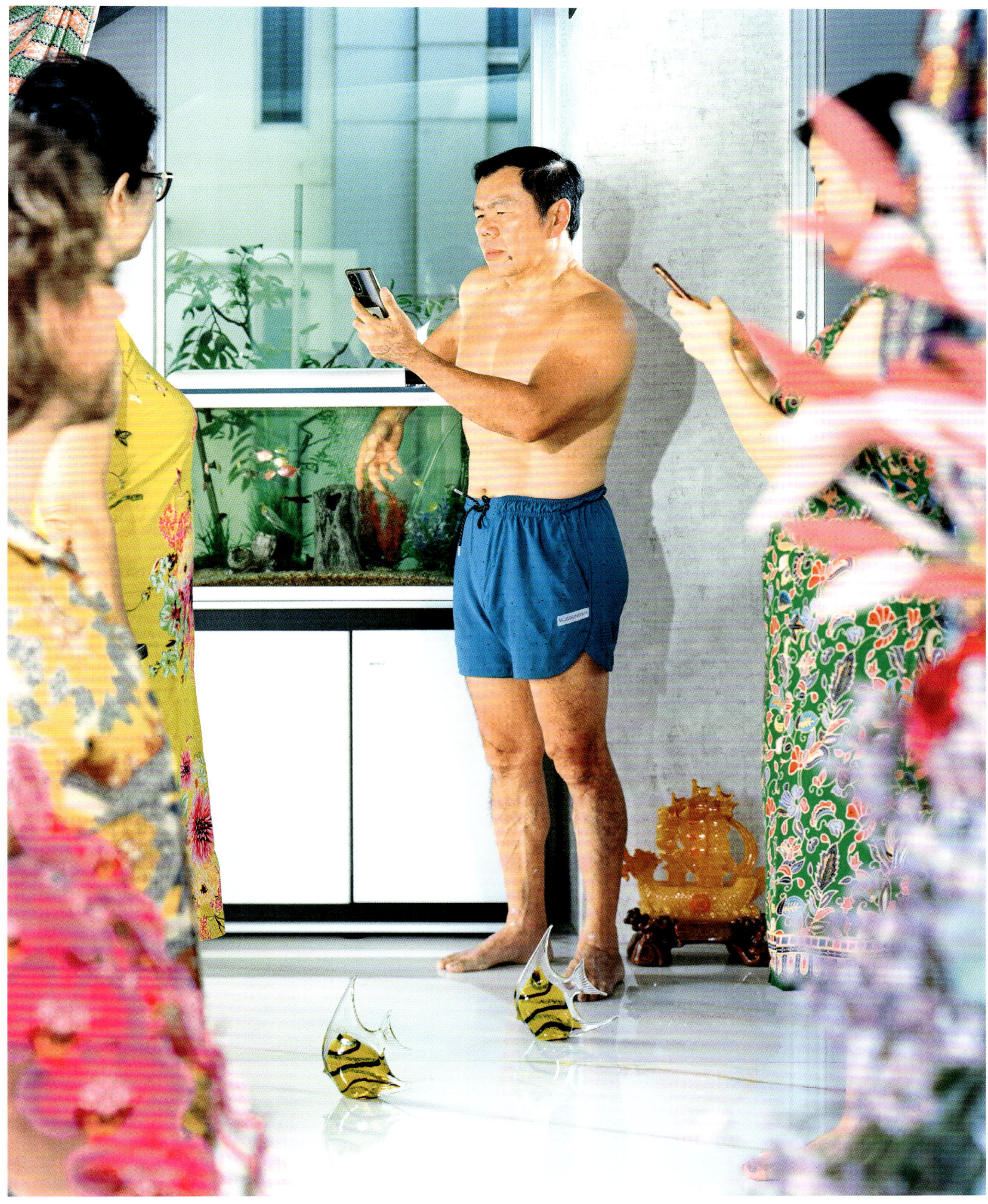

Aperture, a not-for-profit foundation, connects the photo community and its audiences with the most inspiring work, the sharpest ideas, and with each other—in print, in person, and online.

Aperture (ISSN 0003-6420) is published quarterly, in spring, summer, fall, and winter, at 548 West 28th Street, 4th Floor, New York, N.Y. 10001. In the United States, a one-year subscription (four issues) is $75; a two-year subscription (eight issues) is $124. In Canada, a one-year subscription is $95. All other international subscriptions are $110 per year. Visit aperture.org to subscribe. Single copies may be purchased at $24.95 for most issues. Subscribe to the *Aperture Digital Archive* at aperture.org/archive. Periodicals postage paid at New York and additional offices. Postmaster: Send address changes to *Aperture*, P.O. Box 3000, Denville, N.J. 07834. Address queries regarding subscriptions, renewals, or gifts to: *Aperture* Subscription Service, 866-457-4603 (U.S. and Canada), or email custsvc_aperture@fulcoinc.com.

Newsstand distribution in the U.S. is handled by CMG. For international distribution, contact Central Books, centralbooks.com. Other inquiries, email orders@aperture.org or call 212-505-5555.

Become a Member of Aperture to take your interest in and knowledge of photography further. With an annual tax-deductible gift of $250, membership includes a complimentary subscription to *Aperture* magazine, discounts on Aperture's award-winning publications, a special limited-edition gift, and more. To join, visit aperture.org/join, or contact membership@aperture.org.

Credits for "Curriculum," pp. 22–23: Model: © Estate of Lisette Model and courtesy Baudoin Lebon, Paris, and Avi Keitelman, Brussels; Boffin: © Estate of Tessa Boffin and courtesy the University for the Creative Arts, Surrey; Gupta: © the artist and courtesy Artists Rights Society (ARS), New York, and DACS, London

Library of Congress Catalog Card No: 58-30845.

ISBN 978-1-59711-548-3

Printed in Turkey by Ofset Yapimevi

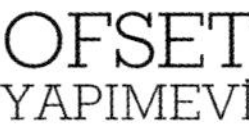

Support has been provided by members of Aperture's Magazine Council: Jon Stryker and Slobodan Randjelović, Susan and Thomas Dunn, Kate Cordsen and Denis O'Leary, and Michael W. Sonnenfeldt, MUUS Collection.

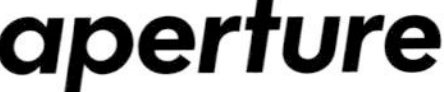

The Magazine of Photography and Ideas

Editor
Michael Famighetti
Guest Editor
Stephanie Hueon Tung
Senior Managing Editor
Brendan Embser
Assistant Editor
Varun Nayar
**Contributing Editor,
The PhotoBook Review**
Lesley A. Martin
Copy Editors
Donna Ghelerter, Chris Peterson
Production Director
Minjee Cho
Production Manager
Andrea Chlad
Press Supervisor
Ali Taptık

Art Direction, Design & Typefaces
A2/SW/HK, London

Publisher
Dana Triwush
magazine@aperture.org

Director of Brand Partnerships
Isabelle Friedrich McTwigan
212–946–7118
imctwigan@aperture.org

Advertising
Elizabeth Morina
917–691–2608
emorina@aperture.org

**Executive Director,
Aperture Foundation**
Sarah Meister

Minor White, Editor (1952–1974)

Michael E. Hoffman, Publisher and Executive Director (1964–2001)

aperture.org

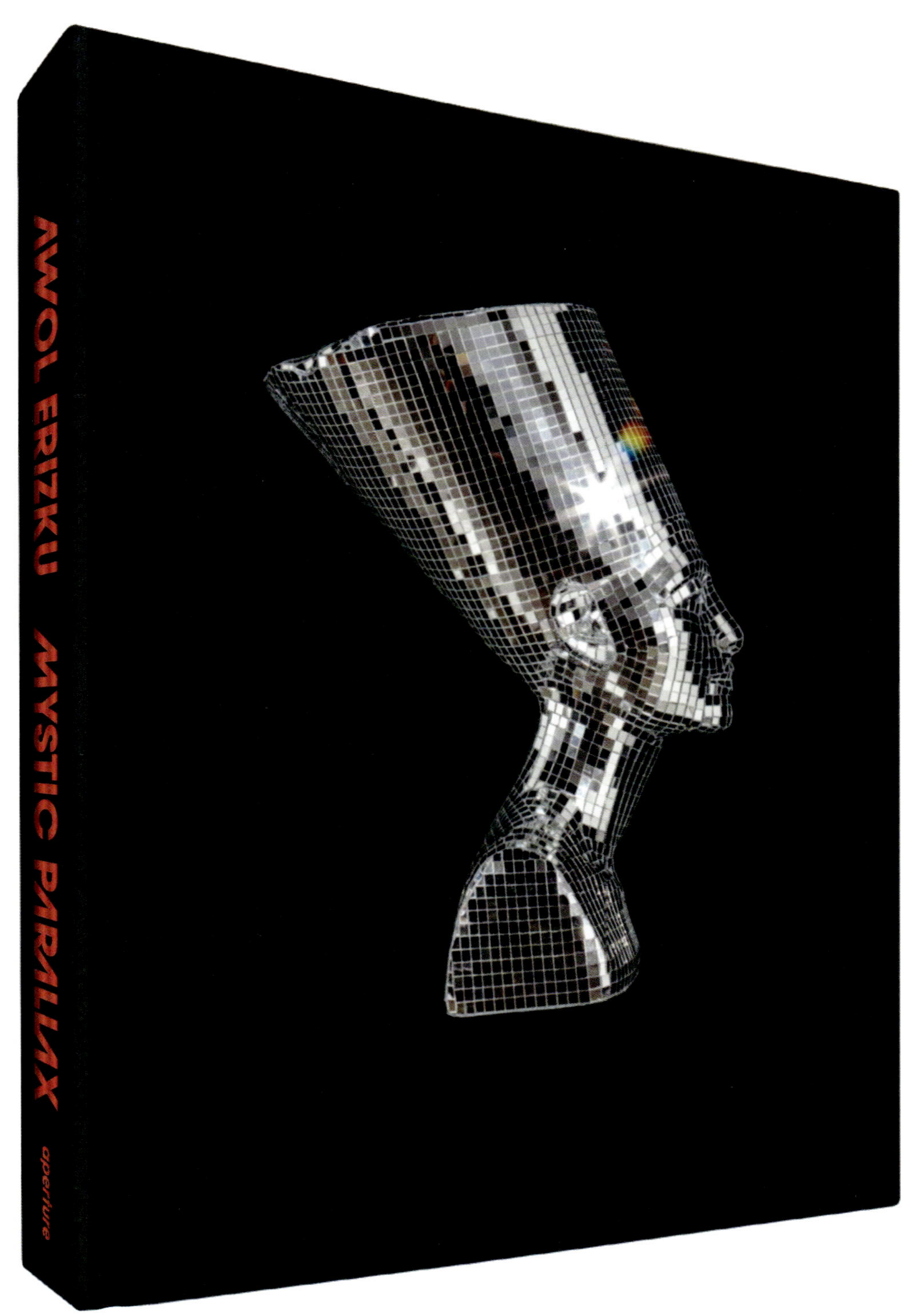

Awol Erizku: Mystic Parallax

Available June 2023

aperture.org/mysticparallax

aperture

Judith Joy Ross

Judith Joy Ross was born in Hazleton, Pennsylvania, and found photography as a student at the Moore College of Art & Design, in Philadelphia, in the 1960s. She made most of her indelible, instantly recognizable portraits in the eastern Pennsylvania towns of Weatherly and Bethlehem, where she discovered in her subjects—teenagers, students, soldiers, a car-rental salesman, a gas-station attendant—a transcendent individuality. "Judith has this immense ambition for the work," says Peter Barberie, a curator of photography at the Philadelphia Museum of Art, the only US institution presenting Ross's acclaimed traveling retrospective, which originated at the Fundación MAPFRE in Madrid. "It's about being alive in our time," he says. Although Ross's concern for the relationship between individuals and social class has been compared to August Sander's portraiture, the more apt analog might be Eugène Atget's documentation of Paris in the early twentieth century. For the Philadelphia exhibition, Ross will curate a room of ten Atget prints from the museum's collection. Ross's "unironic empathy," says Barberie, distinguishes her as one of the greatest American photographers—one whose work tells us "about our role as subjects in history."

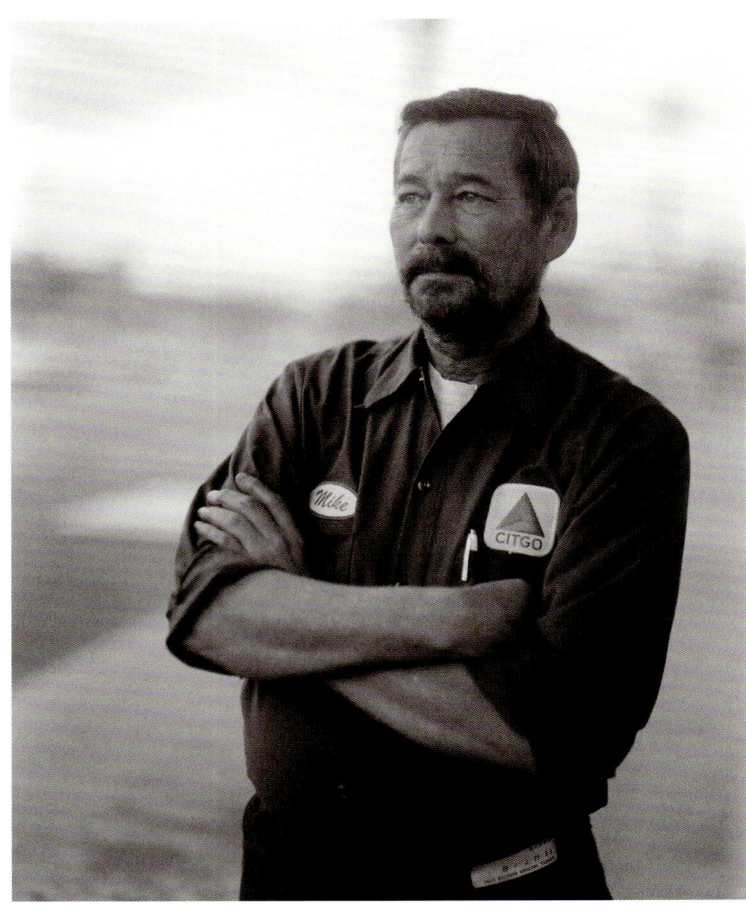

Judith Joy Ross, *Mike, Bethlehem, Pennsylvania*, 1990
Courtesy Galerie Thomas Zander, Cologne

***Judith Joy Ross* at the Philadelphia Museum of Art, through August 6, 2023**

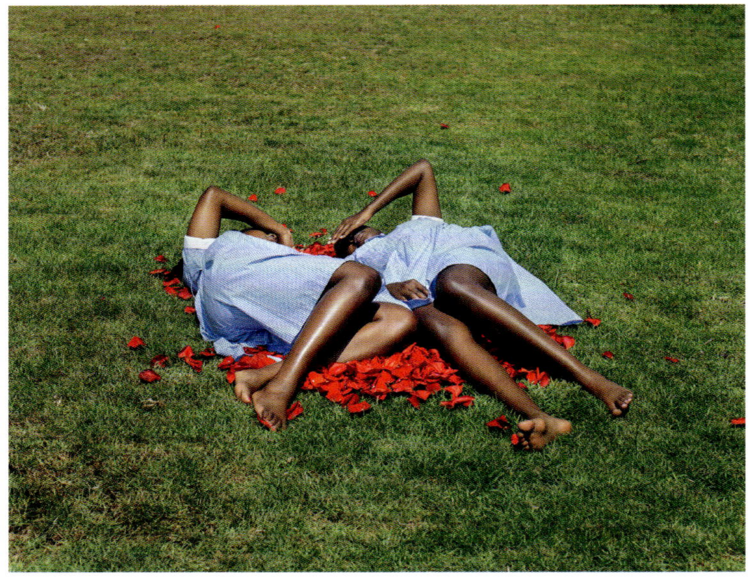

Widline Cadet, *Nan Letènite (In Eternity)*, 2021
Courtesy the artist

Widline Cadet

Widline Cadet was ten years old when her family moved from Haiti to New York. But due to recent political crises on the Caribbean island nation, the first independent Black republic in the world, she and her family can't return. Migration and movement—the shared stories of the Black diaspora and the personal stories of her family—have become the center of her work, which combines enigmatic landscapes, figurative scenes, still lifes, and vernacular pictures. For her solo exhibition *Take This With You / Pran Sa Avèk Ou* at Huis Marseille, Cadet brings together new and recent photographs in an installation that, through architectural interventions, plays on the Amsterdam museum's elegant seventeenth-century canal house. Memory is ambiguous, Cadet implies, more the raw material for a short story than data points in a document. In the photograph *Nan Letènite (In Eternity)* (2021), she re-creates the blue gingham school uniform from her youth, even though she doesn't recall much about school itself. The image, she says, sits "between reality and a dream, or between memories that actually happened, or things I'm making up."

***Widline Cadet: Take This With You / Pran Sa Avèk Ou* at Huis Marseille, Amsterdam, June 24–October 22, 2023**

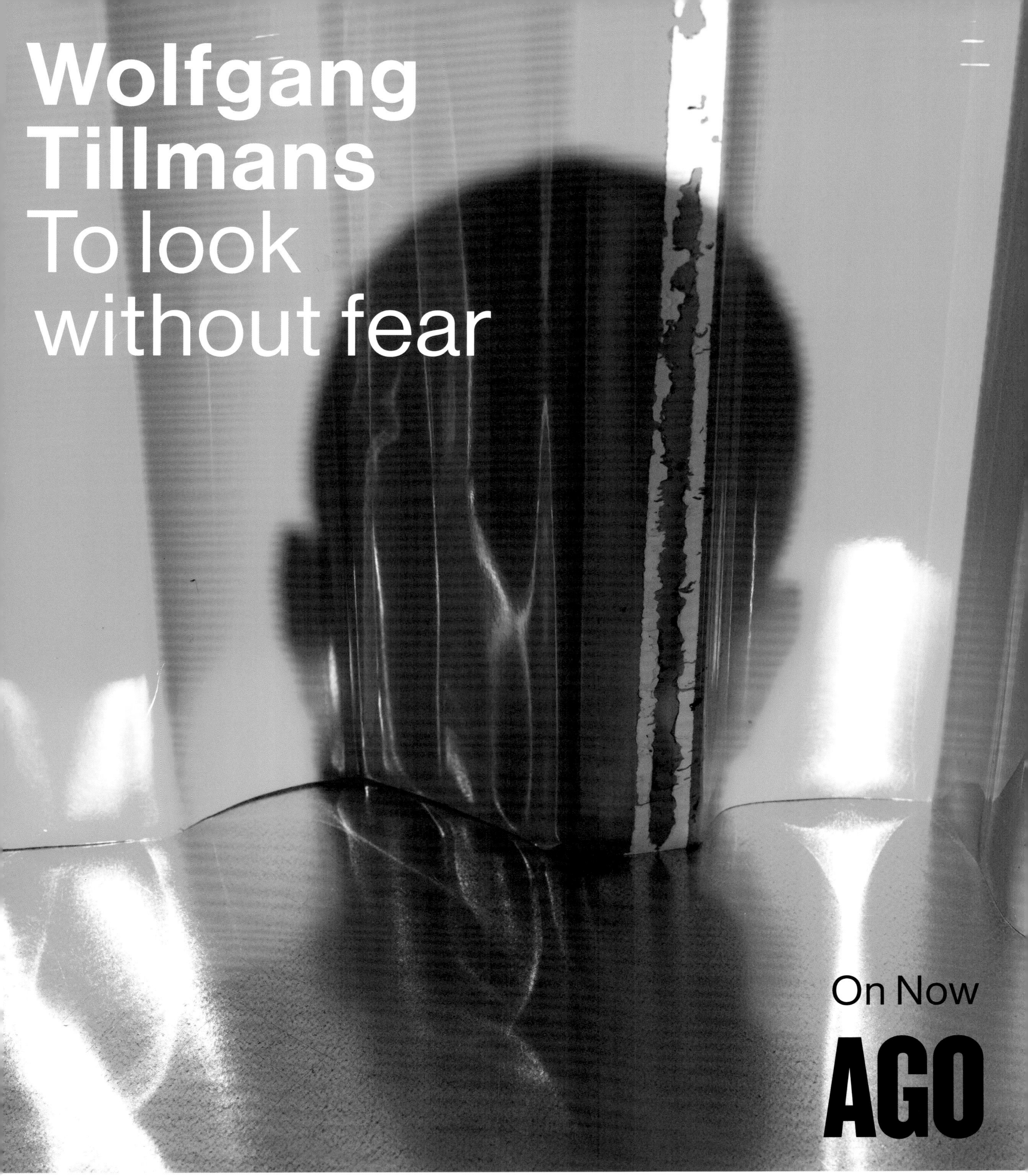

Wolfgang Tillmans
To look without fear

On Now

AGO

Organized by

MoMA

Supporting Sponsor

CIBC◇

Generous Support

**Carol & Morton Rapp
The Schulich Foundation
Eleanor & Francis Shen
Jay Smith & Laura Rapp**

Cor temporary programming at the AGO
is supported by

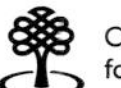

Canada Council   Conseil des arts
for the Arts   du Canada

Presented in collaboration with

**Scotiabank CONTACT
Photography Festival**

The exhibition is organized by Roxana Marcoci, The David Dechman Senior Curator and Acting Chief Curator, The Museum of Modern Art, with Caitlin Ryan, Curatorial Assistant, and Phil Taylor, former Curatorial Assistant, Department of Photography, The Museum of Modern Art. Image: Wolfgang Tillmans, *blue self-portrait shadow*, 2020. Image by Wolfgang Tillmans. Courtesy of the artist, David Zwirner, New York/Hong Kong, Galerie Buchholz, Berlin/Cologne, and Maureen Paley, London.

Gwangju Biennale

The Gwangju Biennale—one of Asia's oldest and largest contemporary art events—returns to the eponymous South Korean city for a fourteenth edition this year. Directed by Sook-Kyung Lee, a curator at London's Tate Modern, the biennale is organized around a non-Western perspective, taking the flow and force of water, and its capacity for transformation and paradox, as the event's central metaphor. The title, *soft and weak like water*, conjures ancient Taoist philosophy and draws connections that span several contexts—regional, transnational, historical. While bringing together nearly eighty international artists, the biennale also engages with Gwangju's rich cultural and political history, particularly the prodemocracy Gwangju Uprising of 1980. The biennale includes a strong showing for photography, including work by Oh Suk Kuhn and Chang Jia, who capture Korean life and history through its colonial legacy and contemporary customs, "rendering society's power structures and their transformations visible," says the assistant curator Sooyoung Leam. Meanwhile, international artists such as Sky Hopinka, Larry Achiampong, and Farah Al Qasimi bring varying perspectives and approaches to the biennale's focus on everyday resistance and solidarity.

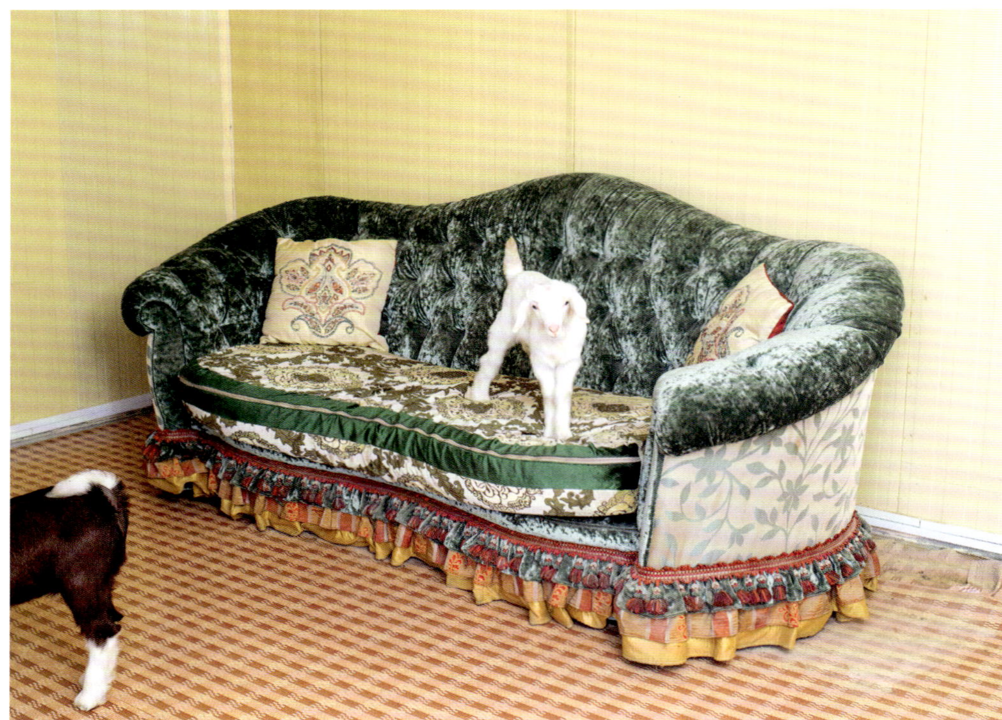

Farah Al Qasimi, *Goat Farm Majlis*, 2021
Courtesy the artist

soft and weak like water at various venues in Gwangju, South Korea, through July 9, 2023

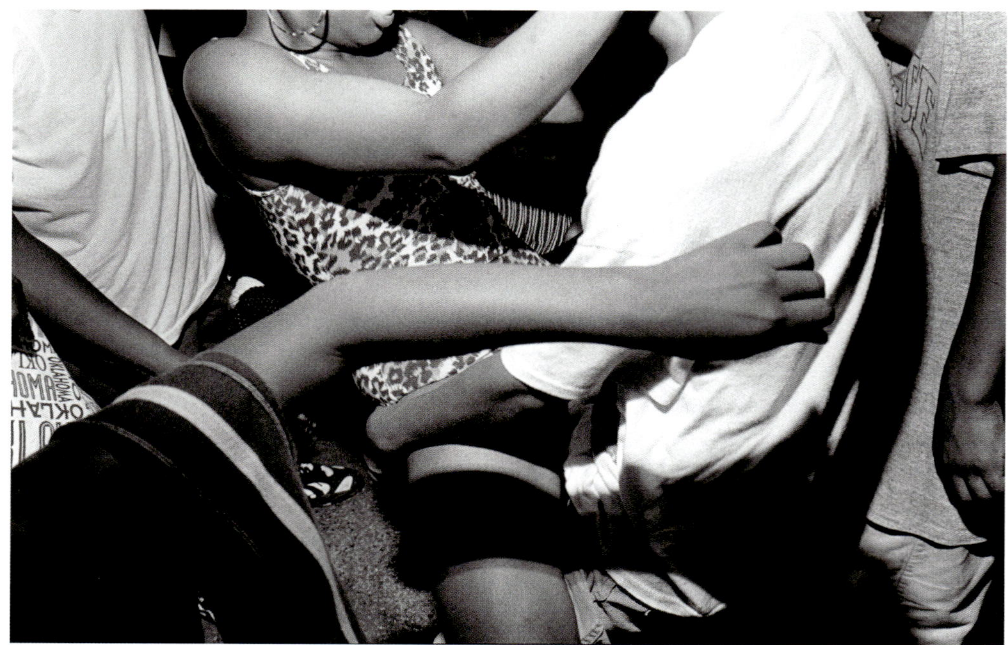

Frank Stewart, *Juneteenth '93, 19th of June Celebration, Mexia, Texas*, 1993
Courtesy the artist

Frank Stewart

Frank Stewart has been around. The Nashville-born photographer captured performances by the Jazz at Lincoln Center Orchestra, photographed the 1984 Summer Olympics in Los Angeles, traveled with a delegation of North American journalists to Cuba in 1977, chronicled the devastation of Hurricane Katrina in New Orleans, and portrayed everyday Black life in Memphis, Harlem, and Chicago, and internationally across Ghana, Senegal, and Ivory Coast. Taught and mentored by Roy DeCarava, Stewart is perhaps best known for his portraits of jazz legends such as Miles Davis and Sonny Rollins, but the subjects that comprise his archive far exceed the stage. *Frank Stewart's Nexus: An American Photographer's Journey, 1960s to the Present*, a retrospective co-organized by the Phillips Collection in Washington, DC, and Telfair Museums in Savannah, charts seven decades of the photographer's work. It includes images as early as 1963, when a fourteen-year-old Stewart made his first photographs with his mother's Brownie camera at the March on Washington for Jobs and Freedom. "Stewart's photographs are never evidence," the curator Mary Schmidt Campbell writes in an essay for the accompanying catalog; "rather they are invitations to remember time, places, people— whether those are circumstances in which people are trapped, liberated, or alone."

Frank Stewart's Nexus: An American Photographer's Journey, 1960s to the Present at the Phillips Collection, Washington, DC, through September 3, 2023

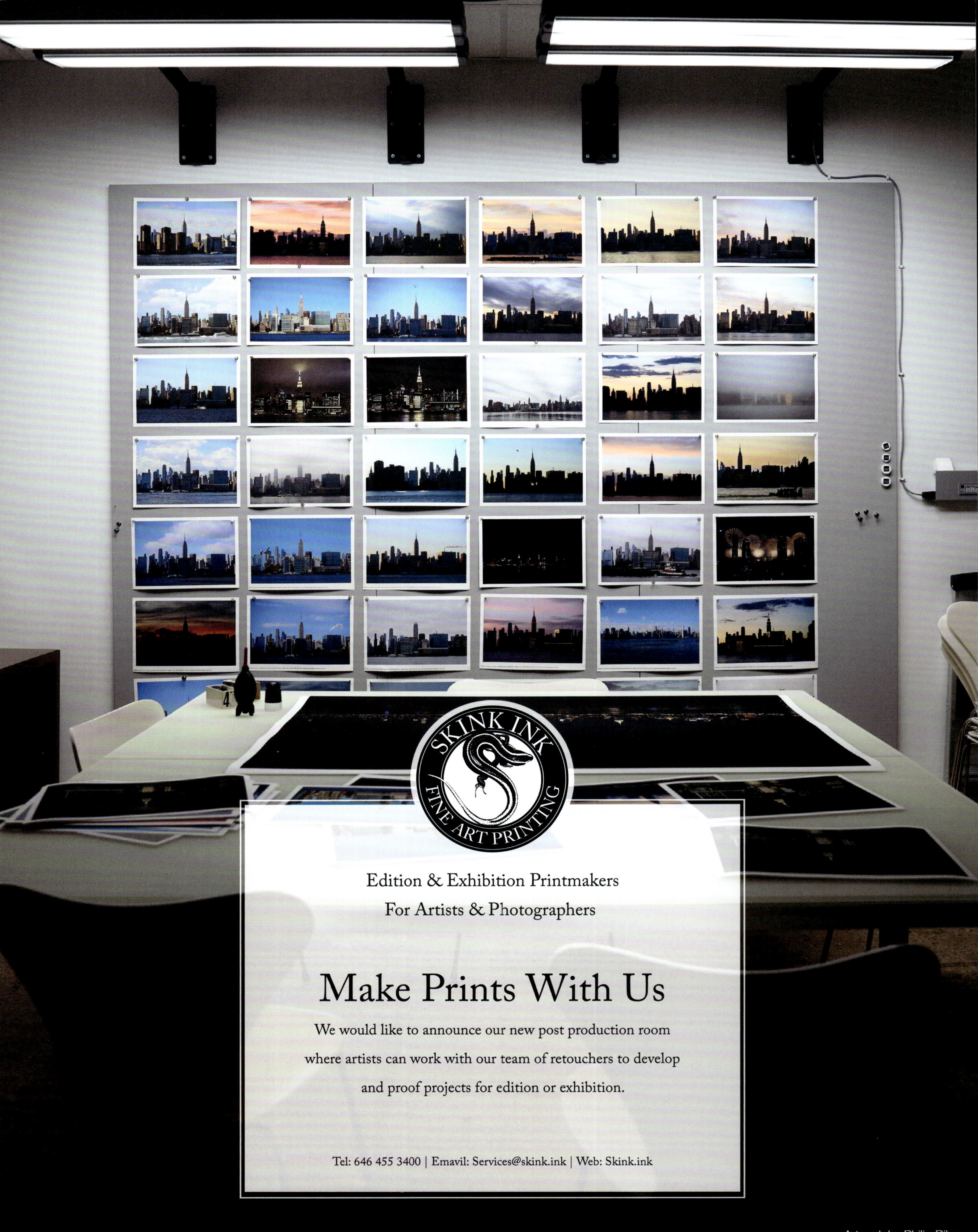
SKINK INK
FINE ART PRINTING

Edition & Exhibition Printmakers
For Artists & Photographers

Make Prints With Us

We would like to announce our new post production room

where artists can work with our team of retouchers to develop

and proof projects for edition or exhibition.

Tel: 646 455 3400 | Emavil: Services@skink.ink | Web: Skink.ink

Artwork by Philip Riley

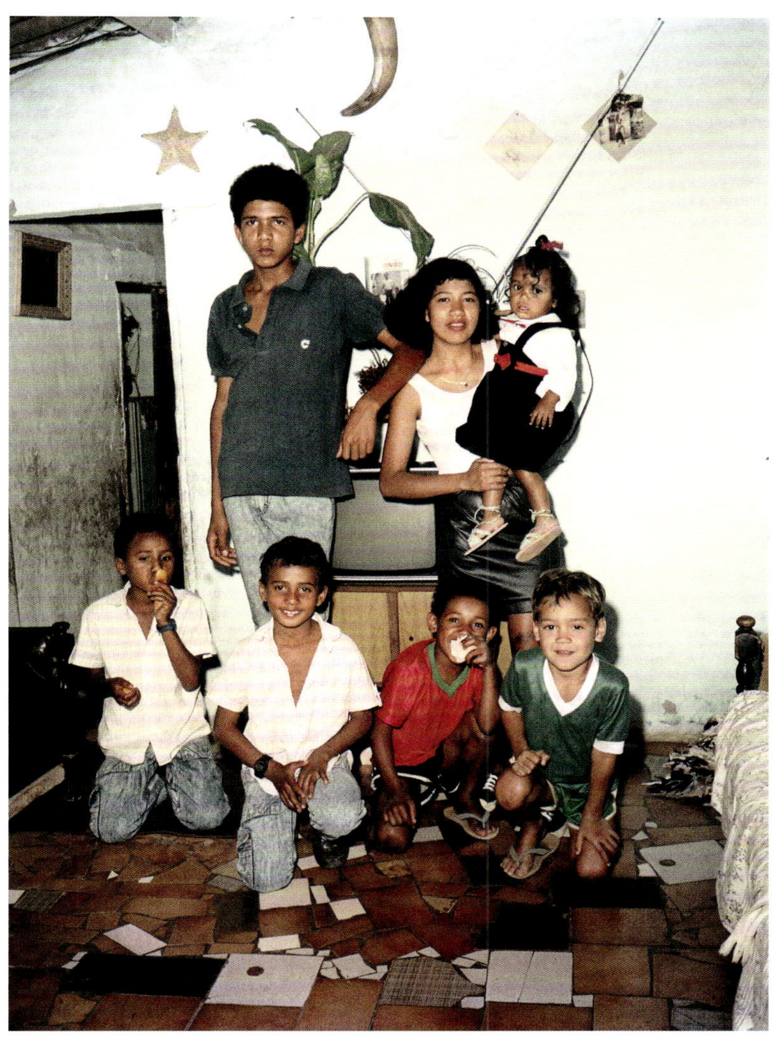

An archive of Brazilian photographs tells the story of a community's celebrations, struggles, and cultural heritage.

Fabiana Moraes

One of my oldest memories is of my sister Patrícia's birthday party. It was the early 1980s, and we were all dressed up around a table with a big cake decorated with colorful whipped cream. Festooned with balloons, the small house was packed with people. It was incredible; it seemed like another world, another life, another potential way of living. More than forty years later, I returned to that smell of new clothes and the brightness of that day when I saw a photograph of a child's sixth birthday party taken in 1988 by Afonso Pimenta. The cake, the simple home, the big bottles of soda, the many Black folk, the few white folk—it's all there, just like it was at Pat's party.

"A photo narrates the finest moment in a person's life. When you take it, it's a moment of glory, of kindness, of good things," Pimenta, a photographer who has been working in the Brazilian city of Belo Horizonte since the 1970s, told me recently. He photographed many families together in their living rooms, including one, in 1990, in which a young couple poses with their daughter and four boys. Their modest home sits in the Vila da Conceição neighborhood on the periphery of Belo Horizonte. Most of the family still lives at the same address, Pimenta recalls, underscoring that he's still in contact with the people he photographed.

Pimenta's images are now part of *Retratistas do Morro* (Portraitists from the Morro), an enormous archive of images captured in Aglomerado da Serra, a favela in Belo Horizonte and one of the largest low-income urban peripheries in Latin America. The archive contains roughly 250,000 images dating from the 1960s, of which approximately 30,000 have been restored. In them, we see celebrations, reunions, weddings, Black dance parties, and family portraits. "In a country where symbolic inequality—or that of visual representation—is as acute as social inequality, these photographs fill a void in our collective imagination through their record of the activities and emotional memories of entire communities whose images were rendered invisible," says Guilherme

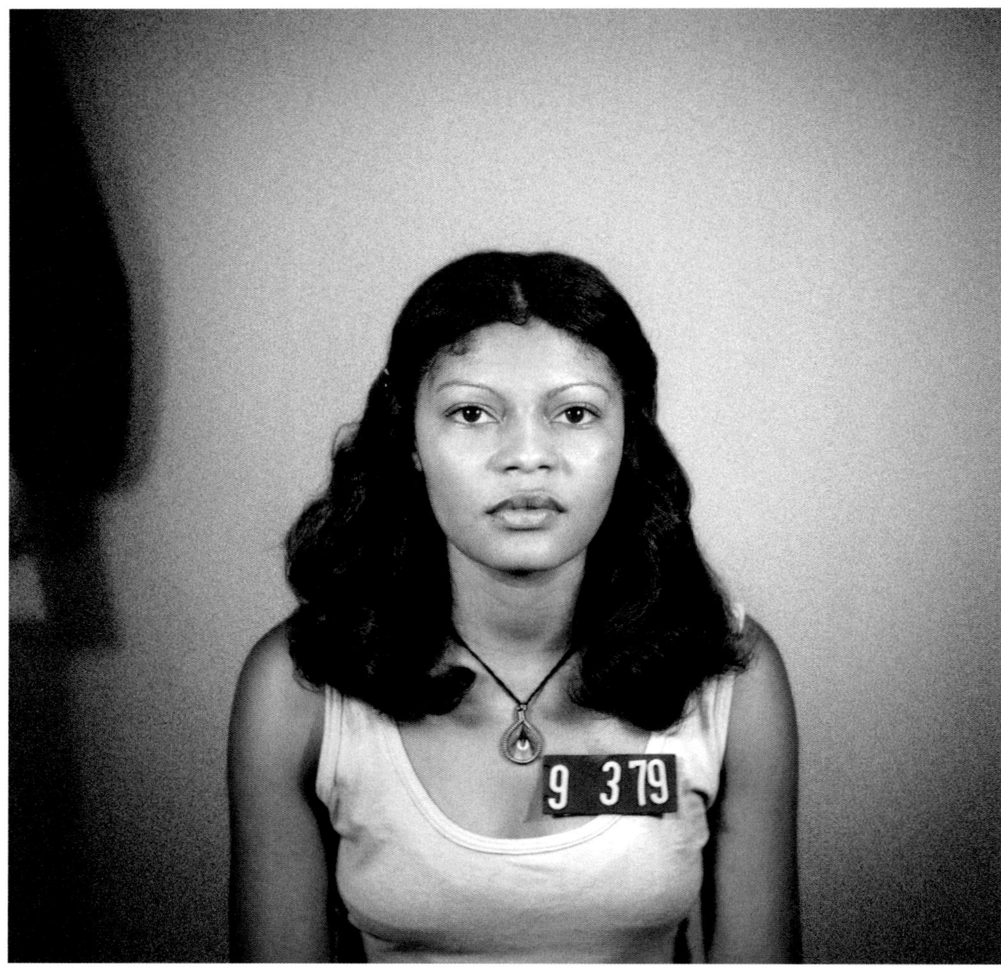

Previous page:
Afonso Pimenta,
*Fernando's Family, Belo
Horizonte,* 1990; this page:
João Mendes, *Fátima's
Portrait, Belo Horizonte,*
1979
Courtesy the artists

With the restored pictures, we are invited to experience the daily lives of people in low-income areas— but not through images of violence.

Cunha, the visual artist who developed the project.

Retratistas do Morro came into being through another project of Cunha's, *Memórias da Vila* (Memories of the Town), which included an exhibition and a book. Through his research, Cunha met Ana Martins, or Dona Ana, as she is commonly known. "One day, she showed us what she called 'her treasures,' various photo-viewers, *monóculos* in Portuguese, tubes similar to a kaleidoscope where one sees a photo at the end. Those *monóculos* offer pictures taken by photographers who worked in the Aglomerado forty years ago, recording local events," Cunha says. "With that material, I went looking for the portraitist she mentioned, Adão. Then he introduced me to João Mendes, who introduced me to Afonso Pimenta."

The images in the archive consist of 35mm and medium-format negatives, and *monóculos* in black and white and color. Cunha developed a methodology to handle the storage, digitization, cataloging, and presentation to the public. (Both Pimenta's and Mendes's photographs were included in the recent exhibition *Negros na Piscina* [Blacks in the Pool] at the Pinacoteca do Ceará in Fortaleza, Brazil, which I curated with Moacir dos Anjos.) "These steps include constructing a biography for the historical figures. Through interviews with the photographers and the people photographed in the community, we gained oral histories related to the images," he says.

With the restored pictures, we are invited to experience the daily lives of people in low-income areas—but not through images of violence, drug trafficking, or pain, as is usually the case. The archive translates life in precarious areas into images of beauty, creativity, pleasure, and even protest, since the people there are shown as the agents of their own lives, not just suffering people waiting for a miracle, or a savior in the form of a priest, minister, journalist, or politician.

Retratistas do Morro also includes the archive of Mendes, who started working at age fifteen as a police photographer in Ipatinga. As a teenager, he recorded forensic investigations. Like those of Pimenta, Mendes's images seem to ask: What is there beyond pain and suffering?

In the 1980s, Mendes began to work at a local school. His 1985 series *Becas* (Finery) shows young children holding their diplomas. They smile, they are happy, they are cared for, and they will go on living; they are following a path different from that of the low-income Black child who so often dies at the hands of drug traffickers or the Brazilian police. "The children's mothers still seek me out," Mendes says. "Now, I photograph the children of those people who I photographed."

Another of Mendes's images is a 1979 portrait of a woman named Fátima. In his studio, Mendes took photographs for identity documents, military IDs, and work cards. He did so for Fátima, who lived in Aglomerado da Serra. "You had to take the photo with the date on the chest, a requirement that was in force until the end of 1985. This image makes me nostalgic for the darkroom I used for black-and-white photos," he says.

For Cunha, the biggest challenge of *Retratistas do Morro* is the abyss between what the photographs reveal and the erasure of what they represent. "João's and Afonso's photographs show us other versions of the recent history of Brazilian images, revealing a cultural heritage and an unrecognized iconography produced over the last five decades," Cunha says. "They represent the life trajectories, the struggles, and the accomplishments of Brazil's favela communities, telling those stories through their own experiences and views of the world."

Fabiana Moraes is a journalist, curator, and professor of social communication at the Federal University of Pernambuco, Brazil.

Translated from the Portuguese by Zoe Sullivan.

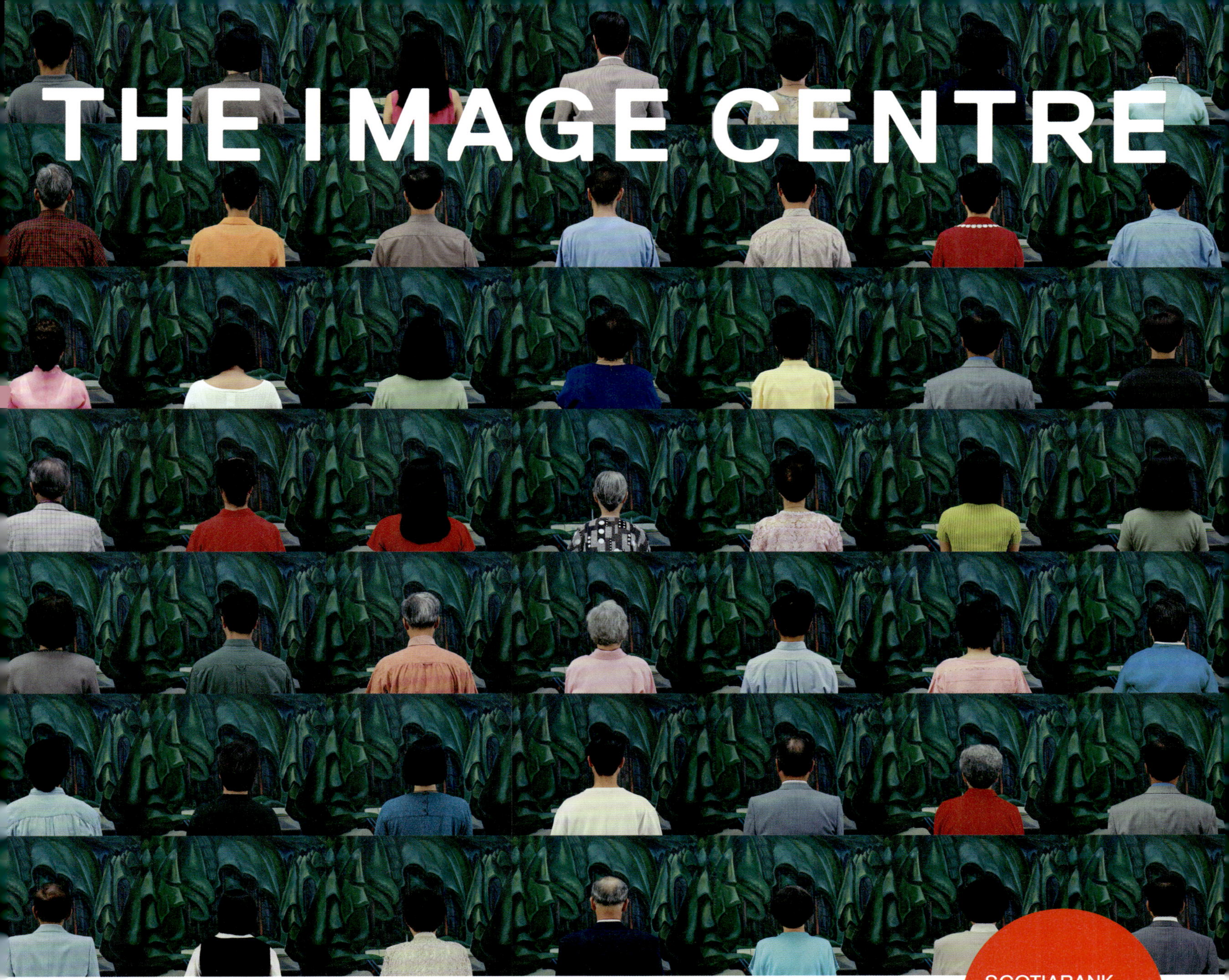

THE IMAGE CENTRE

SCOTIABANK PHOTOGRAPHY AWARD

JIN-ME YOON

**OPENING RECEPTION &
CONTACT FESTIVAL LAUNCH**
APRIL 28, 2023, 7–10 PM

EXHIBITION ON VIEW
APRIL 29–AUGUST 5, 2023

33 Gould Street
Toronto, Canada
416.979.5164

Admission is always free.
theimagecentre.ca

Jin-me Yoon, *A Group of Sixty-Seven* (detail), 1996, two grids
of 67 framed chromogenic prints for a total of 134 prints and 1
name panel. Collection of the Vancouver Art Gallery, Vancouver
Art Gallery Acquisition Fund. Courtesy of the artist

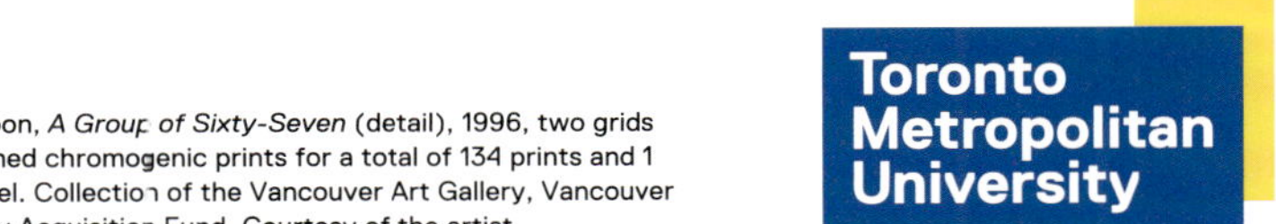

Studio Visit

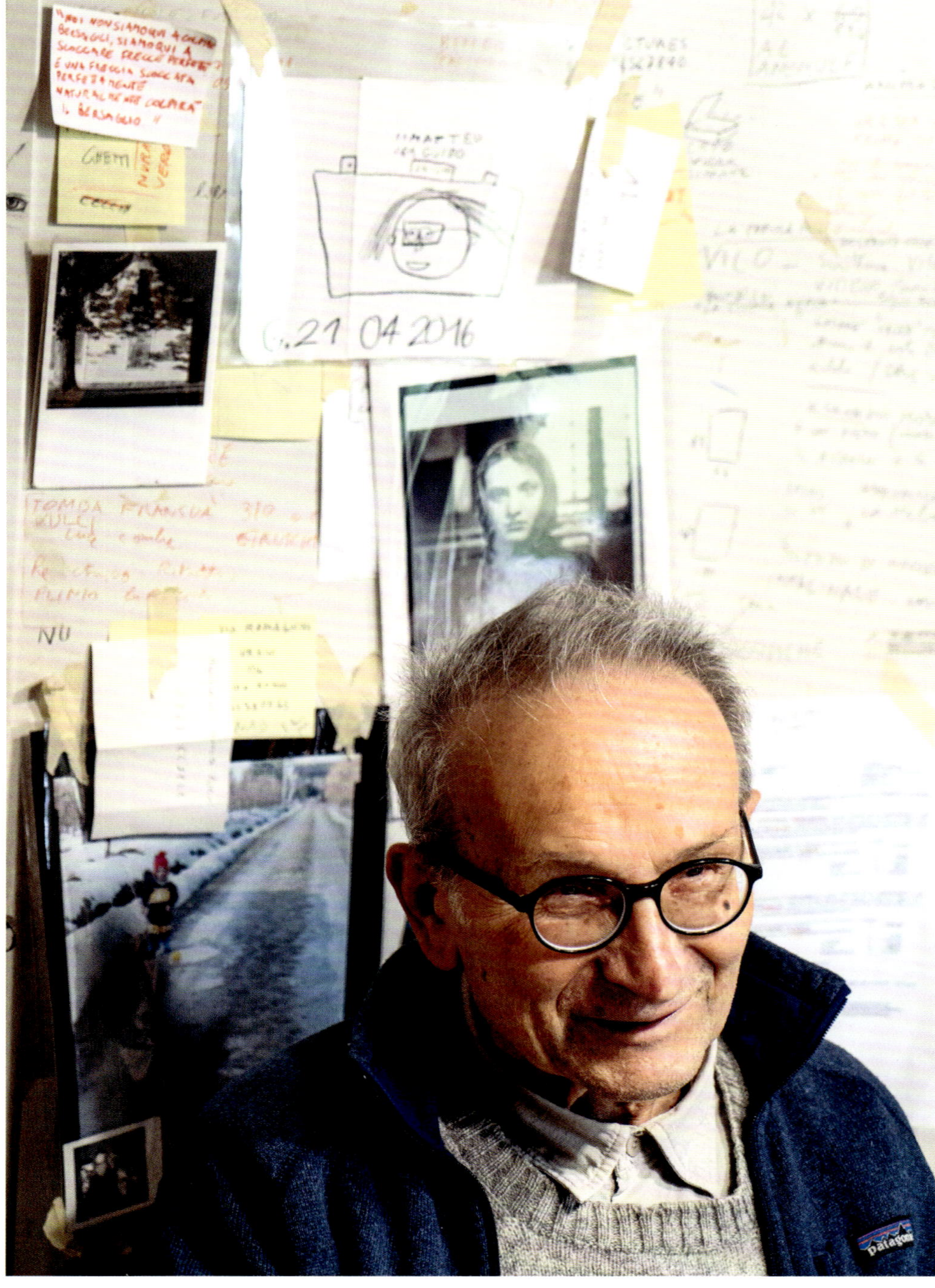

From his studio in the countryside near the Adriatic Sea, Guido Guidi reflects on decades of studying Italy's urban and architectural history.
Luca Fiore

Guido Guidi and his studio, Cesena, Italy, 2022
Photographs by Mike Slack
for *Aperture*

Guido Guidi's studio is located on the ground floor of his countryside house on the outskirts of Cesena, Italy. This is just a few kilometers from the coast of the Adriatic Sea, a half-hour drive from the early Christian mosaics of Ravenna, ancient capital of the Western Roman Empire, and the dreamy atmospheres of Rimini, where Federico Fellini's *Amarcord* is set. To reach Guidi's old building, you follow a dirt road between two long rows of persimmon trees. It is mid-December, and the ripe fruit, full and orange, warms the winter palette. It feels like being inside one of the pictures for which Guidi is famous: a nowhere place, marginal, aesthetically unremarkable. Ruined walls, abandoned tools, vegetation growing wild. What first comes to mind are the photographs in *Per Strada* (2018), his work on the settlements along the Via Emilia, the road that, since Roman times, has connected Rimini to Piacenza. Yet the stillness is what you sense when leafing through his earlier book *Preganziol, 1983* (2013), in which a sequence of images shows an empty room photographed every few minutes: the passage of time, seen in the movement of light and shadows on the walls.

Guidi's parents bought the house in the 1950s, and he moved here in 2000, after living for years in Venice and Treviso. The studio entrance is guarded by a German shepherd, dozing in a worn-out, light-blue wooden doghouse. Taped to the jamb of the front door is a white push button bearing the handwritten inscription "Zoffoli-Guidi." The photographer's handwriting is a constant in the studio's

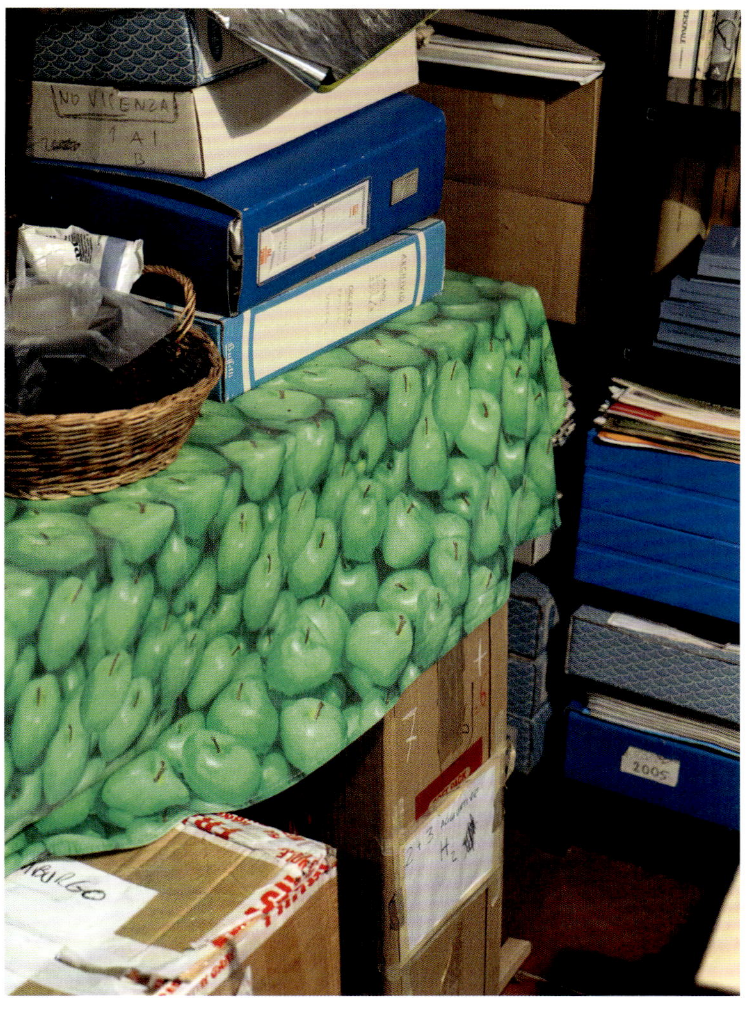

decor; it is found on the boxes in which negatives and prints are stored, on the cabinets, even on the frame of the window next to the toilet. Attached to one piece of furniture is a quote from Henry David Thoreau that not only explains Guidi's idea of the space but is also a poetic disclaimer: "When a traveler asked Wordsworth's servant to show him her master's study, she answered, 'Here is his library, but his studio is out of doors.'" Guidi admits, however, that since passing the age of eighty, his time spent making photographs has been greatly reduced. Now, the activities of organizing the archive and designing new books consume his days.

A joyful disorder prevails in Guidi's studio. Proofs and copies of his many books—including *In Between Cities* (2004), *A New Map of Italy* (2011), and *Carlo Scarpa's Tomba Brion* (2011)—clutter one table. A reproduction of a Robert Adams photograph, another of Lewis Hine's famous image taken at Ellis Island of a young Russian Jewish woman, and some pictures of Guidi's grandson hang on a metal cabinet. Also on the table is a roll of proofs for his latest book, *Di sguincio, 1969–81*, a collection of black-and-white images. Made with small-format cameras, they exhibit the strongly experimental approach characteristic of Guidi's work

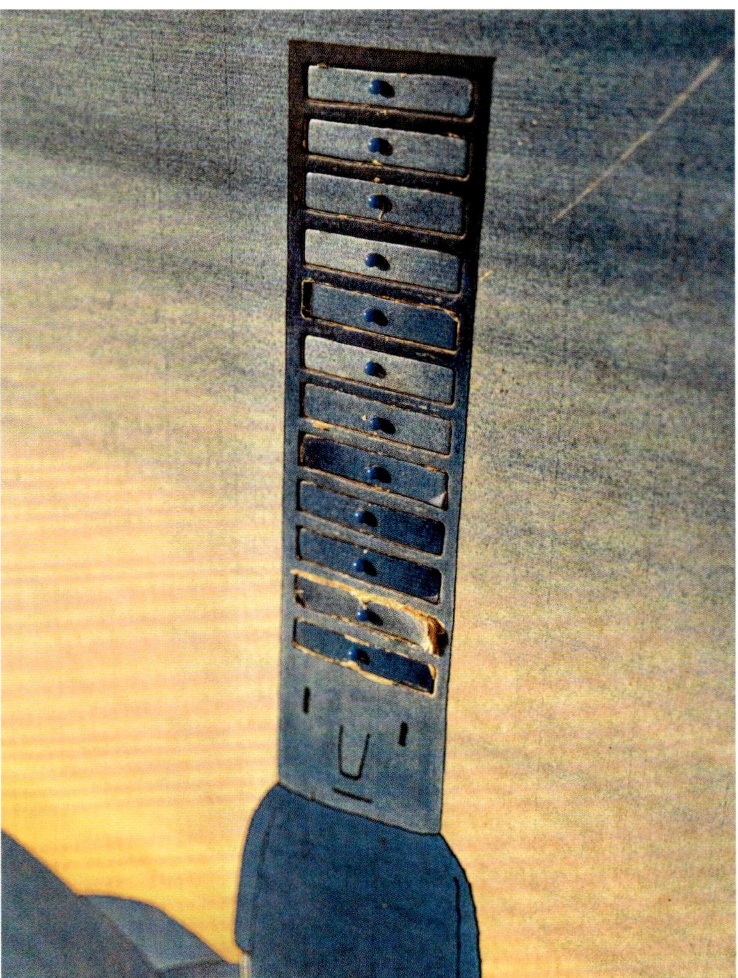

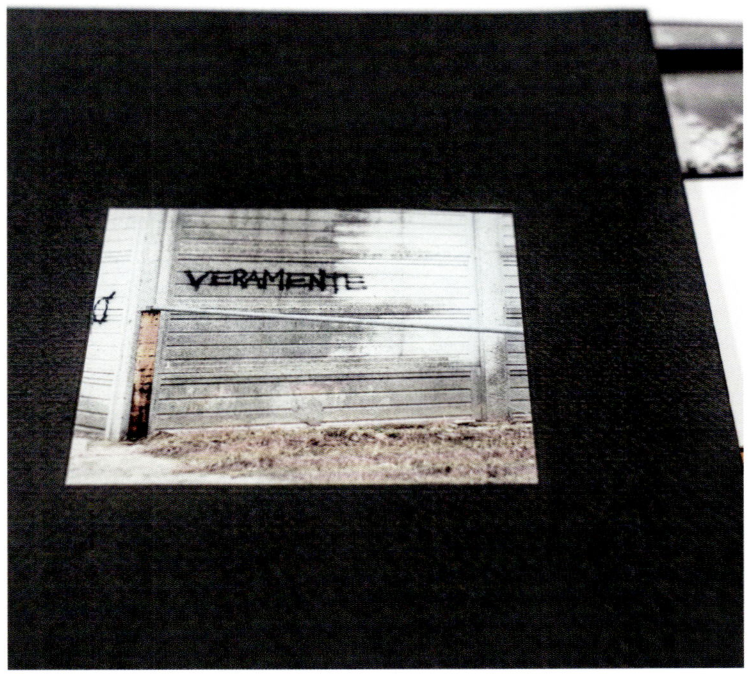

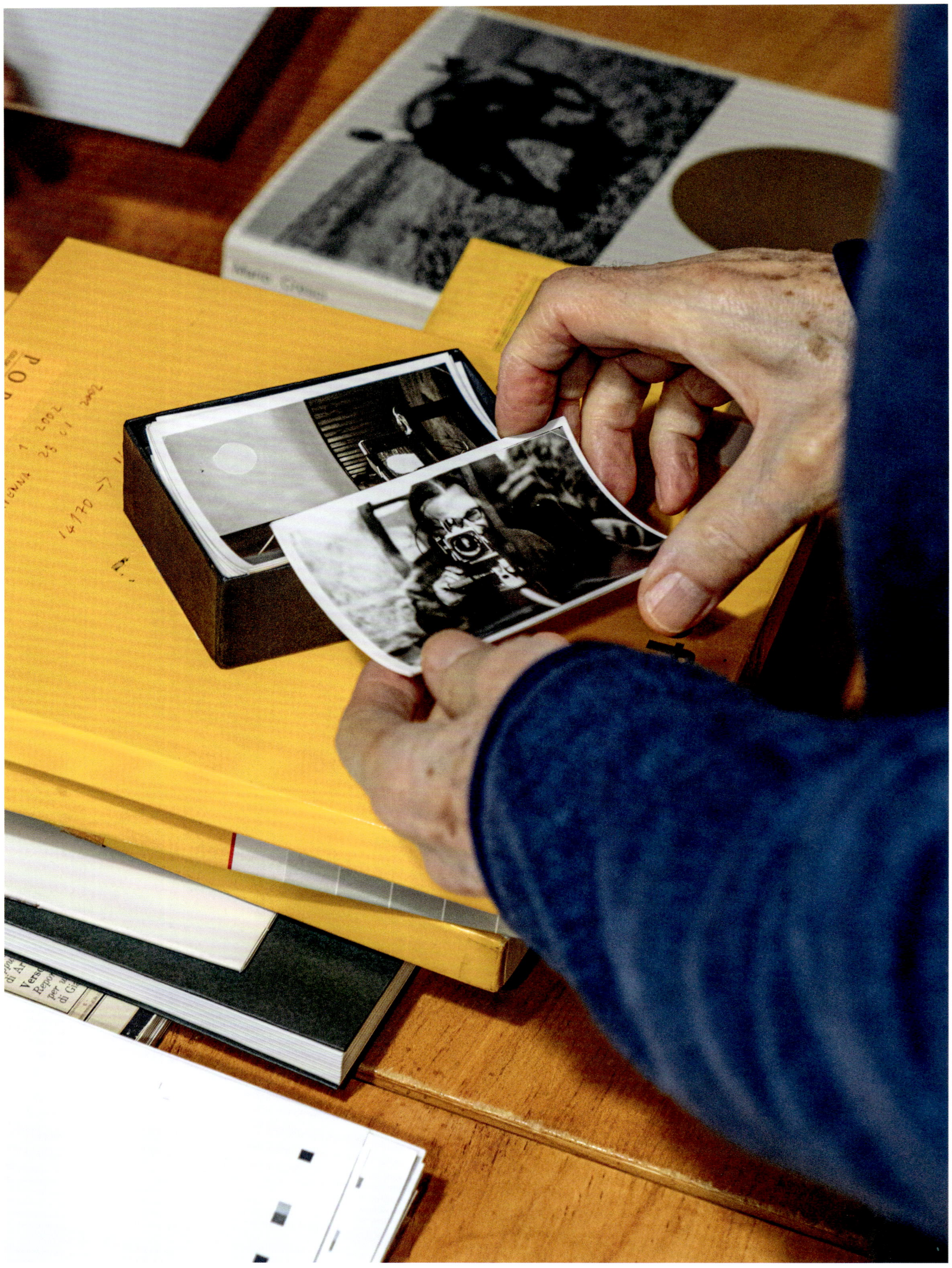

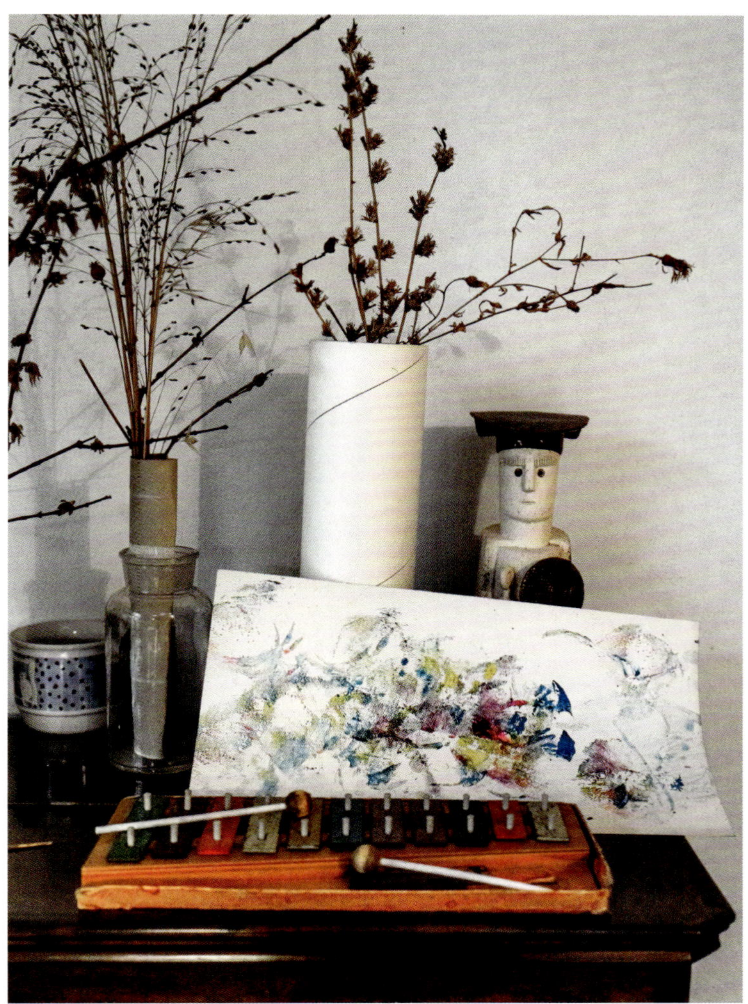

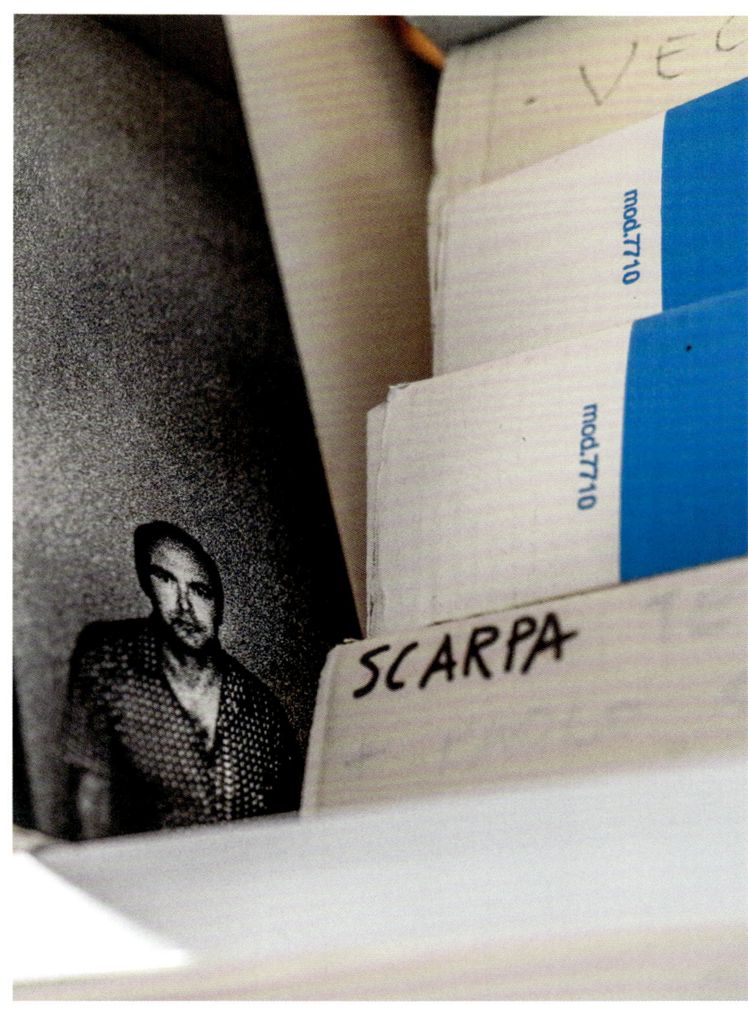

One of the quotes Guidi repeats most often is inspired by the Talmud: "Wherever you look, there is something to see."

at the beginning of his career, before he began working in an 8-by-10-inch format. "In Venice, I took lessons from Italo Zannier, who encouraged us to investigate the potential of the photographic medium," Guidi explains, referring to the Italian photographer and historian. "I was attempting to go in directions different from the neorealist tradition that preceded me. It's as if, in the early years, I tried to retrace the steps of the history of photography. To understand O'Sullivan, Atget, or Evans, one has to put oneself in their shoes."

He would also commit "infractions" against classic photography by placing the camera at ground level. A gray cat jumps onto his lap, and he continues, "What led me to large-format photography was, on the one hand, the impossibility of printing all the material I was shooting—with the large format, you're constrained to making fewer images—and on the other, the impossibility of remaining a 1968 protester all my life."

While Guidi's most recent photographs are, by his own admission, stylistically "classic," a nonconformist bent still drives him. "I remember once showing my pictures at a gathering of the Order of Architects of my region. The president said, candidly, that certain buildings, to which I was passionately attached, were artifacts that he would tear down," he recounts. The curator Agnès Sire notes that Guidi is "conscientiously bringing to light a shifting reality which we do not wish to see, where we think there is nothing to see."

This is not just a quirk; it's an attitude that springs from a specific worldview. One of the quotes he repeats most often is inspired by the Talmud: "Wherever you look, there is something to see." For Guidi, photographing is a gesture of a secular spirituality, a desire to know the world through an identification with subject matter. His precision and care in photographing reflect this desire.

Guidi explains that his current perspective has changed slightly from the past: "In the beginning, I favored a wide-angle lens, as if my ambition was to get everything into the frame. Today, I'm more selective. I'm moving farther from the subject, but I'm doing so, paradoxically, by constraining the field of vision. As Michelangelo Antonioni said, 'As you get older, you gain a distance from things.'"

Luca Fiore is a writer based in Milan.

Translated from the Italian by Mike Slack.

Spotlight

Vân-Nhi Nguyen, winner of the 2023 Aperture Portfolio Prize, offers a bold perspective on the lives of young people in contemporary Vietnam.

Thessaly La Force

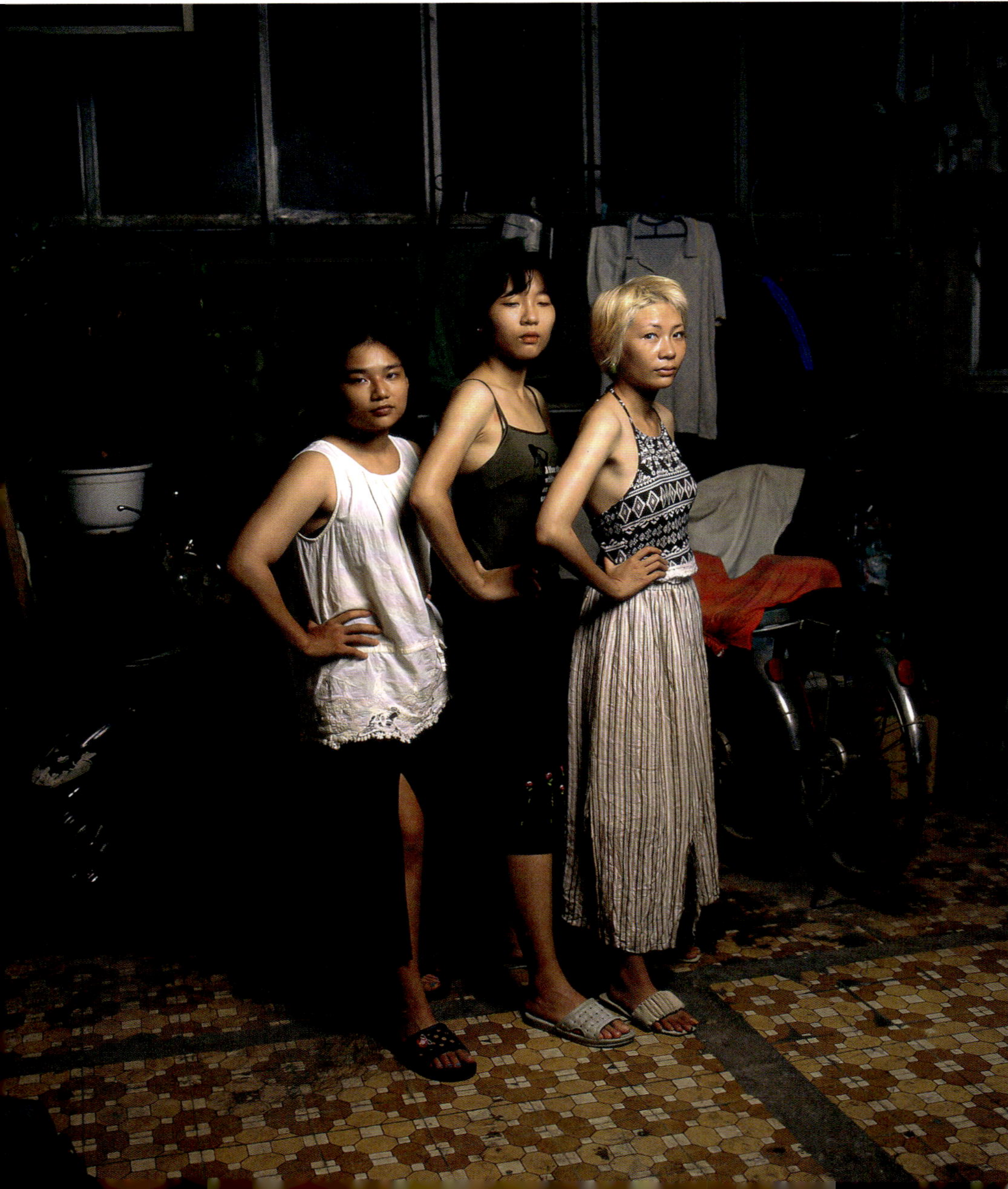

A young woman sits on a plastic-covered bed in a cheap motel room. She is dressed without pageantry or occasion, in a black tank top and a pair of shorts. A small tattoo is visible on the inside of her elbow. She is barefoot. Her gaze is one of neither confrontation nor seduction. "See me as I am," she seems to be saying. "Look at me as I look at you." Behind her, a poster depicting a flat, computer-rendered landscape of a beach is tacked to the wall. This could be Vietnam, but it could also be anywhere tropical.

What does it mean to grow up in a country violently marked by colonization and war? For Vân-Nhi Nguyen, the twenty-three-year-old Vietnamese photographer who took the untitled image as part of her 2022 series *As You Grow Older*, it is a disorientating experience, one that overwhelms her emotionally.

"Our history has been wiped clean every single time from thousands of years of colonization," she told me in a recent conversation. "It strips us of our identity so that, even now, young Vietnamese people don't even know who they are to begin with, to even tell a story. When you actually look at the history of Vietnamese people, we didn't really gain any sense of our own identity until our independence in 1975, which was forty years ago. That's still within a human's lifetime."

Nguyen's relationship to photography has been complicated. Initially, art was more a means to escape a conventional life and less a way to express herself. "Art, in general," says Nguyen, "is not something too important to public education in Vietnam. I think it's fair to say that people need to stay alive first. Not just in Vietnam, but, typically, it's understandable that people can't look for anything else if their stomach is empty or their beer is not cold."

At sixteen, she began taking photographs, and soon, while in college, found a place for herself with commercial and fashion-oriented work. But Nguyen eventually came to see that this type of image making was essentially meaningless. She was equally unimpressed with the clout that the camera lent her socially, and, in a radical gesture, she put it down when she was twenty and stopped producing altogether for two years. "Photography became to me something so shallow and so superficial," Nguyen says. "I hated the emptiness of images I saw scrolling Instagram, and I hated the cleanliness of the fashion images in magazines. Everything was too sterile and dishonest."

That time was a fallow period for Nguyen, who spent it looking at

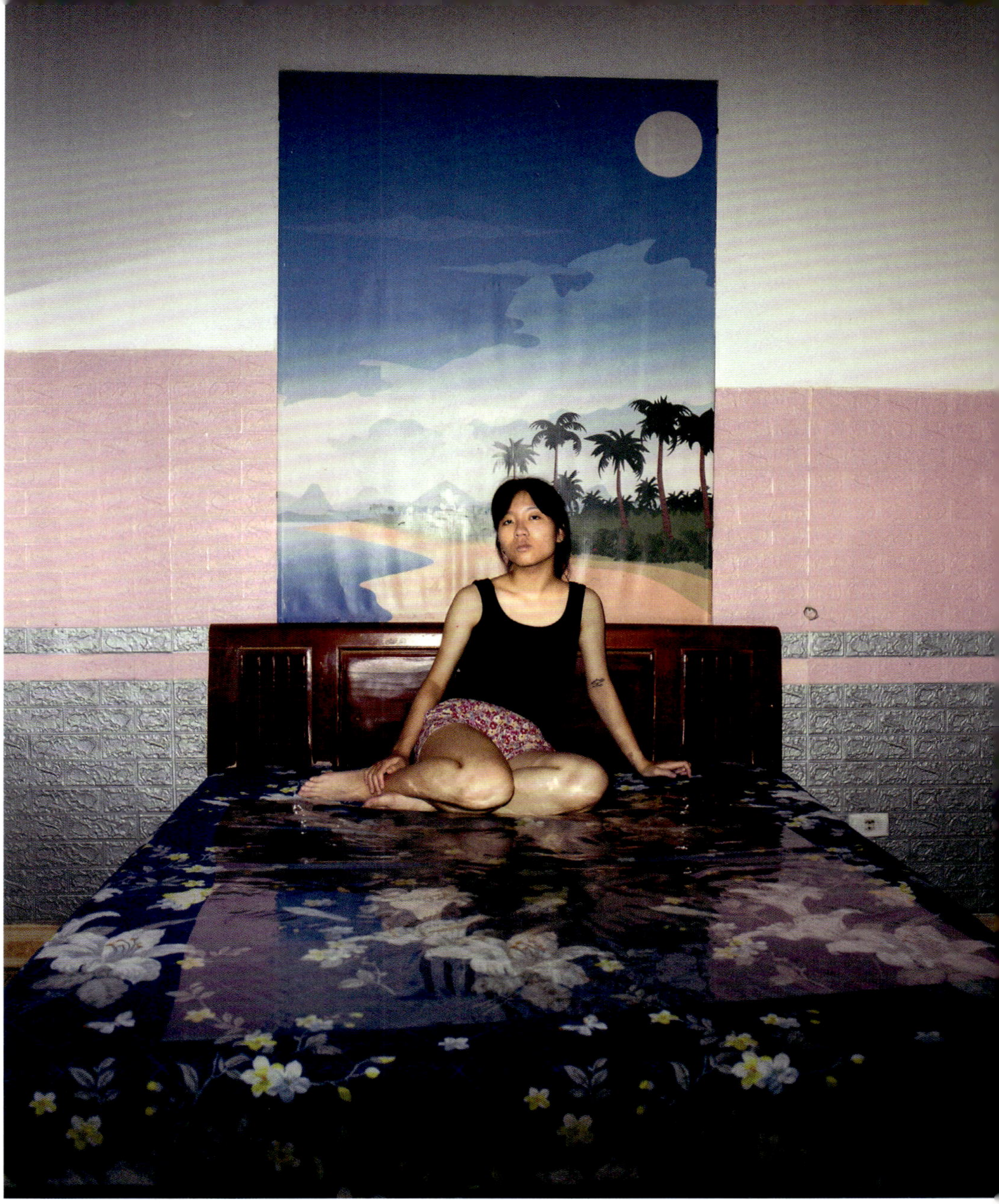

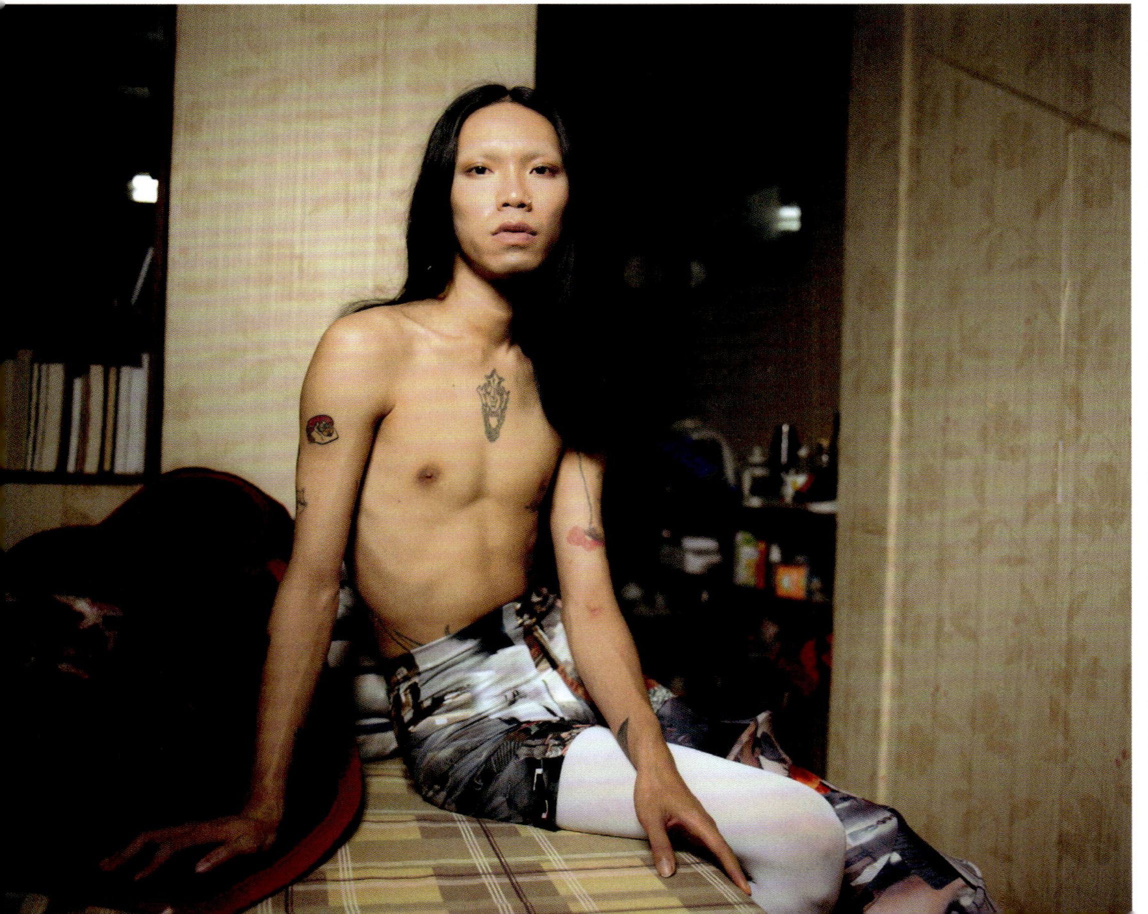

photography books, studying not only
her peers but those who came before
her. One of her biggest influences is the
photographer Deana Lawson, whose
portraits of Black American men and
women, often at home, are striking in
their ability to capture a kind of out-of-
time noble or aristocratic manner.
As Zadie Smith wrote in a 2018 essay
for Lawson's Aperture monograph:
"Deana Lawson's work is prelapsarian—
it comes before the Fall. Her people seem
to occupy a higher plane, a kingdom
of restored glory, in which diaspora
gods can be found wherever you look:
Brownsville, Kingston, Port-au-Prince,
Addis Ababa." To Nguyen, this kind of
framework was a revelation. She asked
herself: What am I even doing if I can't
put my people on a pedestal?

Nguyen's photographs in *As You
Grow Older* are a serious attempt at
exactly that. She asked friends, colleagues,
and acquaintances to pose for her,
sometimes staging them in intimate

Under Nguyen's lens, the flattening stereotypes of Vietnamese culture are never present, even if she is perfectly aware of them.

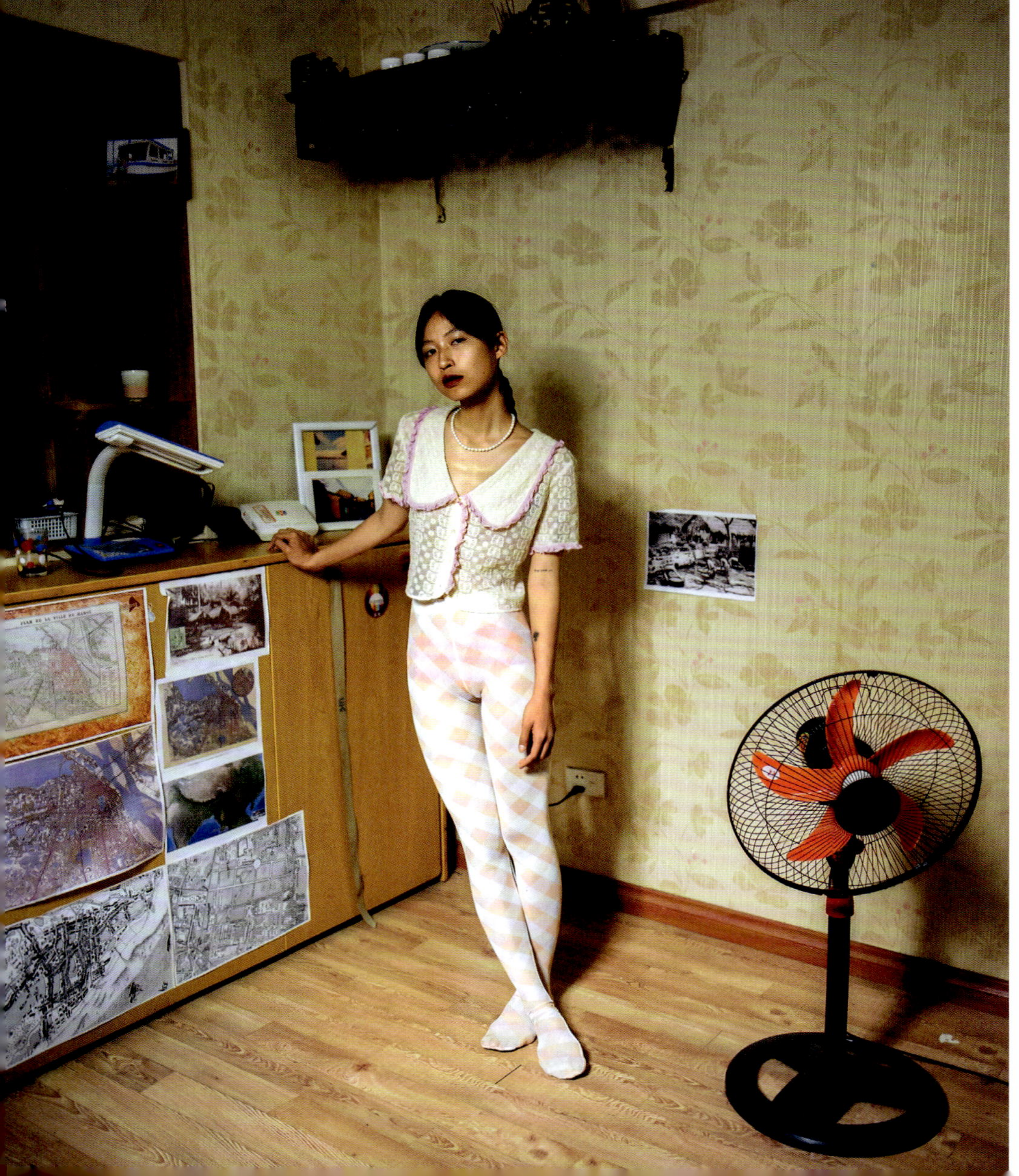

settings such as their bedrooms, other times in unfamiliar spaces. In one memorable photograph, three women stand defiantly in the center of the frame, each striking an identical pose, their hands on their hips, like a line of chorus girls. But the image is unsettling in its power, even though its setting—a dimly lit hallway of an apartment walk-up—is ordinary, almost bland. Nguyen was, in fact, referencing a pose from a historical image she had come across, of three Vietnamese women on the verge of being executed by European settlers, their necks shackled together by chains.

"Even though that image was taken by a white person, a settler, the women looked as though they owned the space," Nguyen observed. In her pictures, masculinity, too, is its own kind of pure beauty: two young men lean against each other at night on the banks of the Hong River; another young man poses calmly on a bed, shirtless. Nguyen has a knack for seeking out the idiosyncrasies of those around her, to find intimacy with her gaze. Under her lens, the flattening stereotypes of Vietnamese culture are never present, even if she is perfectly aware of them.

Lately, Nguyen has been productive, completing the first portion of a series of photographs called *Under the Sun*, taken by the Siem Reap River in Cambodia earlier this year, and is at work on an upcoming show this August with Aperture. Her relationship to photography is still complex. "I feel like I'm in a marriage," she says of her art. "Some days, I can feel intense passion for it that feels like I could survive off photographs and images alone, and some others, I just want to stop altogether and never touch a camera again." But she is spending more time deepening her craft. She allows herself to fall in love with people and places. She is open to where photography will take her next.

Thessaly La Force is a writer based in New York.

Vân-Nhi Nguyen is the winner of the 2023 Aperture Portfolio Prize. A solo exhibition of her work will be on view at Baxter St at the Camera Club of New York in August 2023.

The **LINDA McCARTNEY** Retrospective

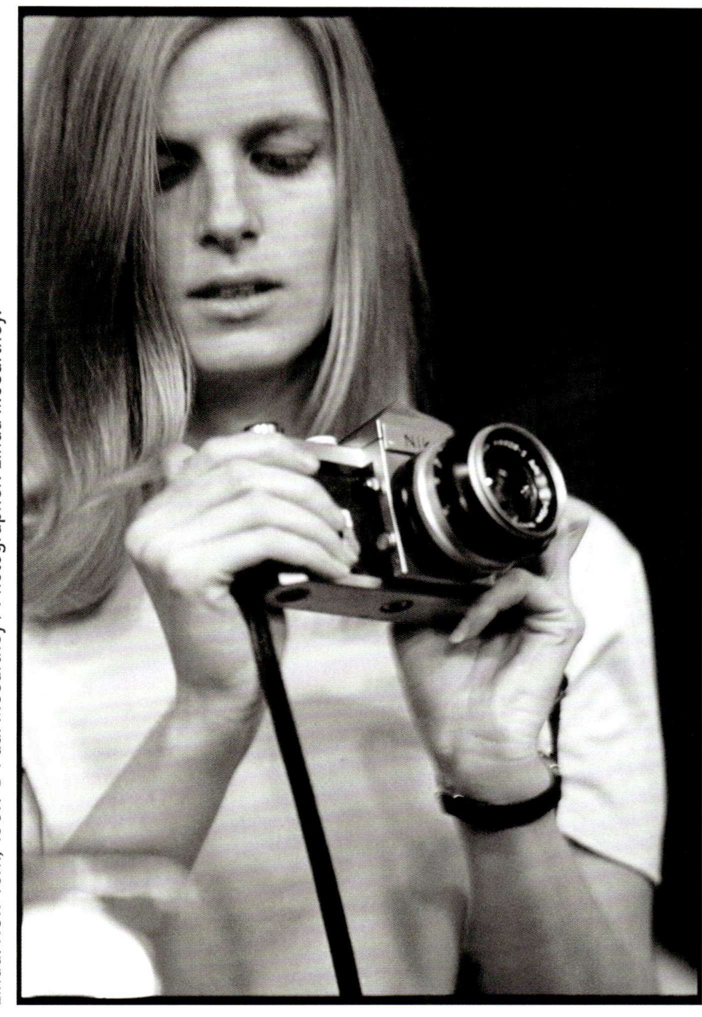
Linda. New York, 1967. © Paul McCartney / Photographer: Linda McCartney.

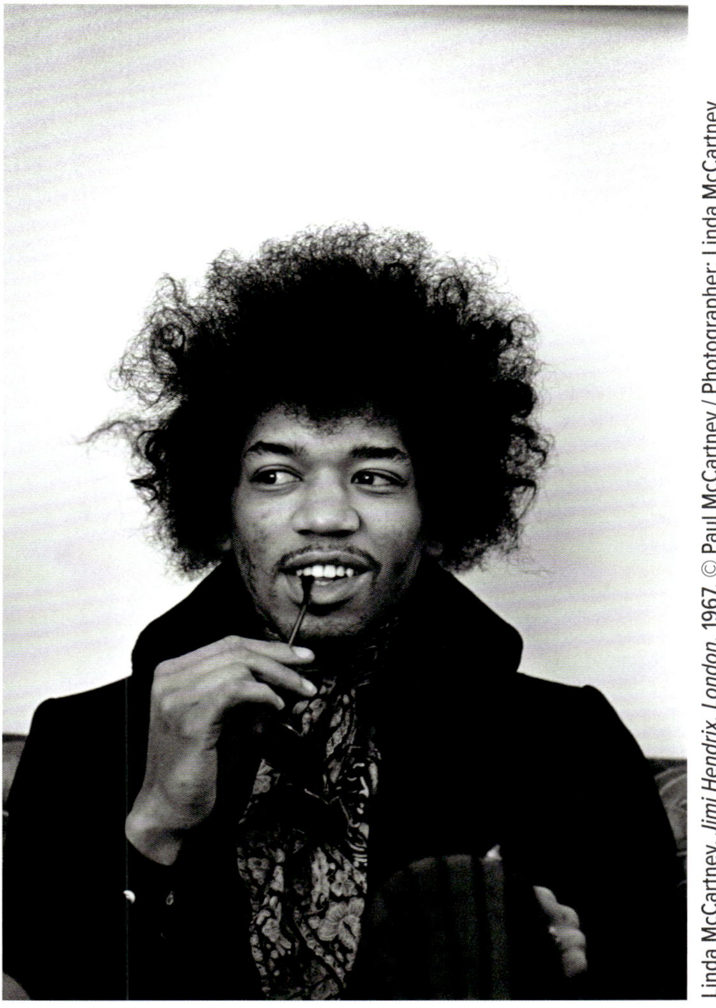
Linda McCartney, Jimi Hendrix. London, 1967. © Paul McCartney / Photographer: Linda McCartney.

The University of Arizona Center for Creative Photography is proud to host the North American premiere of "The Linda McCartney Retrospective," opening Feb. 25!

Celebrate McCartney's 30-year, barrier-breaking career, and her connection to Tucson. Free to all!

ccp.arizona.edu | **Tuesday-Saturday, 10:00a-4:30p**

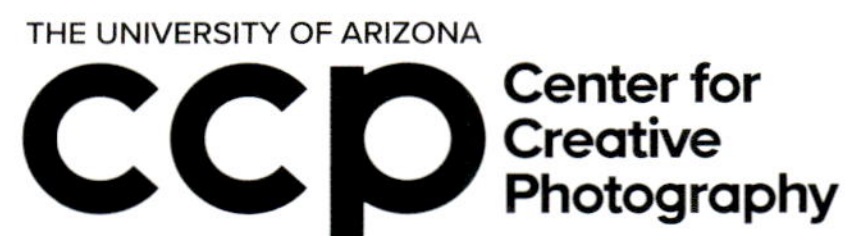
THE UNIVERSITY OF ARIZONA
ccp Center for Creative Photography

Curriculum
Sunil Gupta

In the mid-1980s, soon after graduating with an MA in photography from the Royal College of Art, Sunil Gupta wrote in the pages of the British photography quarterly *Ten.8*: "It's time we reconstructed images of desire by ourselves and for ourselves." Gupta has made sensitive portraits about homosexuality in Indian cities and advocated for more equitable representation in UK art spaces, pushing postcolonial resistance throughout a career spanning life in Delhi, New York, and London. His writing, recently collected in *We Were Here: Sexuality, Photography, and Cultural Difference* (Aperture, 2022), is fierce in its political commitments while attuned to the value of community and togetherness—a range of vision that dwells on the life-altering potential of desire.

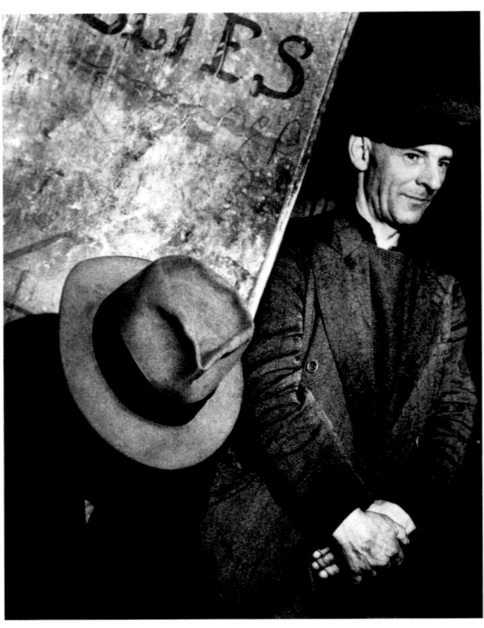

Lisette Model

I took Lisette Model's class at the New School in the mid-1970s, and it completely transformed my life. At her behest, I dropped out of my MBA program and decided to become a photographer. She agreed with me that it would not make me any money. Model was an extraordinary teacher of great passion; she either liked your work or she didn't. Fortunately, she did like mine, and she legitimized my wanderings in the West Village photographing gay men. She was all for doing what you had to do regardless of commissions, money, or fame. My pictures from that time lay untouched until 2018, when they were published in *Christopher Street 1976*.

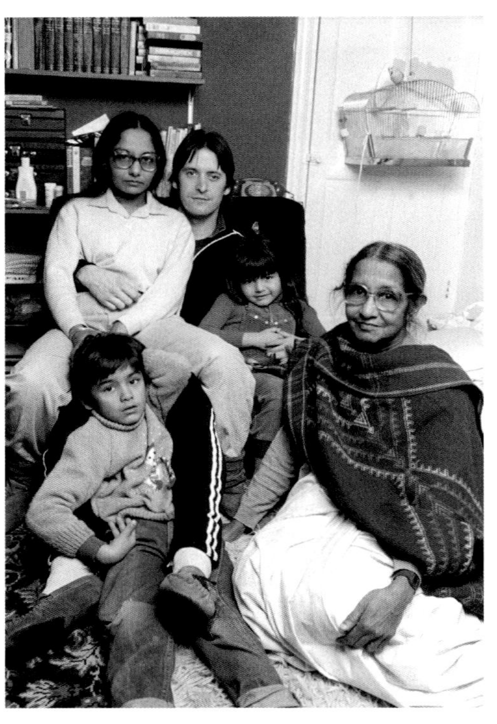

Reflections of the Black Experience

I came to London in the early 1970s fully formed as a modernist photographer from New York, and then, in 1983, I emerged from the full-time study of photography at the Royal College of Art into a postcolonial and postmodern world. A group of us staged a Black student graduation show. Three years later, Monika Baker curated the seminal exhibition *Reflections of the Black Experience*, of a hundred pictures commissioned from ten Black photographers. The project brought us together, not just as photographers but as photographers of African, Caribbean, and South Asian descent. We carried on meeting informally for two more years, and in 1988, a small group of us founded Autograph, the Association of Black Photographers, an organization that continues to this day, with Black as not skin color but a postcolonial position.

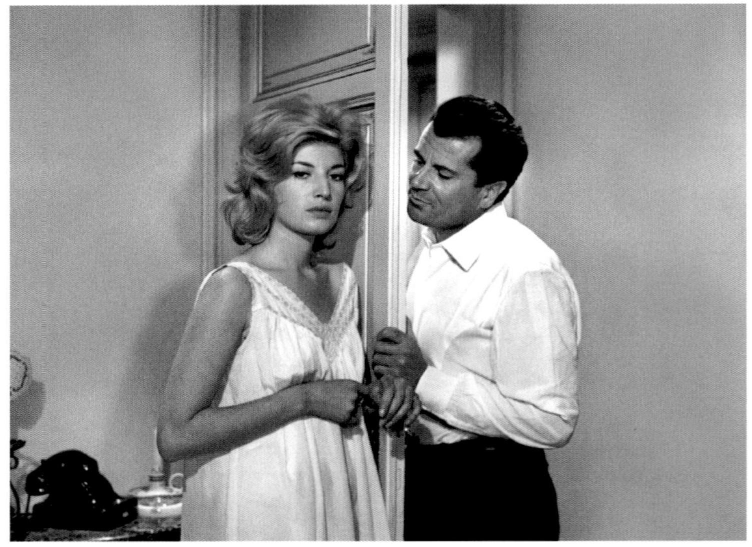

Michelangelo Antonioni

My undergraduate years marked a period when I was busy devouring literary novels and independent cinema. I was blessed with an amazing film society at school and got to see and discuss everything from Jean-Luc Godard and François Truffaut to Akira Kurosawa and Yasujiro Ozu. However, I had a soft spot for the Italian neorealists. One day, I saw Michelangelo Antonioni's 1960 film *L'Avventura*, with its post-neorealist shift away from a narrative emphasis and extraordinarily beautiful cinematography in wide-screen black and white. Not everything has to be in color, I decided, and not everything has to have a story. These were all early lessons, before I found photography. Italy has now come back into my life; I've signed up with a gallery in Rome, enabling future projects there.

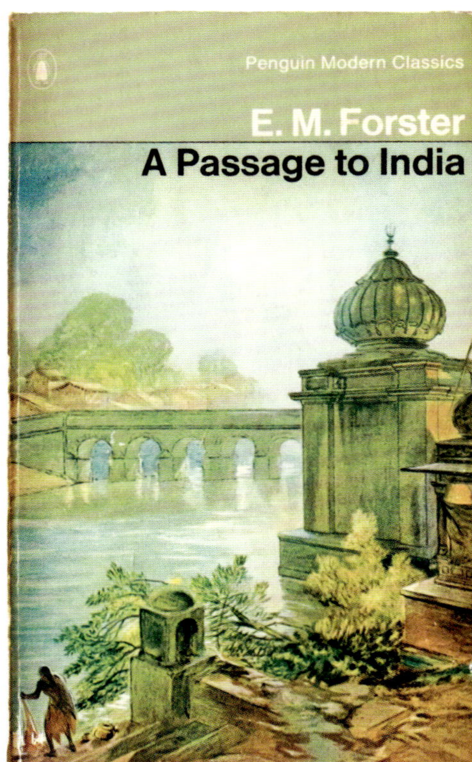

A Passage to India

Landing in Montreal in 1969, I eagerly devoured *gay* as a welcome identity, since the Indian one that I had arrived with appeared to carry no weight. Yet, I was still keen to discover some, indeed any, reference to an Indian gay experience. I found it in E. M. Forster's 1924 novel *A Passage to India*, which is ostensibly about what may or may not have happened to Miss Adela Quested in the cave. But it is actually about the friendship between Dr. Aziz and Cyril Fielding, and how the two men formed a relationship in an impossible setting. Although Aziz feels betrayed by Fielding's return to England and subsequent marriage, there is a fantasy moment when the two men ride off in different directions. It's a tragic image that I've always carried with me.

Pakeezah

I was born and raised in New Delhi on a steady diet of big, colorful Bollywood musicals and glossy picture magazines. Unbeknownst to me, my gay identity was already forming, using a camp vocabulary from the silver screen. Later, in the West, when I encountered rainbows, friends of Dorothy, Judy Garland, and Stonewall, I felt I already knew this subculture—Kamal Amrohi's 1972 film *Pakeezah* embodies it all. The story begins with the voice-over of a courtesan describing her fall from grace and her life in a graveyard. From there the melodrama never lets up. At the core is the romantic idea of a love that cannot be acknowledged by society, something I began to recognize as my own fate before I knew what being gay was.

Tessa Boffin

I met the photographer Tessa Boffin at an AIDS meeting at the London Lesbian and Gay Centre in 1988. We spontaneously suggested to the assembled crowd that we would like to make an art show about HIV/AIDS. This idea became *Ecstatic Antibodies: Resisting the AIDS Mythology*, a very British (we felt the Americans were having a disproportionately large influence on our discourse) and pro-sex take on HIV/AIDS politics in the United Kingdom at the time. *Ecstatic Antibodies* was a photography exhibition that toured almost continuously from 1990 to 1992, with an accompanying book that sold out. Before her death in 1993, Boffin went on to do another project, this one with the photographer Jean Fraser, called *Stolen Glances: Lesbians Take Photographs* (1991).

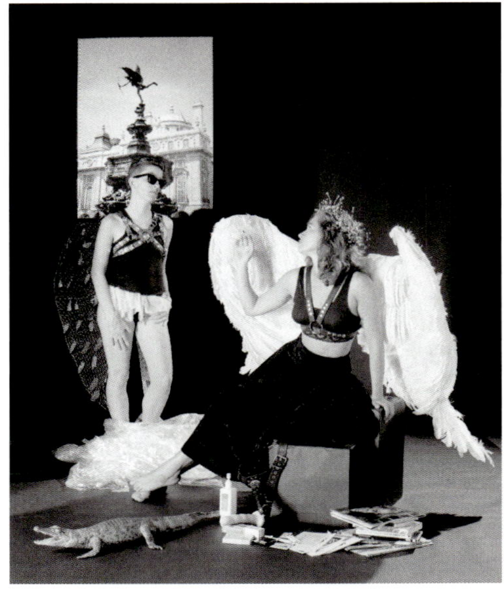

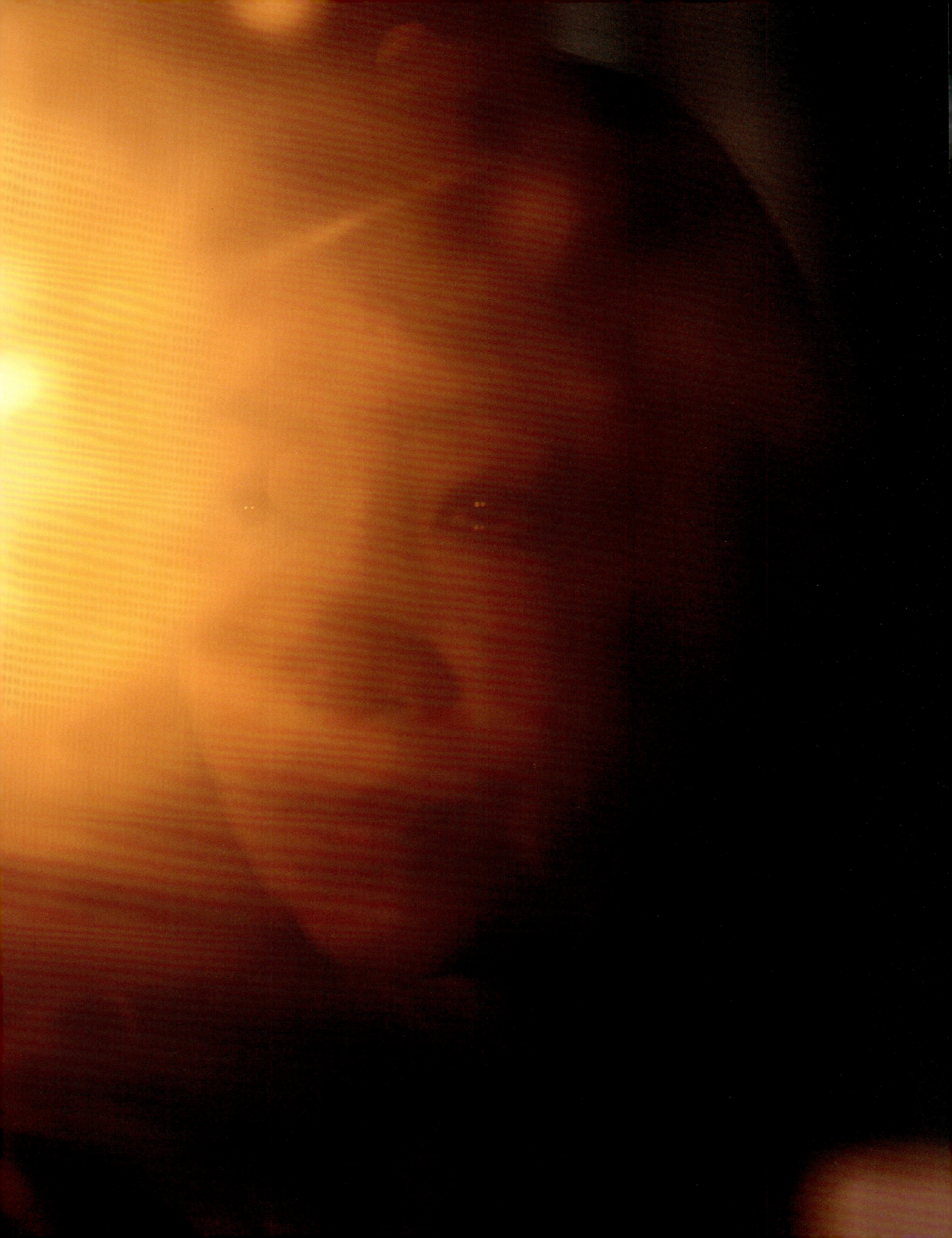

Being & Becoming: Asian in America

How have Asian American artists explored the unspoken tensions between the past and present—and made visible new possibilities for the future?

Stephanie Hueor Tung

In the summer of 1953, Charles Wong's photo-essay "1952 / The Year of the Dragon" was published in the fifth issue of *Aperture*. The impetus for Wong's piece—a carefully designed sequence of photography and poetry—was an extortion scheme that had plagued the immigrant community in San Francisco's Chinatown. The perpetrators peppered vulnerable immigrants with fake notices about kidnapped family members in China. Cut off from communication by the Communist Revolution, many of the scheme's victims opted to pay an expensive ransom, while others made the difficult decision to forsake their loved ones to imagined captors. The themes of Wong's work—immigrant displacement, vulnerability, memory, and intergenerational trauma—reveal wounds of the Asian American immigrant experience that feel no less raw today. Wong's piece might be read as a statement about the impossible choices and pain of forgetting that building a new life in this country continually demands.

As guest editor of this issue of *Aperture*, I have found solace and inspiration, throughout my research, in seeing how generations of artists have used the medium of photography to grapple with questions of visibility, belonging, and what it means to be Asian American. Just as there is no single point where Asian American experience converges, photography produced by Asian American image makers encompasses disparate ways of viewing the world—and demands to be approached as such. But to seek connection and coherence among these perspectives is to acknowledge a shared story of immigration to the United States that relates to a long legacy of exclusionary policies and struggles for recognition and citizenship. Being and becoming Asian in America is an unfixed, constantly evolving, and expansive process, and photography plays an essential role in envisioning it.

Since the first Asian immigrants arrived in America in the mid-nineteenth century, social visibility has conferred vulnerability. Our modern-day system of passport controls was based upon nineteenth-century forms of visual policing developed specifically to regulate the movement of Chinese and Japanese bodies, the first national methods of biometric identification to utilize photography. Falling under the gaze of the camera was an experience shared by most Asian immigrants, not primarily as a hobby of self-documentation or leisure but as a bureaucratic fact of racialized surveillance and policing. Under the threat of deportation or detention, many early immigrants opted for self-effacement and erasure as strategies for survival. A daguerreotype from 1850s California that shows a young, working-class Chinese woman cradling a picture of an absent loved one in her hand is a rare exception. The dearth of historical photographs portraying Asian men and women at ease speaks to contested ideas of place, identity, and belonging that continue to shape our collective image of the United States.

The author Ocean Vuong once identified a generational divide in the aspirations of Asian Americans. To paraphrase

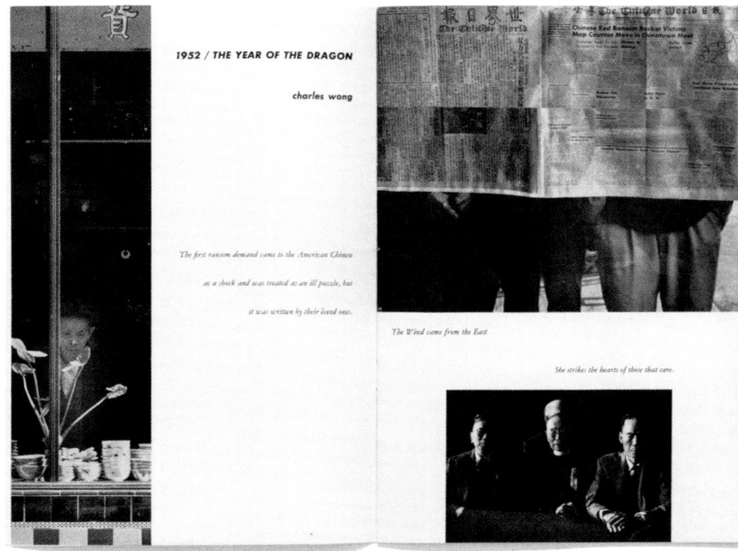

Generations of artists have used photography to grapple with questions of visibility and what it means to be Asian American.

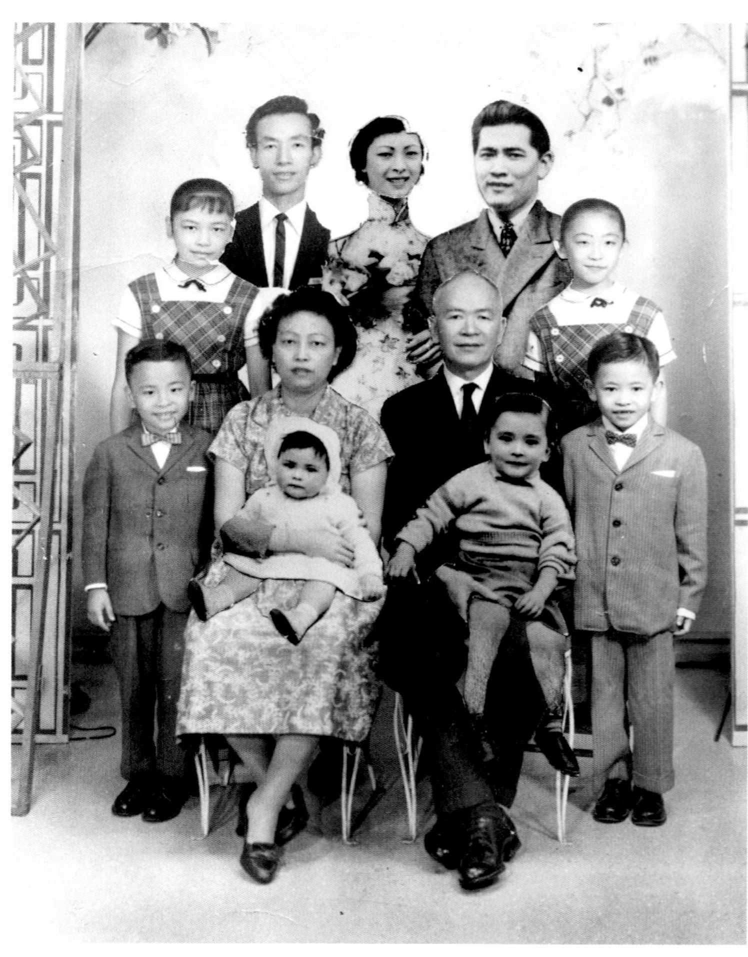

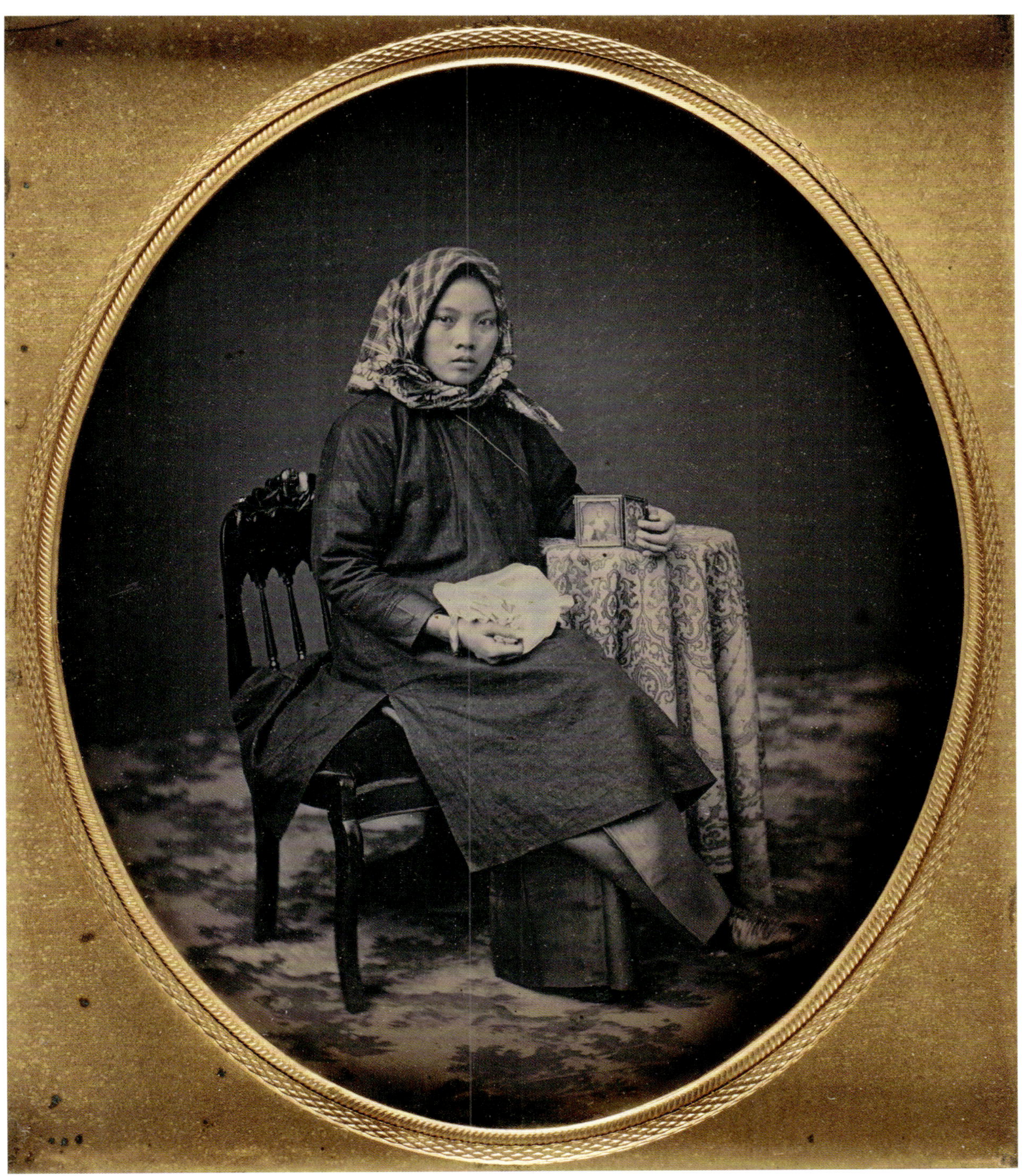

Vuong, first-generation immigrants saw life in America as such a privilege that they were content to put their heads down, work, fade into the background, and live a quiet life—so much so that they expected their children to do the same. But with the second generation, there came a desire to be *seen.* A great paradox for these children of immigrants, many of whom seek agency and self-expression through art, was that they betrayed their parents in order to subversively fulfill their parents' dreams.

For this younger generation of artists and immigrants, the desire for visibility is about more than individual self-fulfillment. It arises from a want to understand a past that continues to act on us and forms part of who we are but remains unspoken and closed off from view. This phantom pain of forgetting creates its own particular sense of loss—so clearly articulated in Wong's piece—that marks where immigrant hopes intersect with intergenerational melancholy. Whether one arrived generations ago or today, being Asian American requires coming to terms with absences, omissions, and silences, as well as with the

complications of human choices that entail various acts of abandonment. It involves negotiating the in-betweenness of here and there, past and future, breaks of language and culture—or, as the creators of the recent film *Everything Everywhere All at Once* imagine it, multiverses that can fracture a sense of self across infinite chains of unrealized possibilities.

This issue of *Aperture* explores the myriad ways in which Asian American image makers have approached questions of visibility and belonging on their own terms. They create works that reveal the full complexity and diversity of stories that make the experience of being Asian in America. They creatively navigate the tension between being seen and unseen as strategies of survival, play, and reclamation, from the pursuit of anonymity or effacement during times of exclusion to self-fashioning and commemoration. And in the spirit of the late photographer and activist Corky Lee, they are working toward what he called "photographic justice" by exploring areas of hope, celebration, and connection alongside doubt, uncertainty, and sorrow across generations. What comes into view in these pages is not a single

This issue provides an opportunity to discover generative ways of seeing that are rooted in connection and empathy.

story or image but a kaleidoscopic refracting of shared patterns and impressions that is connected to the specifics of an evolving Asian American identity and its potential.

How might we acknowledge the invisible wounds of US warfare and imperialism in Asia? Artists have employed diverse approaches to reflect the trauma inscribed on our bodies and psyches, from landscape to portraiture, abstraction, and conceptual practices. Toyo Miyatake's photographs show the mundane highs and lows of Japanese Americans' daily lives while interned during World War II at the Manzanar concentration camp in California. They are testaments to the resilience of a community and the ways in which art perseveres even in the darkest hours. In reenactments of Vietnam War battles, An-My Lê draws on the landscape tradition to investigate how history seeps into the present. Yong Soon Min explores the emotional terrain of displacement in self-portraiture that marks the body as a repository for personal and national histories. And while both Annu Palakunnathu Matthew and Stephanie Syjuco turn to archives for source material, their projects pursue different ends: Matthew's animations collapse time by merging immigrant family photographs from different generations in an act of suturing or repair; Syjuco calls attention to the evidence gathered to quantify, categorize, and understand the Philippines in order to question the unseen power structures still embedded in national archives and museums today.

Family is central to the stories of Asian American lives, but what new visions of our loved ones—what entirely different multiverses, of what could have been and what is possible for the future—might emerge from the push-pull of picture making? In the early 1960s, the Low family in New York City used cut and paste to create an ideal world in which family members

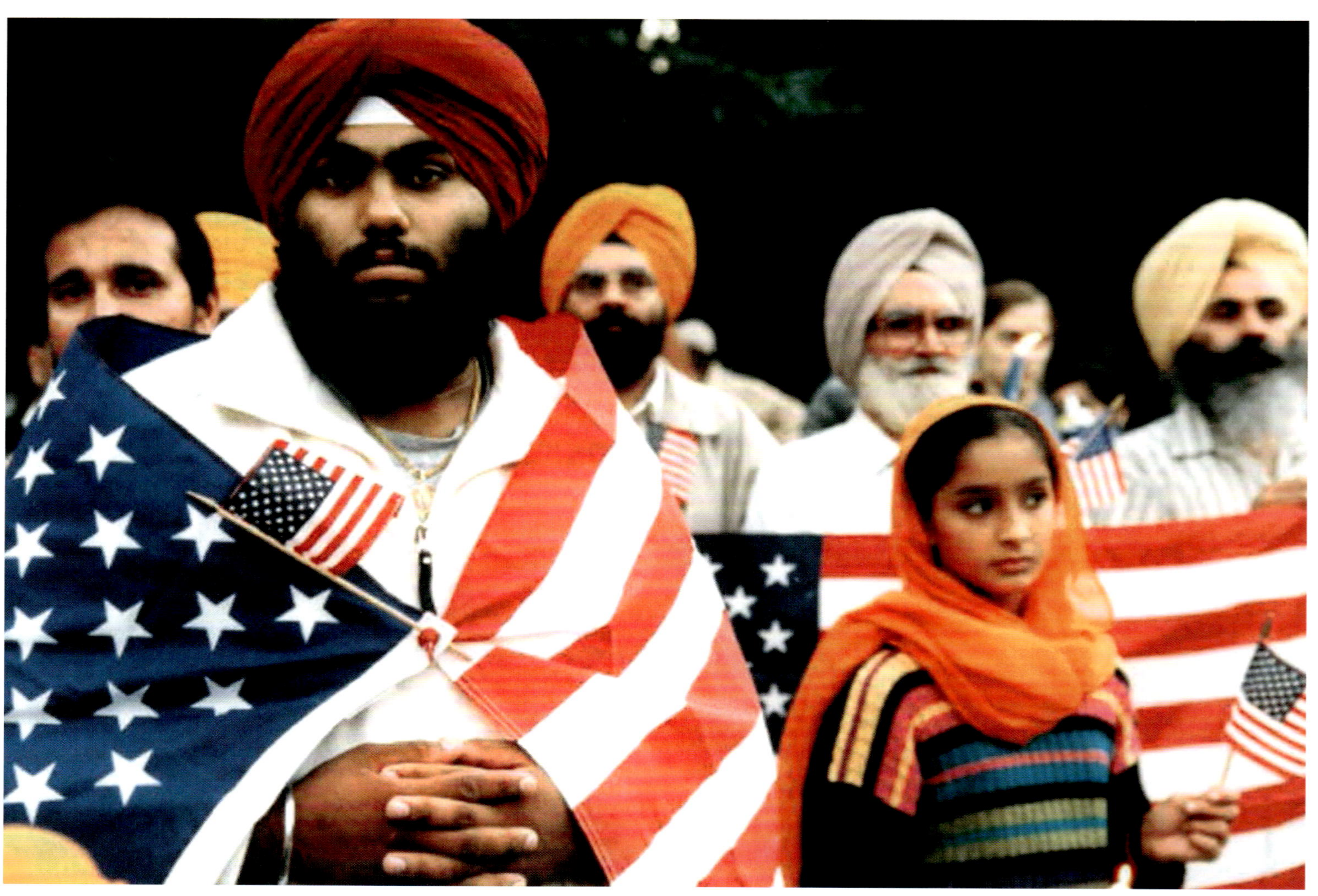

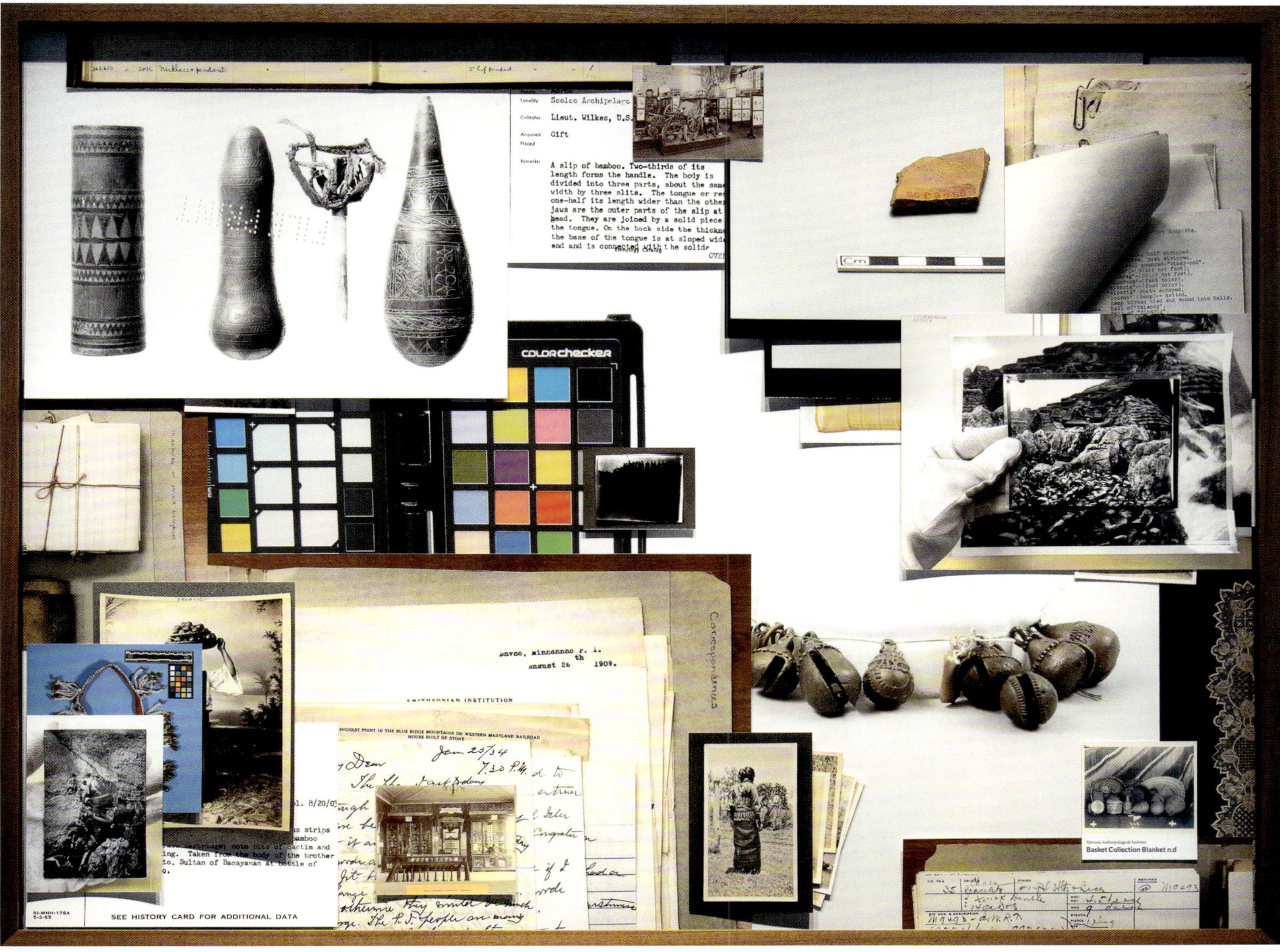

separated by immigration policies are reunited in one image. In the same vein, Leonard Suryajaya's theatrical tableaux and Guanyu Xu's layered domestic spaces are filled with symbols of hope, history, and affection. From the vibrant, dignified portraits taken at May's Photo Studio in the early to mid-twentieth century to Michael Jang's wryly observant photographs of his suburban family in the 1970s and the haunting series *Half Self-Portraits* made collaboratively by Tommy Kha and his mother in the beginning of this century, photography acts as a prism, allowing us to glimpse the dazzling humor, ambitions, desires, and regrets of our expanded families and ourselves.

Reconciling this yearning to be seen—to find meaning, be acknowledged, and, finally, belong—with the habits of opacity is part of the process of being and becoming Asian in America. It has taken me time to realize that there is agency and subjectivity in both positions. That there are emotions that cannot be expressed or articulated but are deeply felt. Photography has the ability to help us navigate what we choose to bring to the surface and what we hold back. It can address losses that are difficult to name by making visible, with attention and respect, the actions and concerns of previous generations. Perhaps it is this fundamental act of care that will aid us in moving from personal experience to greater collective action and solidarity.

It is my hope that this issue provides an opportunity to discover generative ways of seeing that are rooted in connection and empathy. It is through the work of artists that we can change our perceptions of the past and heal generational wounds.

In seeing one another and recognizing the beauty and creativity of these endeavors, we take part in a project of reclaiming agency and humanity.

Charles Wong is now over a hundred years old and still living with his partner, the photographer Irene Poon, in San Francisco. It has been seventy years since his photo-essay was published in *Aperture*. The two don't have cell phones or email, but Wong sent a handwritten note on the occasion of this issue: "This is a brave project, and is heading into the 2024 elections. We are with you."

Stephanie Hueon Tung is the Byrne Family Curator of Photography at the Peabody Essex Museum.

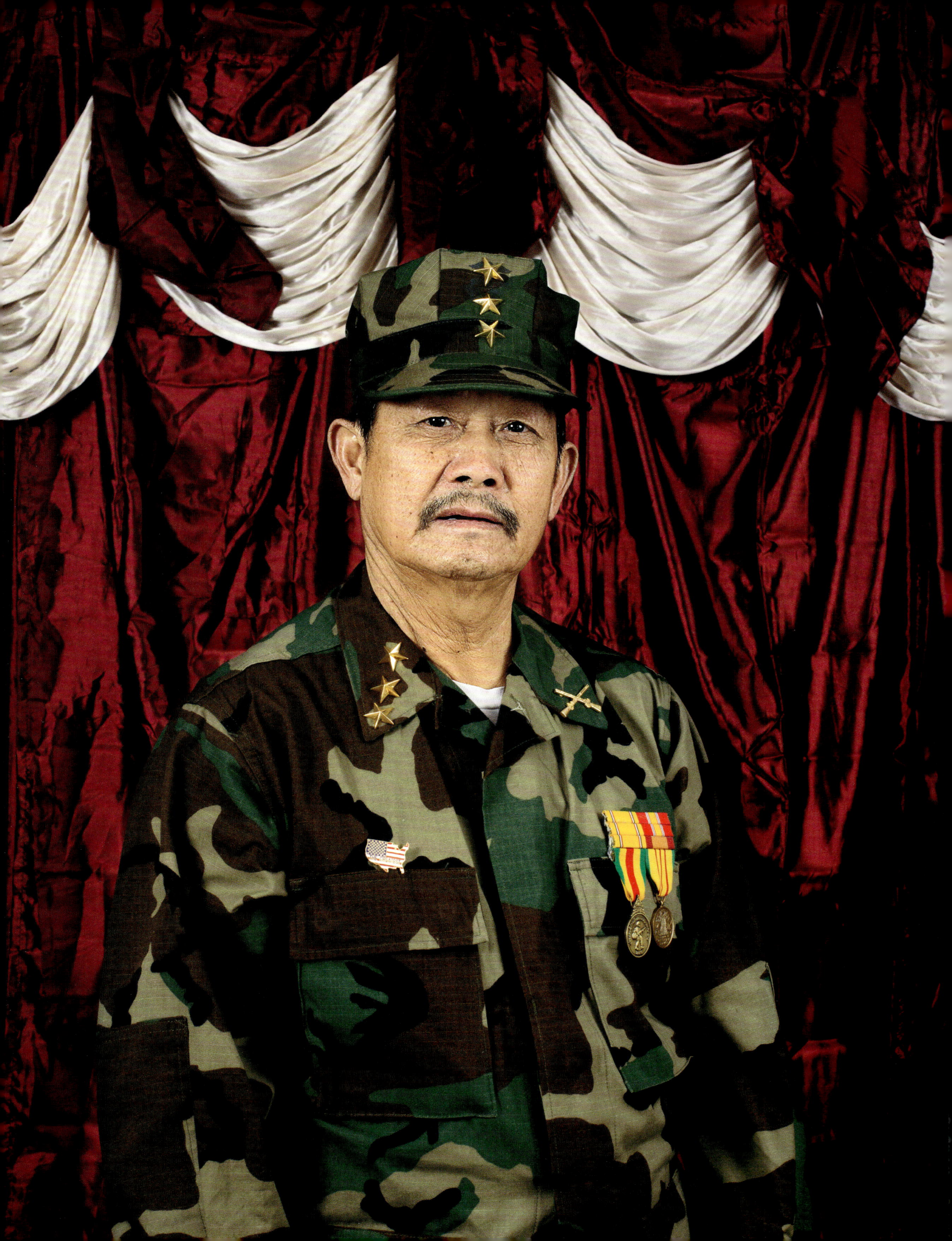

Landscapes & Memories

An-My Lê and Pao Houa Her in Conversation with Ryan Lee Wong

An-My Lê and Pao Houa Her are two photographers addressing fiction and truth in war and its aftermath, and the marks—or lack of them—left by migrant and refugee communities on the American landscape.

Lê's series *Small Wars* (1999–2002) restages scenes from the Vietnam War with reenactors, creating images that, at first, seem to offer journalistic evidence, but on examination open a strange conversation about that war and its memorialization. Her's series *Attention* (2015) shows Hmong veterans in military regalia, and if they look a little showy that might be because the regalia was purchased online or given to each for their service in the Secret War in Laos—a community honoring itself for contributions the US government refuses to recognize.

More recently, Lê's series *Silent General* (2015–ongoing) visits farms in California, pipelines in Texas, yards and churches in Louisiana, and the United States–Mexico border—sites of contested historical and political discourse, especially after the 2016 election, where open skies and sunshine only underscore how hard it is to make a single meaning of them. Her's latest series, *Mt. Shasta* (2021–22), capture traces of Hmong farmers' makeshift marijuana cultivation sites in that harsh and beautiful California landscape—not unlike the mountains of Laos. Both photographers, of different generations, take something we think we know about the United States and ask us to think deeply, to not only expand what's recorded as history but examine the lenses through which we define history.

I am always hoping to be surprised in ways that I think only art can deliver.

Ryan Lee Wong: **You both consider landscapes and histories of warfare, bringing forth what we don't see— the inner workings of the military, migrant labor, the constructions of political imagery. What areas of Asian America, and I invite your specifics within that broad term, do you think remain unseen? Or are seen and misunderstood?**

An-My Lê: Are we speaking about what remains unseen in art, in the news, in academia, in Hollywood?

I am mindful about representation, but at the same time I am weary of consumerism and demographics. I am always hoping to be surprised in ways that I think only art can deliver, because it can defy expectations. There are stories that need to be told, but I do care about how they are told. I am interested in artists, individuals who reach for new expressive forms that are an amalgamation of their background and influences.

These days, there is so much priority placed on the subject alone at the expense of everything else. I am not a topic person, which might have to do with my supercognizance of the tension that exists between art photography and editorial photography. Artists don't feel the need to illustrate an idea or neatly wrap a narrative; they can be messy. I am always looking forward every year to a new crop of Asian American artists, hoping that these emerging voices are as concerned with form as they are with their personal stories and perspectives.

Pao Houa Her: For me, the Hmong American refugee narrative has largely been one of perseverance and adaptability in the United States and seen from the perspective of Hmong men. What is missing are voices of Hmong women and the struggle of what it means to live in America and be a part of the legacy that is America. While perseverance and adaptability are very much part of our Hmong American narrative, I'm interested in the unseen and untold.

RLW: **On one hand, the wars in Southeast Asia are the most "seen" in the US imagination—they defined the baby boomer generation and continue to define the nation's image of itself in the world. On the other hand, as both of your work shows, those histories and the people they continue to impact are profoundly "unseen." What do you feel are the states of these unseen stories today?**

AML: Well, South Vietnamese flags were seen flying among the mob attacking the Capitol on January 6, 2021. I recognize that history matters, and as artists, we are after things that we know are not going to build consensus. Art engenders different types of responses, some of which can be dividing. It is important to think historically, and official narratives need to be revisited, but we need to tread lightly. Inclusivity can also lead to purgation. I believe in facts—it is dismaying to see that there is a very fine line between political rhetoric and mythmaking. History can easily become a moralizing and galvanizing tool.

PHH: Recently, on a trip to Laos, my father talked, for the first time, about his involvement in the American war. I knew that he fought with the Americans but that was the extent of my knowledge. He revealed that he had a really bad childhood, that his stepfather beat him and left him hungry, and that the only way he could

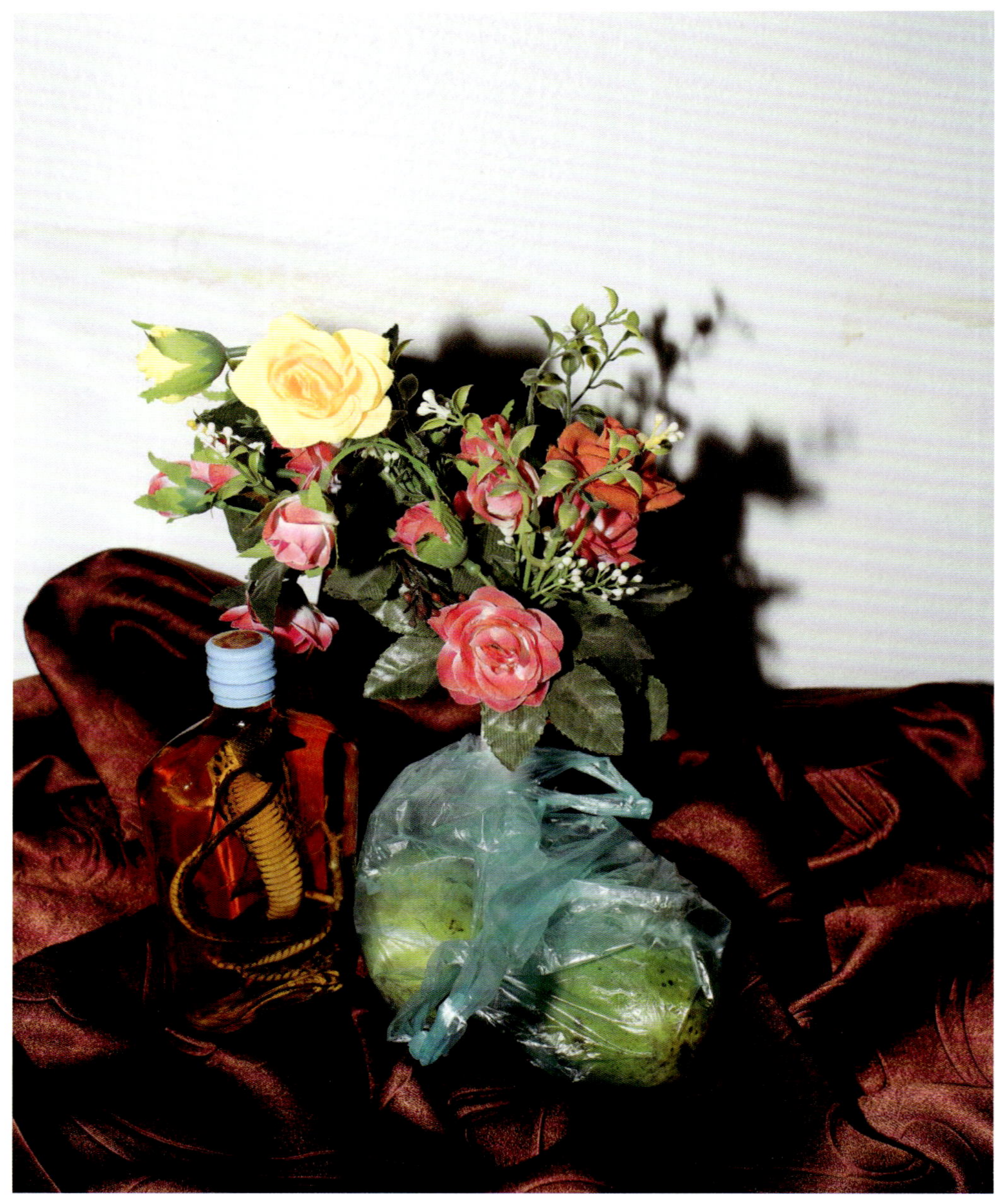

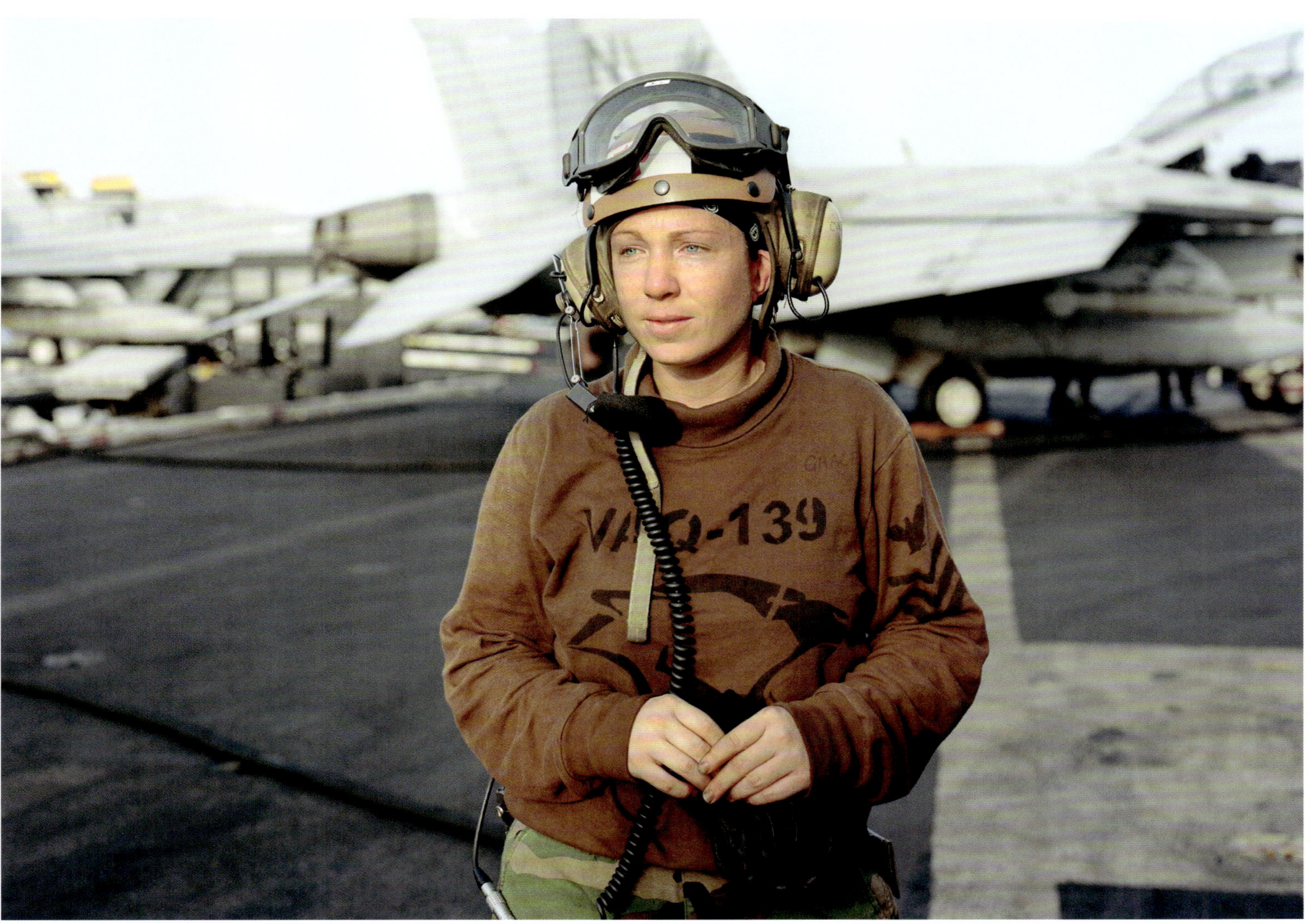

survive was to help the Americans. For a lot of the Hmong boys and teens fighting, this was the sentiment. All of my life, I've been told and led to believe that the reason why I am able to live a life in America is because of the American government. But what about the *whys* and *hows*?

RLW: Both of you have recently been photographing American landscapes, in particular the vastness of the West and South, in Pao's *Mt. Shasta* series and An-My's *Silent General*. For me, as a Californian, it's impossible not to think of photographers I was brought up with, such as Carleton Watkins and Timothy O'Sullivan and Ansel Adams, whose images shape not just the photographic discourse but the popular imagination of the American landscape. How do you find yourself contending with, or in conversation with, those photographic histories?

PHH: As a photographer, I feel it is important to know and to study the photographers who've come before me. So, when looking at images of California and the West, I was looking at Watkins, Adams, O'Sullivan, and others. The reason for this was to understand the kind of photographs that were being made and why they were being made. In the spirit of these photographers and the photographs, I'm also interested in utilizing these tools to bring complexity to my *Mt. Shasta* project. It's a mix of tribute, wanting to do something different, and rebellion against that tradition. I'm leaning on them as photographers who've made pictures, and I'm also leaning on the images made by these men to inform my images.

AML: When you fall in love with a medium, you want to look at everything, study everything. The photographic landscape tradition is important to me, but tradition does not necessarily equal influence and category does not equal tradition. I am equally interested in photography's construction along ideological lines as along aesthetic lines. I am not preoccupied by photography's loaded relationship to truth; a construction is a construction.

Watkins and O'Sullivan are worthy of our attention because they were innovative in the way they contended with and described the Western landscape. But they were working on governmental commissions. The photographic surveys they contributed to eventually helped facilitate land claims and displacements of Indigenous people. It is problematic to appreciate their works without being cognizant of the fact that they were commissioned by ideology, but I wonder how much they really delivered. Many have accused photography of being a tool for colonialism and imperialism, but I think guns and money were much more effective.

RLW: When we're talking about Watkins and Adams, I sense both historically and aesthetically that their social locations place them in a position of power within those landscapes and US history. How do your own social locations—as women, as migrants and refugees, as Asian Americans—inform how you move through those landscapes, what you look for, and what you see?

AML: Photography speaks in a language of scale and contested abstractions. You read the landscape for what it is, what it was, and what it might be. I think that this coming together of different narrative layers creates fault lines that lead to a conversation about site and dweller, about possibilities.

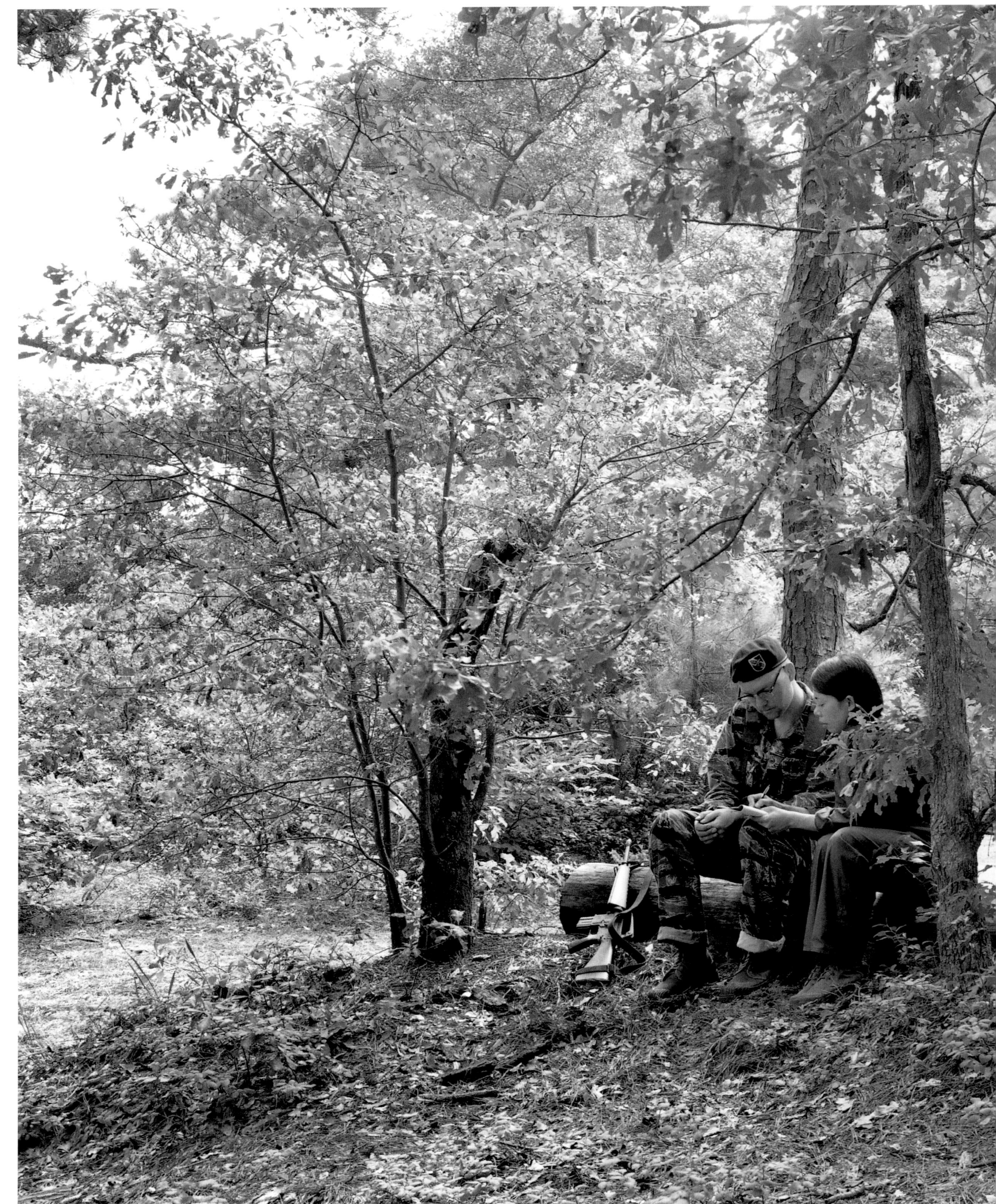

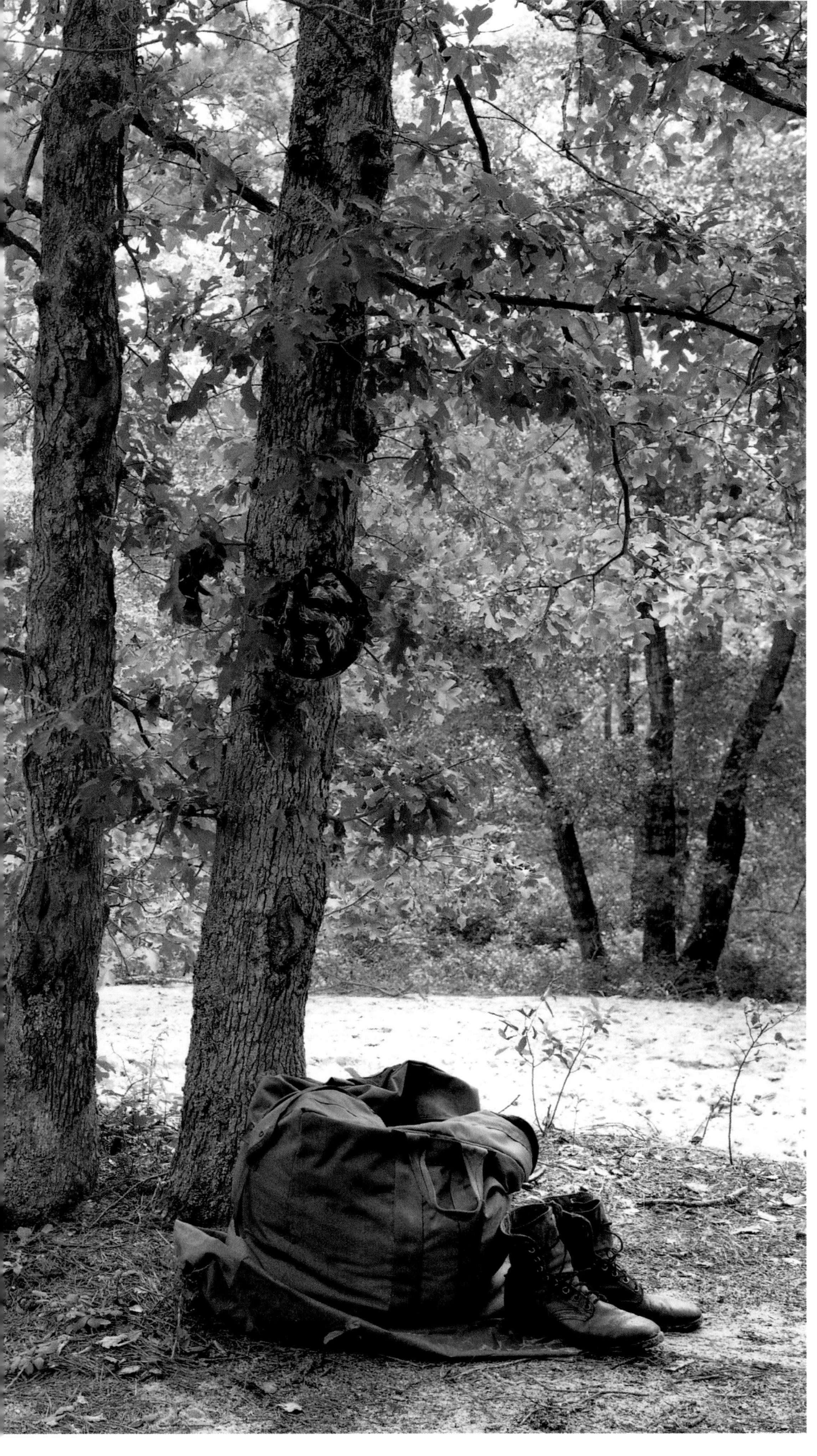

I am mindful that the people I photograph know way more about the place where they live than I do. I try not to apply a formula when I photograph. It is unfair to amplify my process beyond the minutiae of what I do. I don't walk around with ideas about control in my head. I don't think about an agenda to impose. For me, being an artist means being solitary, being in the minority. I think my work is an exploration of the powerlessness I feel.

PHH: Understanding the landscape and who's been there before me and my people becomes really important in trying to build a visual language of the space. But also, how is this land different from or the same as the land my people come from? How have my people made this place home? How has community been built here? I'm thinking about all those things when I'm in these landscapes and making images of them.

RLW: **Pao, looking at your *Mt. Shasta* photographs, it takes a second to realize that we're seeing not just a landscape but evidence of the Hmong farmers who make their living there. They're often slight, but we see tubing lines, netting, greenhouse hoops. Trying to describe them immediately becomes political, given the migrant labor these items symbolize: Are they eyesores or beautiful adaptations, intrusions or additions? How did you frame these images? What about these objects spoke to you?**

PHH: So many of the conversations around Mt. Shasta have been environmental, i.e., lack of water, overuse of pesticides, excessive use of plastic. But the land is so barren that in order to use it, soil, water, and other materials need to be brought in. In the history of Hmong people, cultivation of land is nothing new. The tubing lines, netting, greenhouses, and swimming pools are all of the things you mentioned: beautiful adaptations, intrusions, and additions. They are often not the center of the image; you are meant to search for them, to see them on a second or third pass.

RLW: **I read in an interview that you are always carrying a camera, always ready to capture snapshots of the Hmong communities in the Minnesota Twin Cities or in Laos. This feels appropriate, because you photograph communities in flux through migration and modernity. At what moment do you know when to pull out the camera? And can you talk about approaching and building**

Understanding the landscape and who's been there before me becomes important in trying to build a visual language.

trust with the communities you photograph?

PHH: It's always instinctual. There are periods where I will not take out my camera at all. Trust is really important in my work and especially in my portrait work. Returning to the same place over and over again is, for me, building trust. I make images of the same people or things or landscapes again and again.

I have gone to Laos a lot in the last ten years. When I was there the first time, I felt out of place. It wasn't my community. The people were suspicious of me, and I was suspicious of them. Ten years later, after multiple trips back to the same town and being with the same people, finally, this year, I've felt like we've built trust with each other.

RLW: **An-My, our political moment is marked by an erosion of shared truths, from the United States' racial history to the climate, which makes a conversation nearly impossible. Your ongoing *Silent General* series wades into fraught spaces of Civil War monuments and the United States–Mexico border. How might photography**

build a shared understanding when more often it's being abused in order to destroy it?

AML: In my experience, art is polarizing. It's not about consensus. The better the art, the more polarizing it is. I am not sure if my work is contributing much to the stockpile of shared truths. Photographers know that truth is elusive. My work is often understood in different, even contradicting, ways by different people, and that's okay. I am not so interested in explicating. Like many artists, I am drawn to what is fraught. I like the open questions; I love finding the fault lines that allow for ambiguities. I try to make the most of the fact that photography has a special relationship with truth in the popular imagination, and I love to operate within that framework. Artists are also not often fact-checked. Sadly, it is more and more common to see politicians taking the liberties I do, not just trafficking in the gray zone but literally making things up.

RLW: **I'm curious about your process with a large-format Deardorff camera. For an image of a protest in New York**

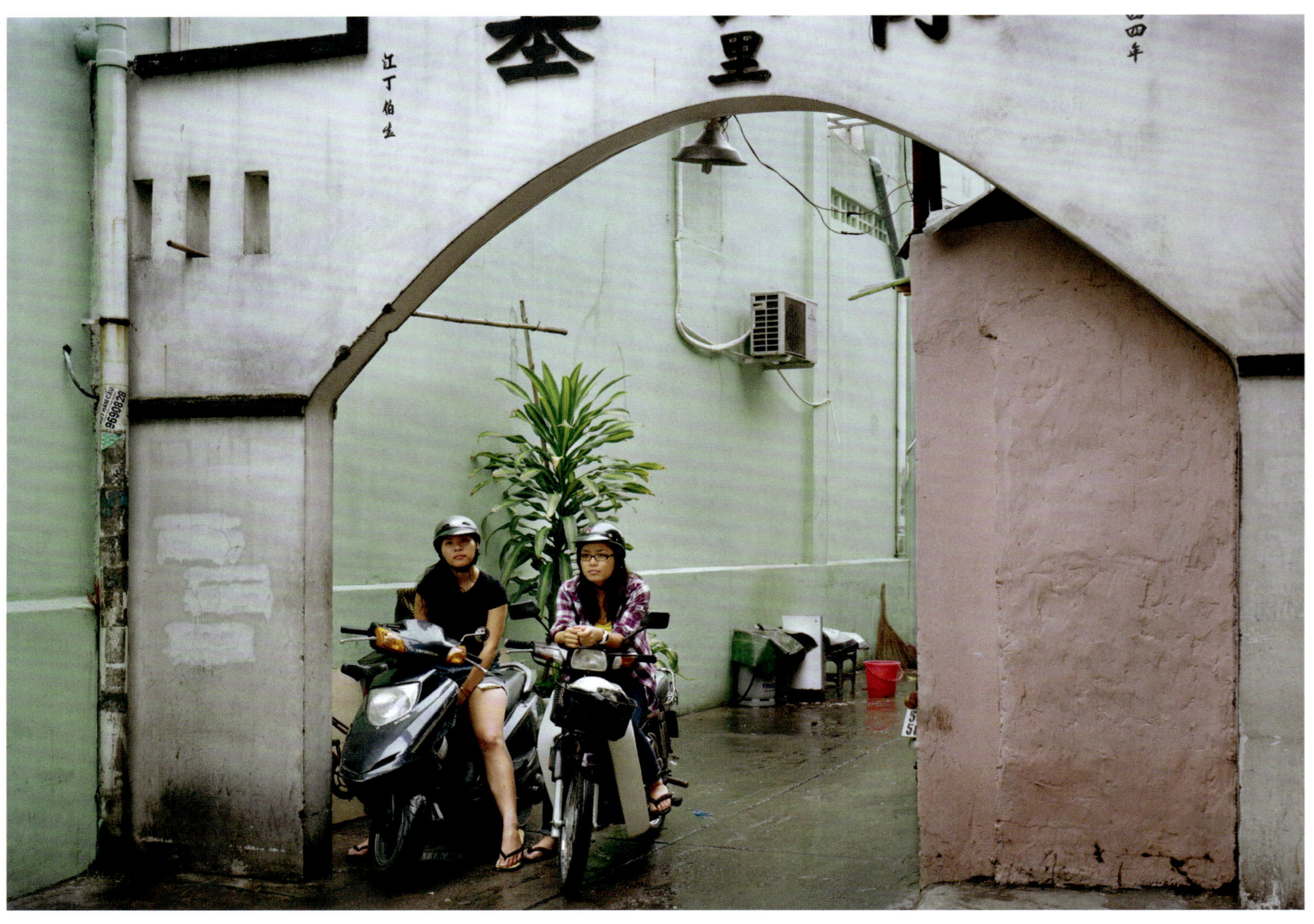

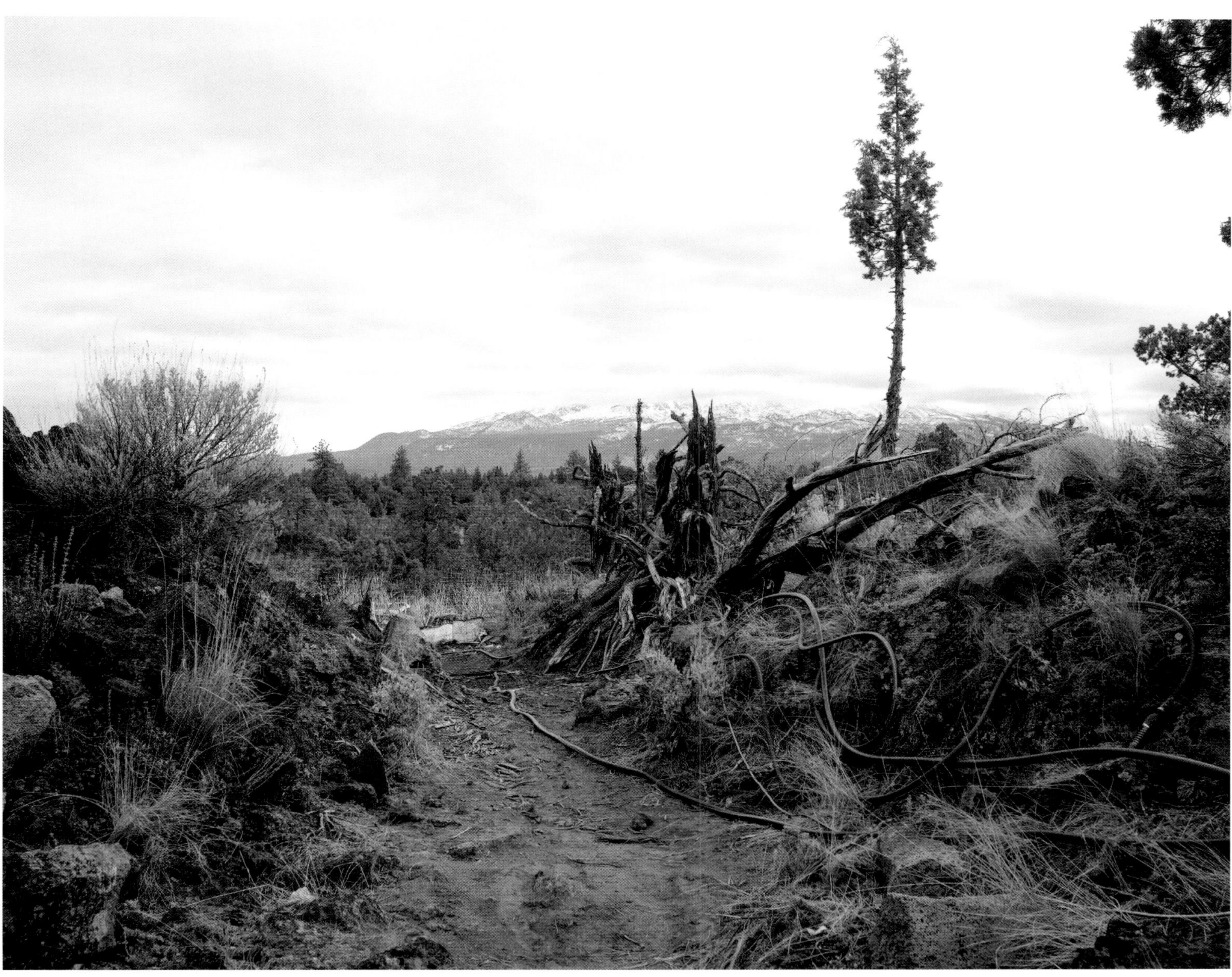

against gun violence, you set up a tripod, and slid in a 5-by-7-inch negative, when there were probably a hundred images being taken of the same moment with phones smaller than that negative. It's an aesthetic choice with political and even ethical resonances. What's important about capturing the level of detail you do, about the slowness of the process? How has technology changed your understanding of your camera compared to, say, five or ten years ago?

AML: The challenge is to find something to photograph, something that I don't understand or have not seen before. The event is, in fact, a pretext, because it draws groups of people out, it carries a particular tone, it exudes tension, anger. I hope to find someone, something specific that my film and camera can describe in a surprising way. I have never been interested in generalizations.

How did I arrive at this process? Which came first, the chicken or the egg? Is that the right expression? The camera is slow and cumbersome. I have embraced it as my tool because I love the way the large negative describes the world, and the way it provides an essential physicality to my prints. In return, I have had to contend with its limitations. They have forced me to be more resourceful, to search for oblique ways to look at an event that is fast-paced and predisposed to being photographed with a handheld camera. I am interested in new technology. I am always looking to lighten up my load and simplify my process. The large-format negative I use may not provide the sharpness that the largest digital file can, but it describes space, the air between things, in a way that only film can. I am not 100 percent analog. I have my negatives drum scanned and printed as ink-jets.

I would like to think that I have integrity as a person, as an artist, but ethics play no role in the way I approach my work. I am an art photographer, not a role model. I am not so invested in photography as truth.

Ryan Lee Wong is the author of the novel *Which Side Are You On* (2022).

Gina Osterloh
Pressing Against Looking

Phoebe Chen

In Gina Osterloh's photographs, there are subjects but no faces. Bodies are pitched at sly angles or obscured by sundry materials, boxed into sparse rooms with impossible vanishing points. These abstract scenes and their solitary figures are usually staged more as tableaux than conventional portraiture, but even to wonder at which point the former arrangement becomes the latter is to ask: Where, in this image, does the subject end and the world begin?

If visual abstraction is about flirting with the limits of recognition, testing our ability to name what we see, in Osterloh's work it becomes a way of questioning how we parse identity at such thresholds of perception. Her interest in what she has called "the flickering between legibility and illegibility" is informed by her experience as a mixed-race Filipinx American raised in Ohio, but her images rarely contain overt markers of identity. Only those in the series *Somewhere Tropical* (2005–6), one of which is on the cover of this issue, exhibit any cultural specificity: figures clad in denim and camouflage assert the textiles of Americana against a saccharine sunset in the frond-filled tropics.

Made during graduate school at the University of California, Irvine, Osterloh's early images from *Somewhere Tropical* introduce her fascination with camouflage as a way of testing boundaries—of an unsteady self, of a subject's racial legibility. She's drawn to the edges of physical materials, where one texture guards its unity against another; she has been animated by a "desire to intimately press and touch photographic space itself," she told me recently. Perhaps it's unsurprising that she first came to art making through performance and installation, modes to which she occasionally returns.

Paper has long been Osterloh's material of choice: in the piece *Rash Room* (2008), it is used as an epidermal extension, a "membrane, a kind of second skin," the artist says. It becomes a textural surface for mark making, too, pushed to abstraction in her many drawing series or entwined with performance in installation projects including *Group Dynamics and Improper Light* (2012). Even as Osterloh cycles through more tactile modes of practice—recently, steel sculptures—what persists is her use of photography as a tool for staging visual contradictions, a strategy for playing with the perceptual mysteries of depth and flatness.

In *Holding Zero* (2020), for instance, a gridded backdrop invokes constraint while its freehand lines tease at sketchy disorder. Centered in these pictures is another paradox: Osterloh's figure is anonymized and doubled, one mummified in black tape and reinserted in the frame as a printed mount while the other hides behind its monstrous duplicate, an absence that becomes a kind of shield. Here, Osterloh wanted her entire body facing the camera, "cloaked in refusal but also wrapped in something that is protecting it, preserving it," she explains.

This, she reminds me, is what photography does: it flattens, captures, regulates—but also protects, preserves. What riper medium is there for exploring such perceptual borderlands, when the very act of framing is also a kind of touch, a means of pushing subjects and forms into one another and seeing what they can withstand? The photographs in *Pressing Against Looking* (2019) are perhaps the keenest expression of this approach: Osterloh's figure, sitting fully frontal, bars her vision with a long pole in each hand, two stark vectors slicing up the frame. Eyes pressed against their blunt heft, she thwarts her own vision along with the viewer's, denying us the intimacy of seeing *her* seeing. The camera and its frame might press her into a structure of visibility, but she, too, presses, against its gaze and our insistence on making her legible.

Press and Ease #2, 2017

Phoebe Chen is a writer based in New York.

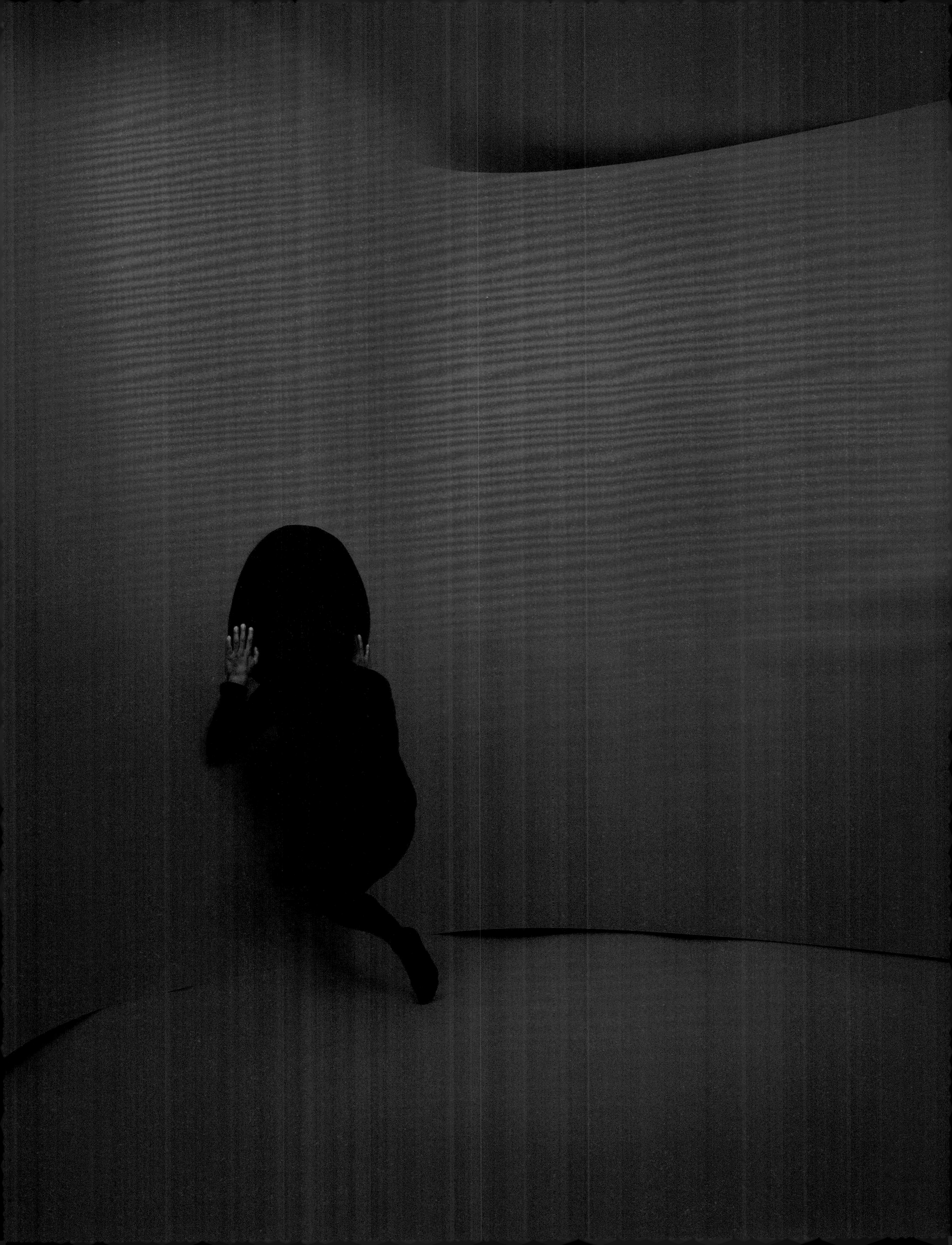

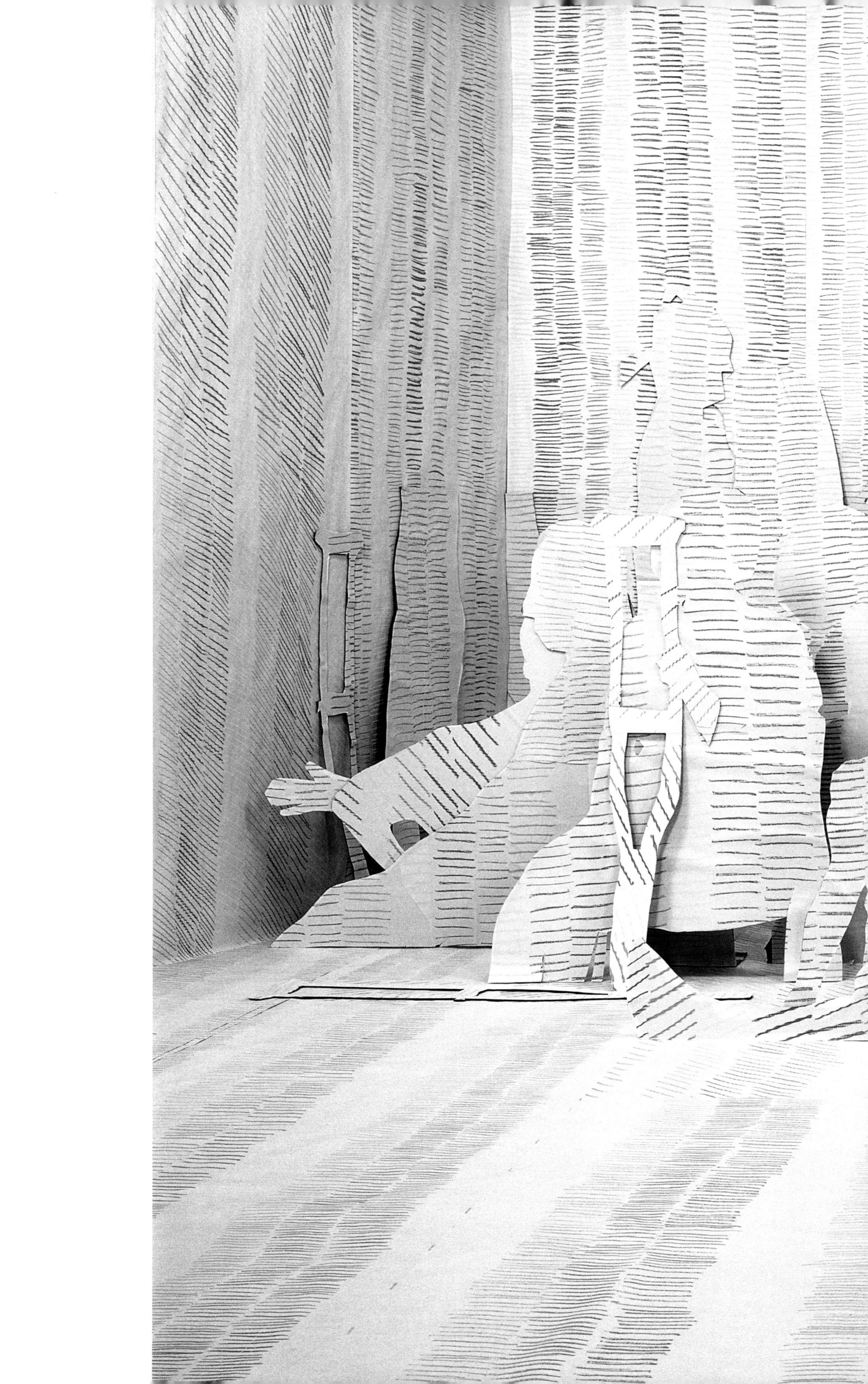

Group Dynamic, 2012

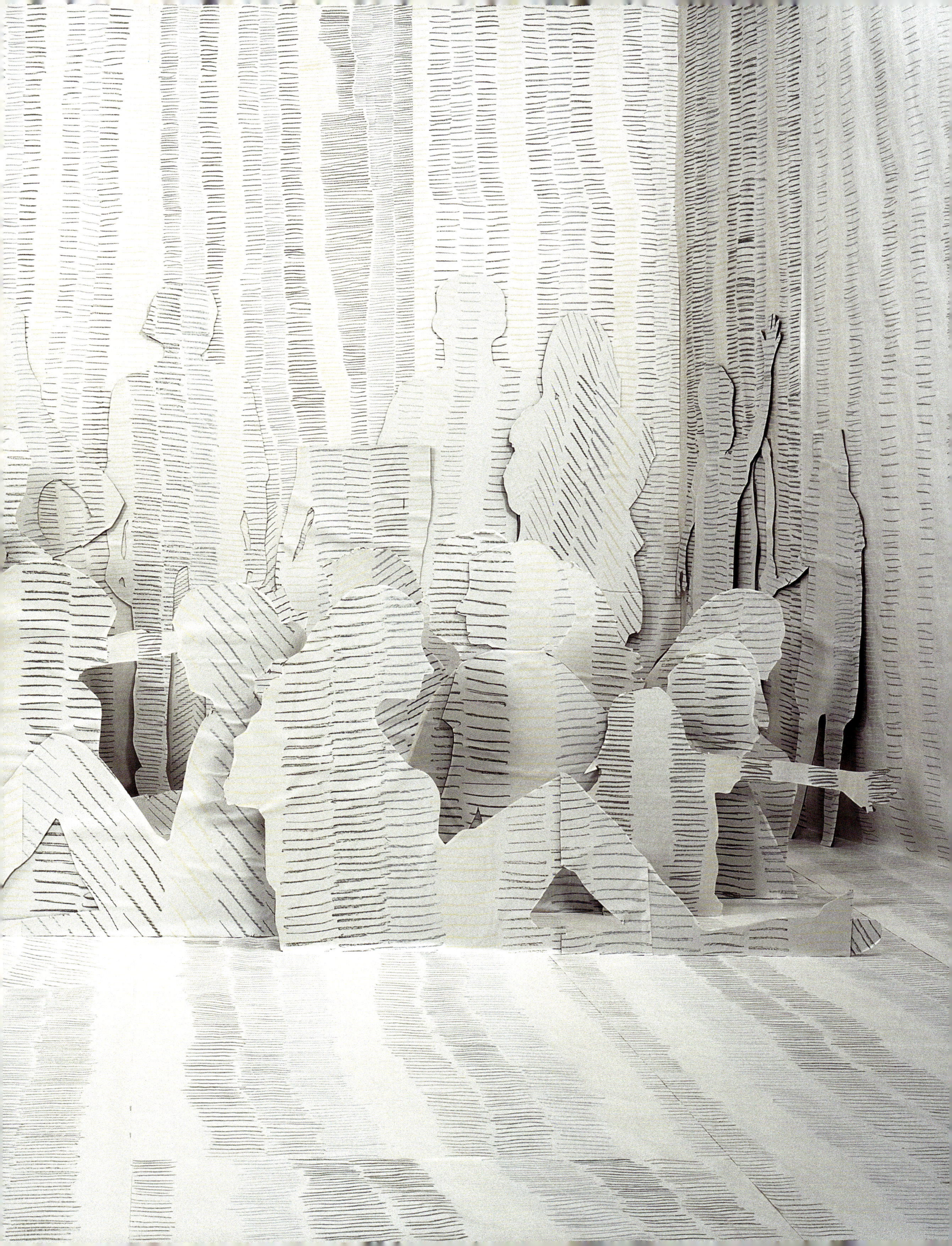

Blind Rash, 2008

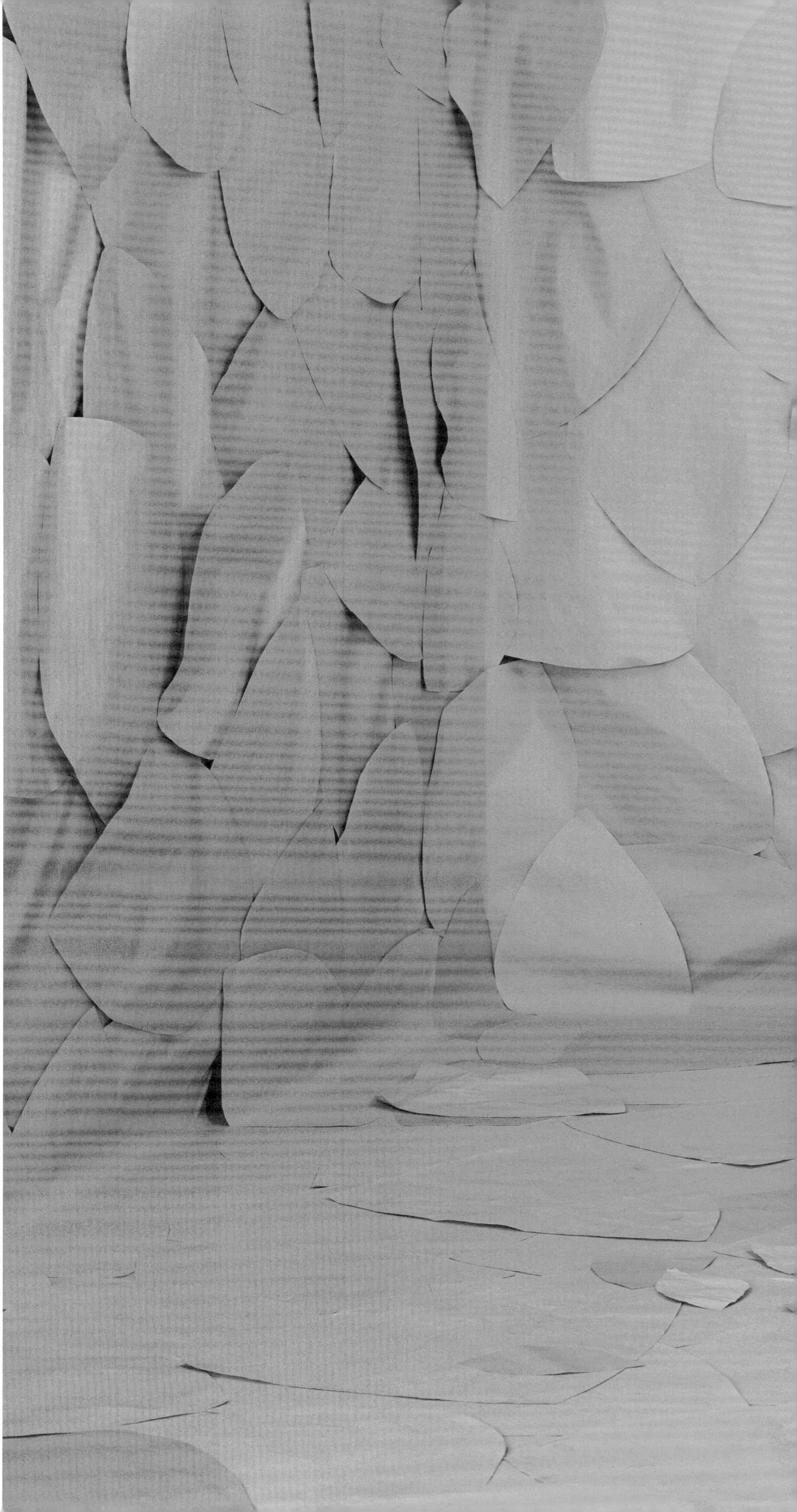

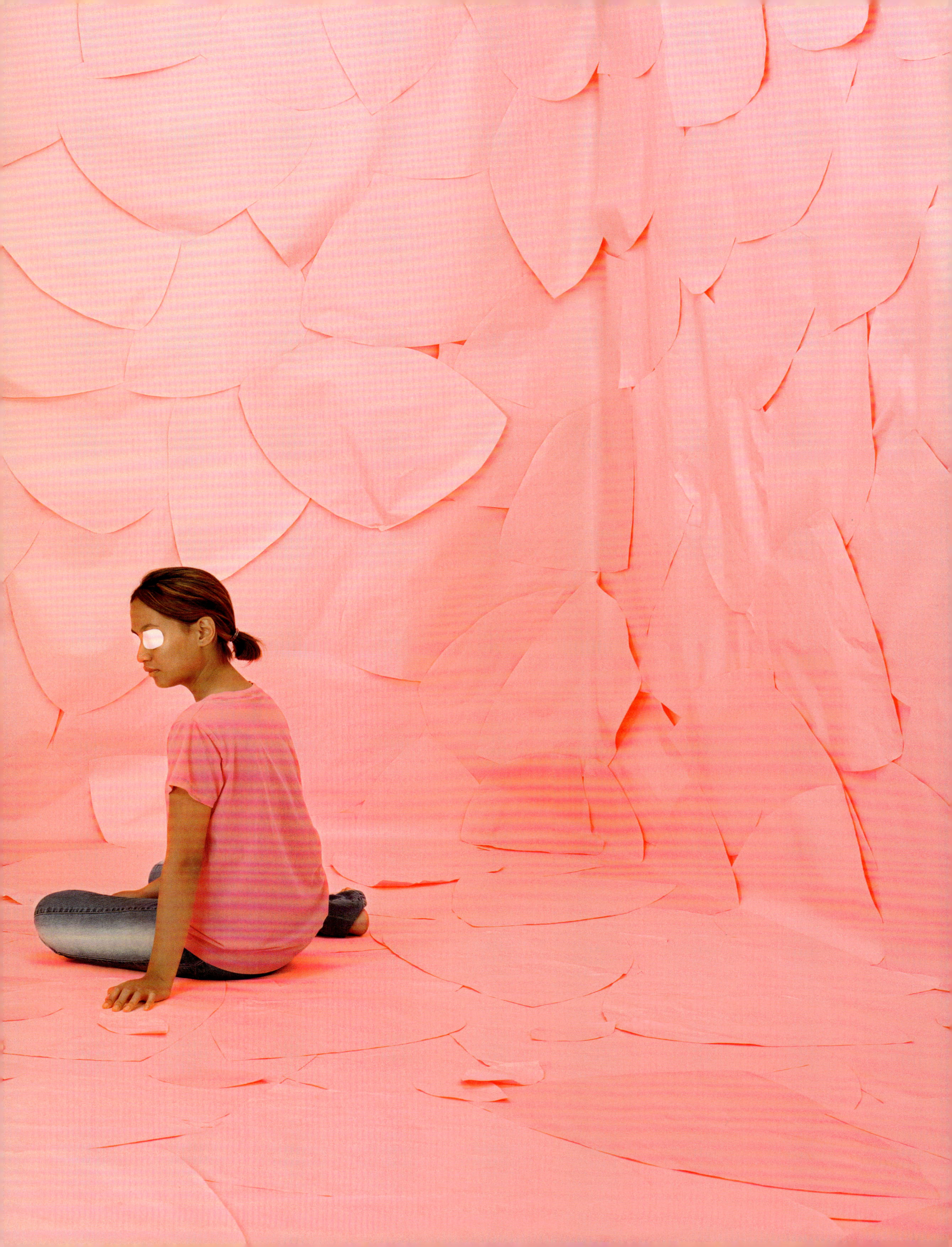

Pressing Against Looking, Fixed, 2019
All photographs courtesy the artist and Higher Pictures Generation, New York

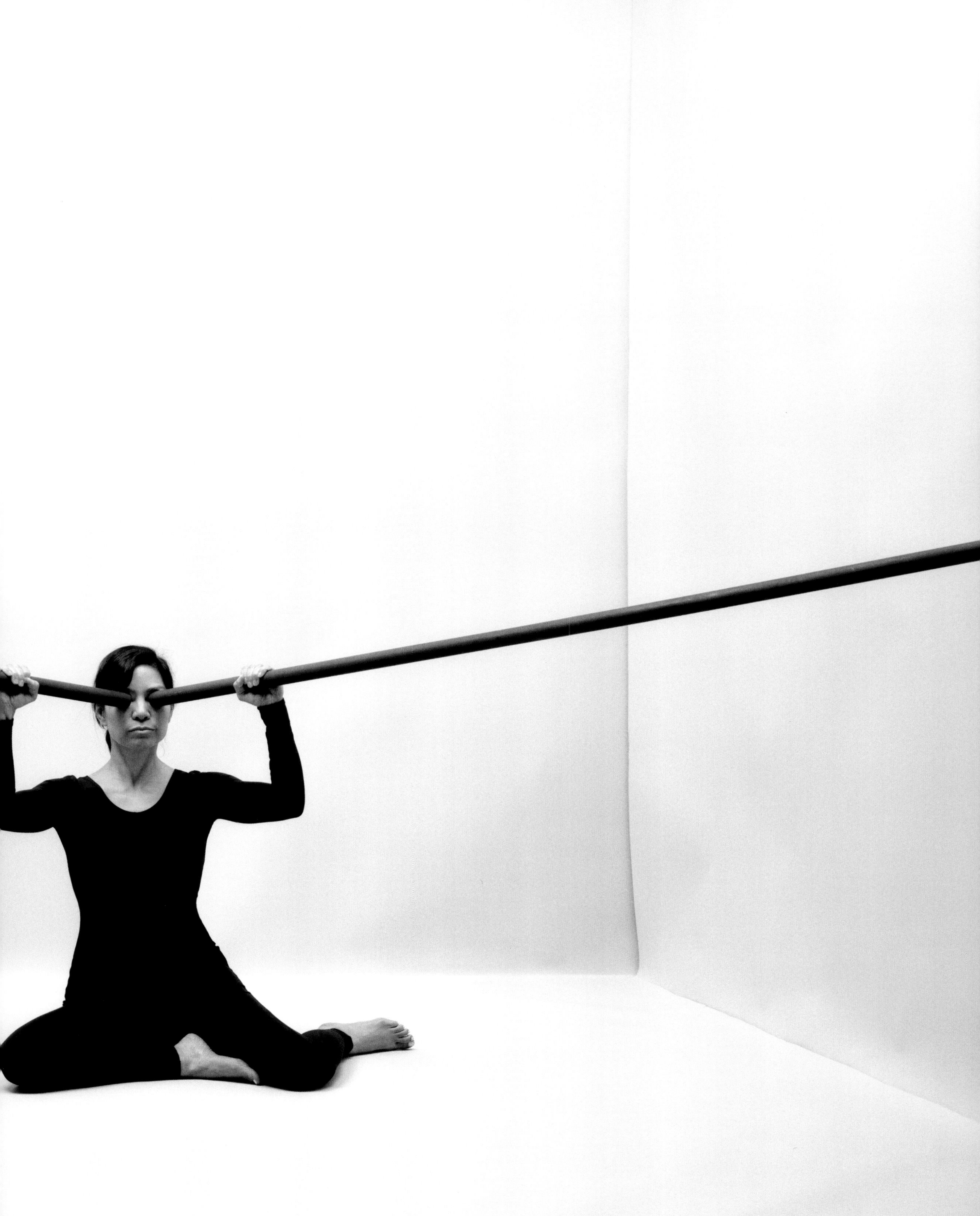

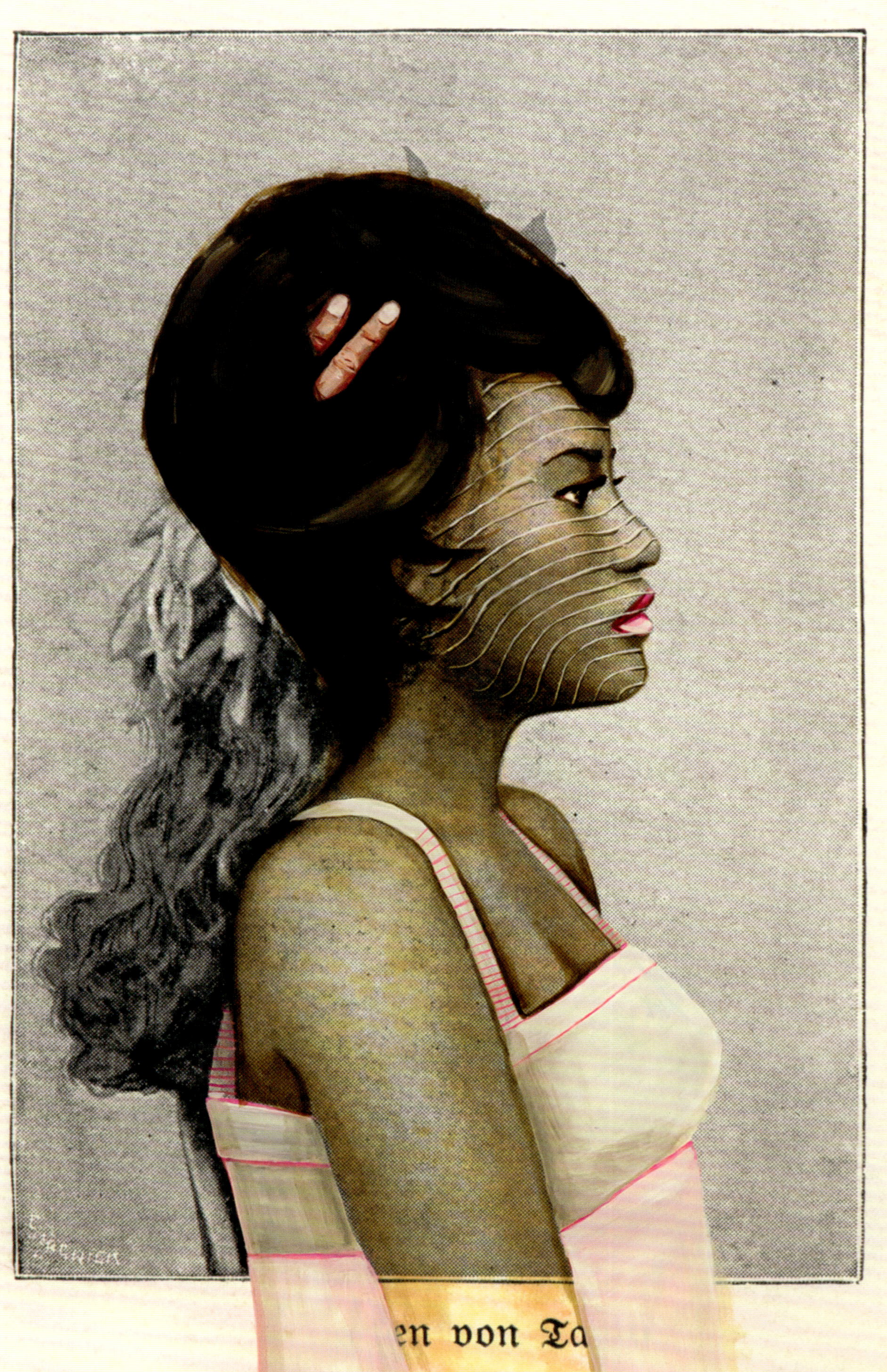

The Living Archive

For many artists, collections contain the future of Asian American representation.
Bakirathi Mani

Photographic archives are repositories of possibility. For myself, they are a store of images that appear to narrate, in ways unmatched by any other historical record, the trajectories of my own family's migration from Kerala to Bombay to Tokyo, and later my immigration from Japan to the United States. For immigrants of East, Southeast, and South Asian descent in the United States, archives are where we turn to see ourselves reflected and preserved in the historical record. But what we often find in public archives are images that render us as strangers, or as spectacles on display. We see objects to be gawked at, our dark faces obscured in portraits where immigrants are identified by turbans, topis, braids, and kimonos.

By contrast, the family photo-album operates as a kind of domestic archive, an accumulation of pictures that intimately documents immigrant life outside of the public eye. At the same time, family photographs can fail to mirror our experience of belonging, within the family as well as in the nation. For Asian American viewers, encountering familial and national photography archives can secure a sense of historical origin and identity but also its inverse—a feeling of alienation and precarity, an inability to recognize ourselves within these carefully preserved images.

In the twenty-first century, how do we perceive Asian Americans in the photographic archive?

In the series *An Indian from India* (2001–7), Annu Palakunnathu Matthew, an artist born in England, raised in Britain and India, and currently based in Rhode Island, pairs late nineteenth- and early twentieth-century portrait images of Indigenous people taken by white settler photographers, such as Edward S. Curtis, with her own self-portraits, which mirror the poses, textiles, and jewelry worn by the Indigenous sitters. Each diptych duplicates the sepia tones and torn edges of the historical prints; they also reproduce the aesthetic form along with the anthropological focus found in Curtis's work *The North American Indian*. Where Curtis identifies his subjects not by name but by tribe, such as "Navajo woman," Matthew also identifies herself as an ethnographic type, as "Malayalee woman."

Matthew's diptychs initially appear to redouble the racial fantasies that shape the earlier prints: yet looking closely at her self-portraits, we notice how her posture, her glance, and her wry smile puncture both the ethnographic pictures as well as our own expectations of what it means to see "Indians." For Matthew, these portraits activate another archive of images: nineteenth-century

The family album, in these artists' hands, becomes an archive of diaspora: a repository of pictures that runs backward and forward in time and in space.

British colonial portraits of men and women on the subcontinent, who were also identified as "natives." If *An Indian from India* initially appears to tell a story about Matthew's immigration as a young adult from India to the United States—how she became "native" to this land—observing the diptychs from left to right and back again opens out a different story of representation, a story about how colonial depictions of racialized people, from Asia and the Americas, persist to this day.

The legacy of ethnographic photography crosses history and nations, as Rajkamal Kahlon, a Berlin-based artist, shows us. Born and raised in Northern California, Kahlon encounters photographs of Black, Indigenous, and Asian subjects in German photographic archives. In the series *Do You Know Our Names?* (2017–ongoing), she reproduces and paints over images and text from *Die Völker der Erde* (People of the Earth), a 1902 German anthropological treatise compiled by Kurt Lampert. Kahlon's painting practice retraces the popularity of hand-colored photography in the early twentieth century, but in this series, she produces a radically different vision of selfhood. Through her intimate engagement with the women and men featured in these prints—many of whom were originally photographed as representations of Germany's imperial ambitions in Asia, Africa, and the Pacific—Kahlon uses brushwork to adorn their bodies, reclaiming their humanity and, for Asian Americans who catch glimpses of ourselves in these photographs, our own.

Yet Kahlon's intervention into this archive is not simply recuperative. Her identification with these unnamed photographic subjects, her depiction via painting of the violence of colonial conquest onto images that are themselves material evidence of empire, provokes us, the artist states, to consider relations of "restitution, reparation, and 'repair'" toward Black and Indigenous people in our present day.

Far removed from national archives, family albums offer a private, intimate documentation of immigrant life. But the family

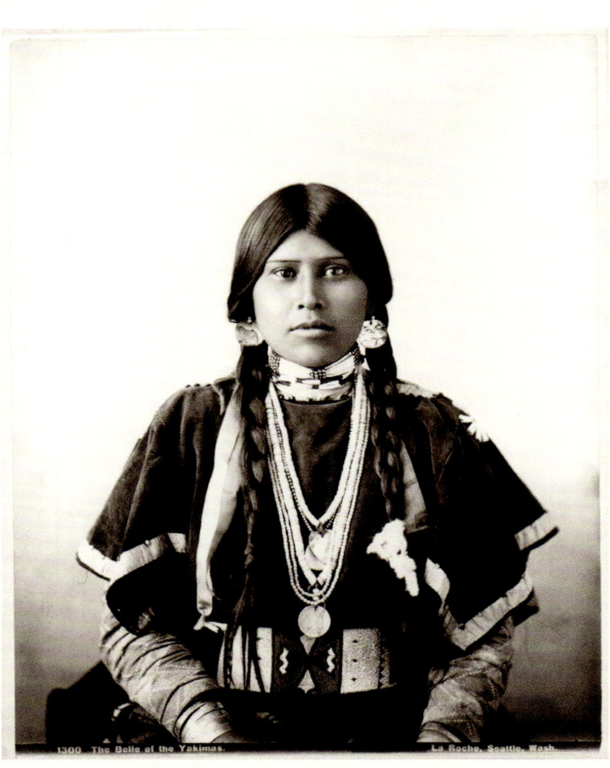

THE BELLE OF THE YAKIMAS

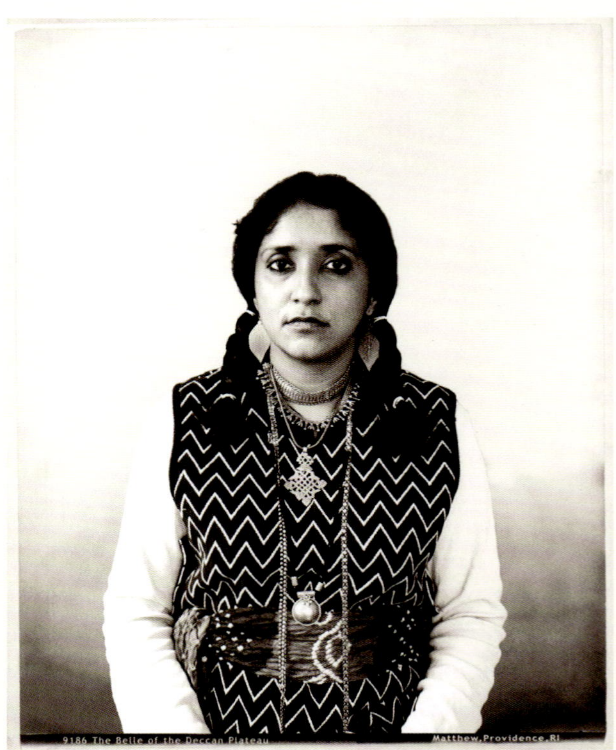

THE BELLE OF THE DECCAN PLATEAU

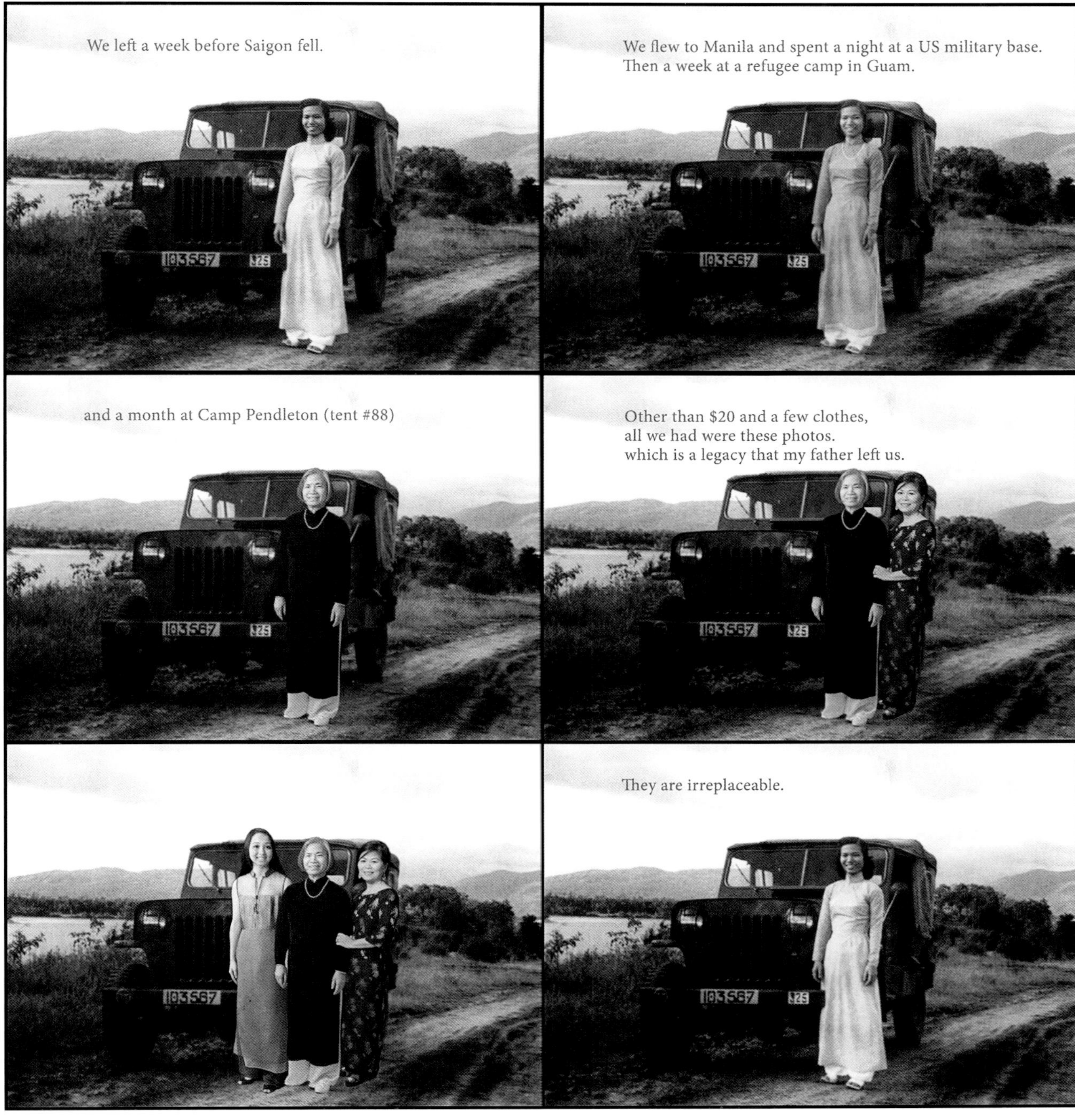

Annu Palakunnathu Matthew, *To Majority Minority, Thuan, Vietnam*, 2013–16. Stills from photo animation, 1 minute, 26 seconds
Courtesy the artist and sepiaEYE, New York

photograph is also an archival object, one that affirms and at times destabilizes our understanding of who we are and where we come from. Matthew, in her digital portrait animation series *To Majority Minority* (2013–16), begins with a single archival print of an immigrant family and photographs its subject decades later, sometimes in the presence of their children and grandchildren. The viewer encounters what looks like a still photograph and experiences, instead, the mobility of the image. Across brief animations that compress decades, we watch between portraits the transition of youthful beauty to the graceful embrace of old age, with accompanying texts that narrate the geographic trajectories of Asian migration, from origins as diverse as Vietnam and the Philippines to the United States. At first glance, *To Majority Minority* visualizes Asian American assimilation. But if we stay with the animations longer, what we begin to see are objects that represent US wars in Asia: a military jeep in Vietnam, identification photographs and placards for Hmong refugees who fought in the secret war in Laos. The quiet, insistent presence of these objects into the final frames of Matthew's animated photographs reminds us of the histories of war and empire that continue to shape Asian American lives.

Sa'dia Rehman, an artist born and raised in New York, uses the visual archive of their Pakistani immigrant Muslim family (including family photographs as well as found images and audio/ visual clips) to create works that refract against ongoing military interventions in South Asia and the Middle East. In *Family* (2017), Rehman re-creates an image of their family as a large-scale silhouette, using powdered charcoal across five scrolls of newsprint. As the fine dust of the charcoal settles to produce an opaque image of domestic life, the image cannot be recuperated as a transparent representation of selfhood. Instead, in the artist's words, the viewer must "activate the work," contending with both the invisibility of Muslim American immigrant histories as well as the hypervisibility of US wars in South Asia and the Middle East in the twenty-first century.

The family album, in these artists' hands, becomes an archive of diaspora: a repository of pictures that runs backward and forward in time and in space. This is also true of the work of Sunil Gupta. In his series *Social Security* (1988), he compiles portraits and snapshots—a studio portrait of his parents in Delhi, a lakeside picnic with his parents and sister on the outskirts of Montreal, himself holding hands with his boyfriend on a hike—to capture

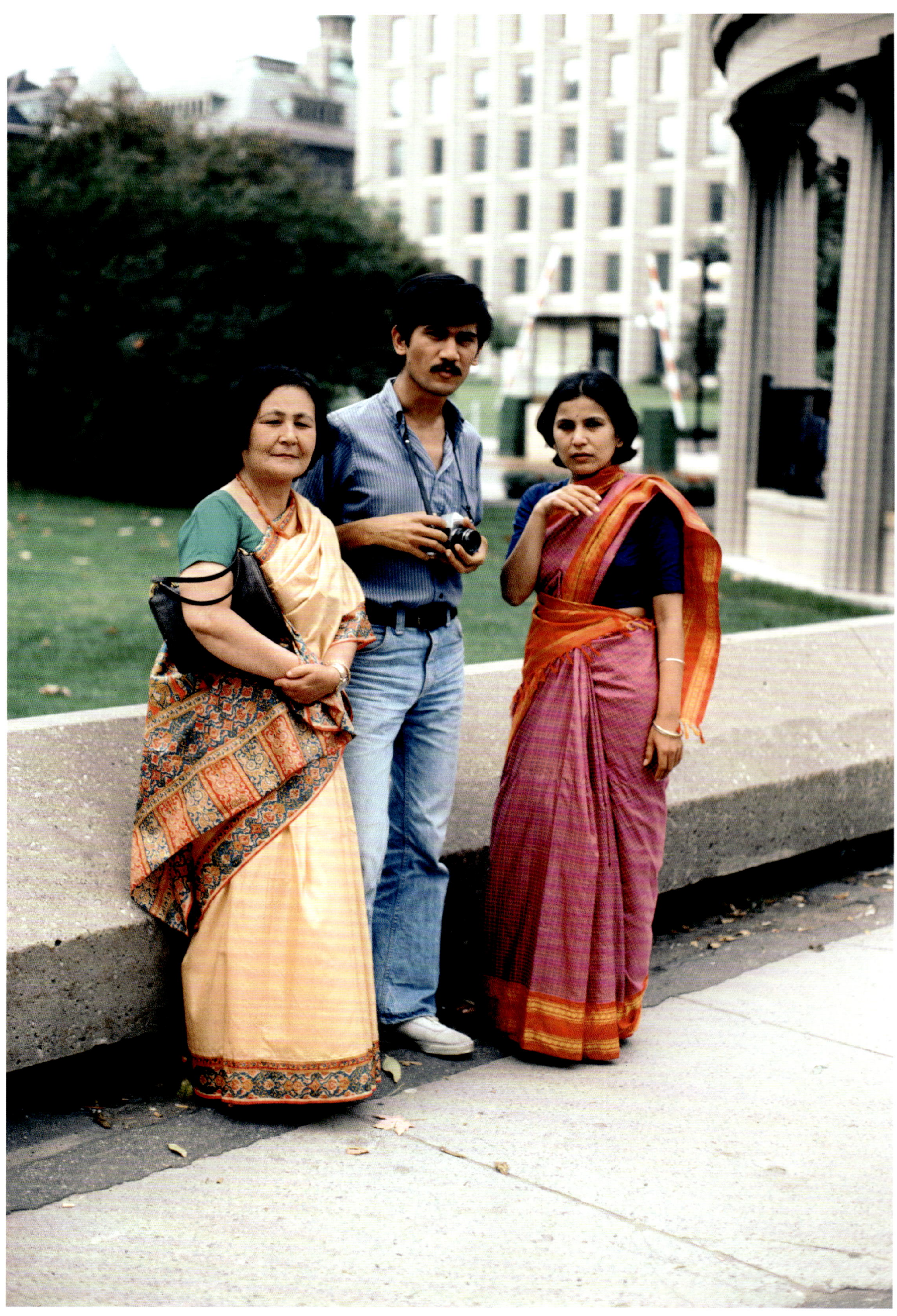

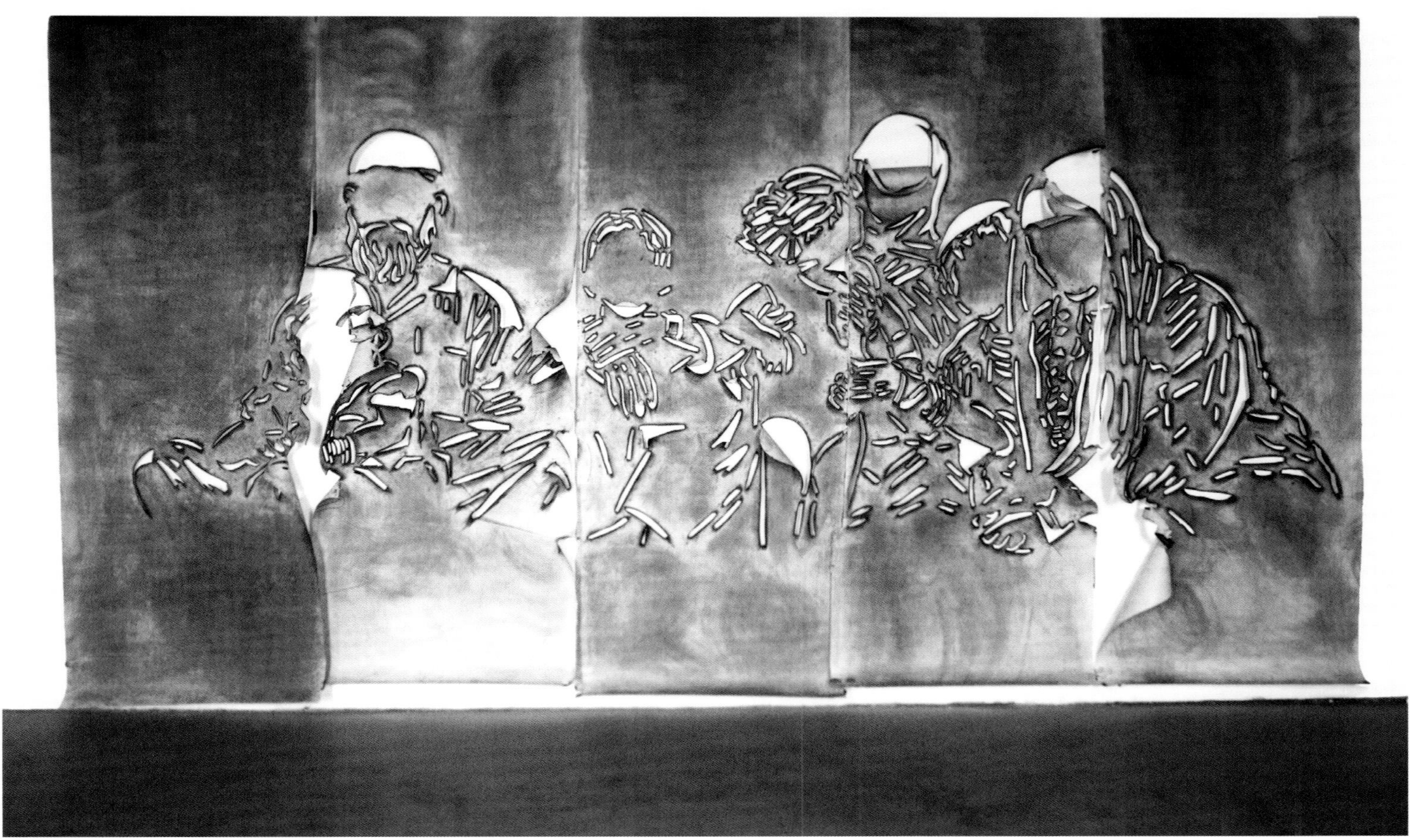

the possibilities that migration to North America initially appeared
to offer his middle-aged parents. But as we follow the series
through images of Gupta's father, who, after immigrating,
worked overnight shifts as a security guard, as well as of his sister,
who left Canada, and Gupta's mother, who is pictured alone
on her apartment balcony in Montreal, we witness the dissolution
of family.

The series concludes with a photograph of Gupta's father's
corpse laid out for mourners at his funeral, followed by an image
of the possessions recovered from his body: cash, a watch,
a Canadian social security card, neatly cut in half. Even as Gupta's
mother, whose voice emerges through the captions, presents the
family's migration from South Asia to North America as having
been a personal choice, Gupta's curation of his family photographic
archive shows us how the lack of economic opportunity in
postindependence India precipitated his parents' emigration,
and how the family's experience of downward class mobility
in Canada contributed to his father's untimely death.

In these artists' hands, the archive contains the futures of
Asian American representation. Even within national archives
that continue to accumulate photographs that distort and constrain
what it means to be a racial minority, Matthew's and Kahlon's
strategies of photographic reproduction and painting enable
Asian American viewers to come closer to the image, to see
something that feels like the experience of our everyday life.
For those who turn to the family album to gain clarity about our
own experiences of migration and belonging, Gupta's work,
Rehman's charcoal drawings, and Matthew's portrait animations
lead us to speculate on who we are, and what we want to be.
As Asian American artists and as observers, we look and look
again at these photographic archives, as if they can offer us the
promise of representation.

This page:
Sa'dia Rehman, Installation
view of *Family*, 2017.
Powdered charcoal on
cut newsprint
Courtesy the artist

Opposite:
Sunil Gupta, *Penny,
Sunil, and Shalini*, from
the series *Social Security*,
1970–73
© the artist and courtesy
Artists Rights Society (ARS),
New York, and DACS,
London

Bakirathi Mani is a professor of English
at Swarthmore College and the author
of *Unseeing Empire: Photography,
Representation, South Asian America* (2020).

It *almost* feels like too much. You can practically hear the gaudy crystalline beads dripping from the ceiling and smell the heady jasmine scent from the floral arrangements. Their slightly stilted expressions, eyes often looking directly into the camera, offer a sharp contrast to their elegant gestures. Some of the poses appear to be plucked from a Busby Berkeley dance sequence, or riff on the vernacular of wedding photos. These scenes of riotous congregation are from *Parting Gift* (2022–ongoing), a series of Leonard Suryajaya's signature tableaux, which lovingly render the strangeness of ordinary people and everyday life.

The Indonesian-born, Chicago-based artist regularly conscripts family and friends as subjects for his highly stylized constructions. For *Perennial Blossom* (2022), the artist enlisted student collaborators to serve as a multiracial chorus that frames his mother and sister, who were visiting from Indonesia. Suryajaya is methodical in building juxtapositions in his scenes, to dazzling, and often disarming, effect. In *Roots (Mom in 7 Years)* (2022), for instance, the artist positioned his mother in front of a portrait he had made of her in 2015, in which she is being fed a bag of milk from a straw by the disembodied hand of her husband; Suryajaya had instructed her to wear every single piece of jewelry she had purchased for herself with her own money. His mother, a frequent collaborator, also makes an appearance in *Mom and Everything She Bought in America* (2022), which Suryajaya made in his Chicago apartment.

"The control is what gives me a sense of power," the artist told me in a video conversation in January. "When I first started taking pictures of my family, I realized that I am myself with my camera: I am nobody's son, nobody's brother. That role of being in charge supersedes my expected social role. This is my life. I get to create new images that feel more honest and closer to who I am, in all my fire and my complexity."

In defamiliarizing the relationships that define weighty concepts such as family or belonging, Suryajaya engages in queer world-building drawn from his experiences of being marked as "other." Suryajaya grew up in a Chinese Buddhist household in Medan, Indonesia, when ethnic minorities were not treated as full citizens. He became aware of the devastating psychological effects of discrimination in 1998 when his family fled to Malaysia, escaping a period of violence against Chinese during a time of economic uncertainty in Indonesia. When Suryajaya moved to the United States in 2006 to study theater in California and, later, photography in Chicago, he found a means to integrate the visual signifiers of the many cultures and religions that shaped the layers of his identity—Christian education, Muslim caretakers, Chinese heritage, and Indonesian upbringing.

Those signifiers find full expression in *Red Envelope* (2023), taken during his sister's wedding, where members of Suryajaya's family offer auspicious red-and-gold envelopes—traditionally used to distribute cash during celebrations—to a tank-top-clad figure reclining in the foreground: the artist's husband. The family's staged gesture is ambiguous: Are they welcoming Suryajaya's husband affectionately, or instructing him in a cultural custom reserved for Suryajaya's sister's more traditional straight union? Making these photographs is a means for the artist to process the complex and often fraught nature of family, to assert the visibility of his existence in society at the intersection of alienation and connection, and to transform painful memories into spaces of exquisite beauty and refinement.

"I have been the recipient of a lot of data I never knew how to process fully, and this fear of being exiled, shunned, or killed off has always been the foundation of how I think of the world," Suryajaya notes. "I want to create a universe where people like me not only feel part of the frame, but where I can share all of the things I have experienced, including trauma. I can't quit photography, because it allows me to make sense of my life."

Leonard Suryajaya
Parting Gift

Tausif Noor

Roots (Mom in 7 Years),
2022

Tausif Noor is a curator and critic whose work has appeared in *Frieze*, the *New Yorker*, and the *New York Times*.

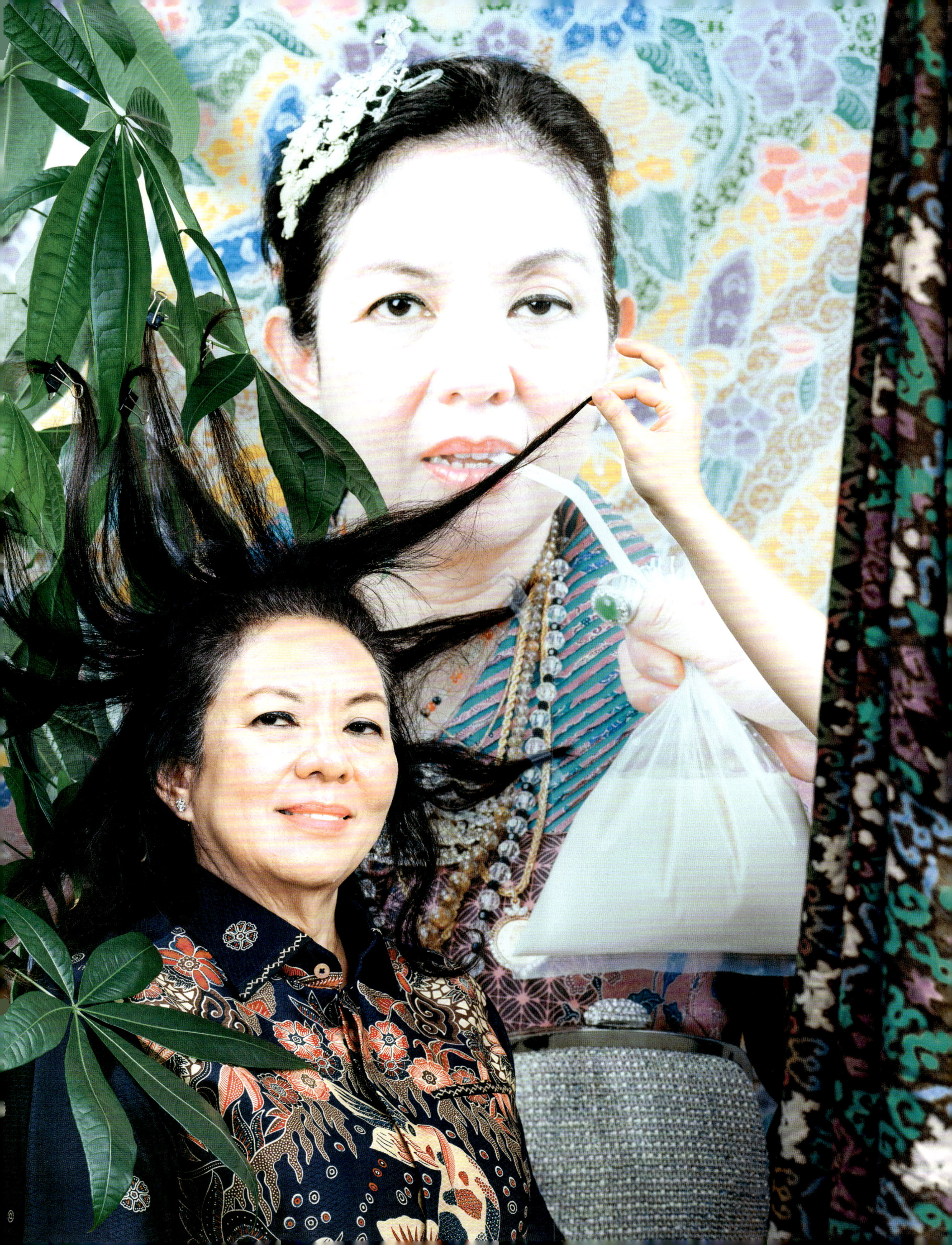

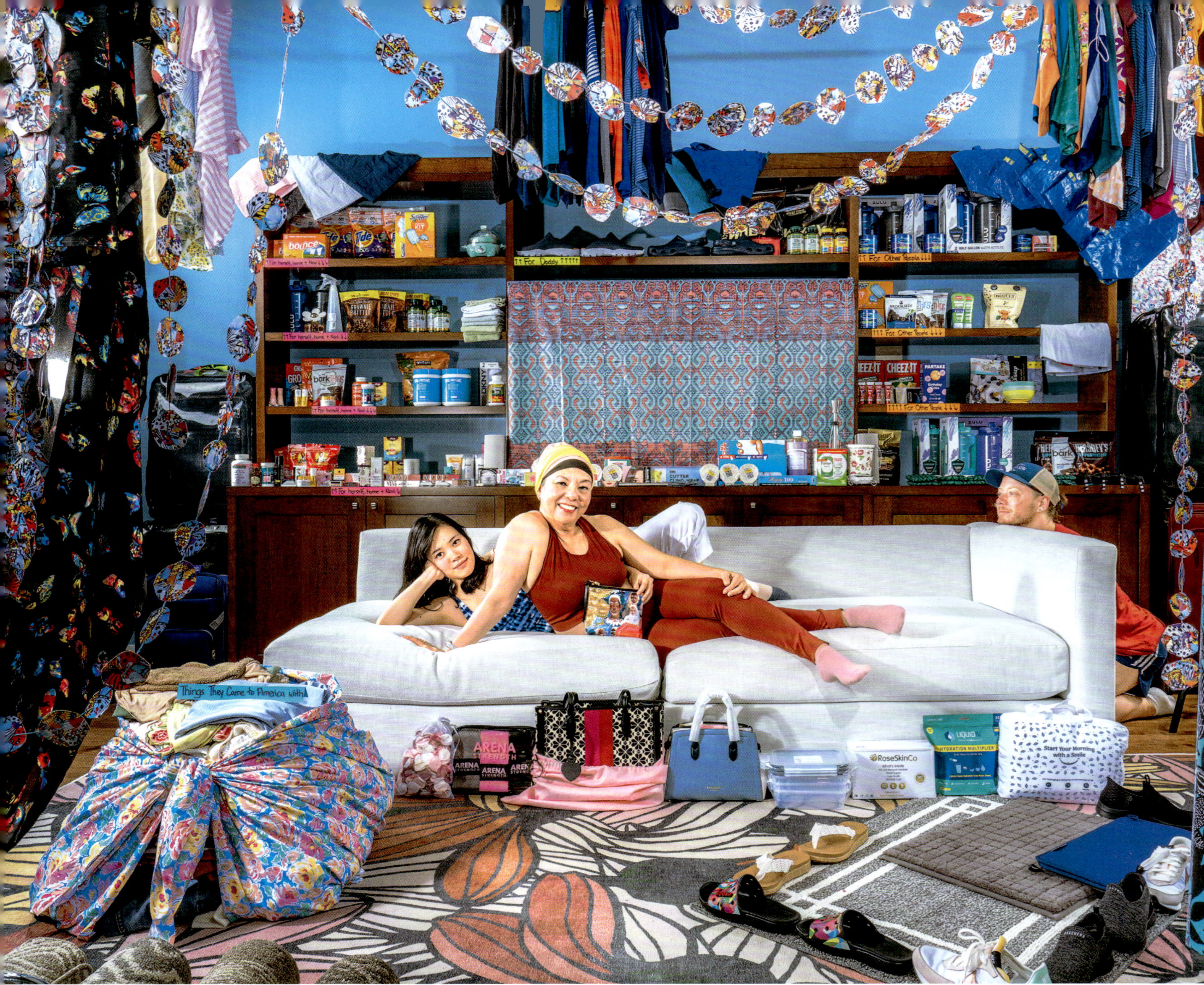

*Mom and Everything She
Bought in America*, 2022

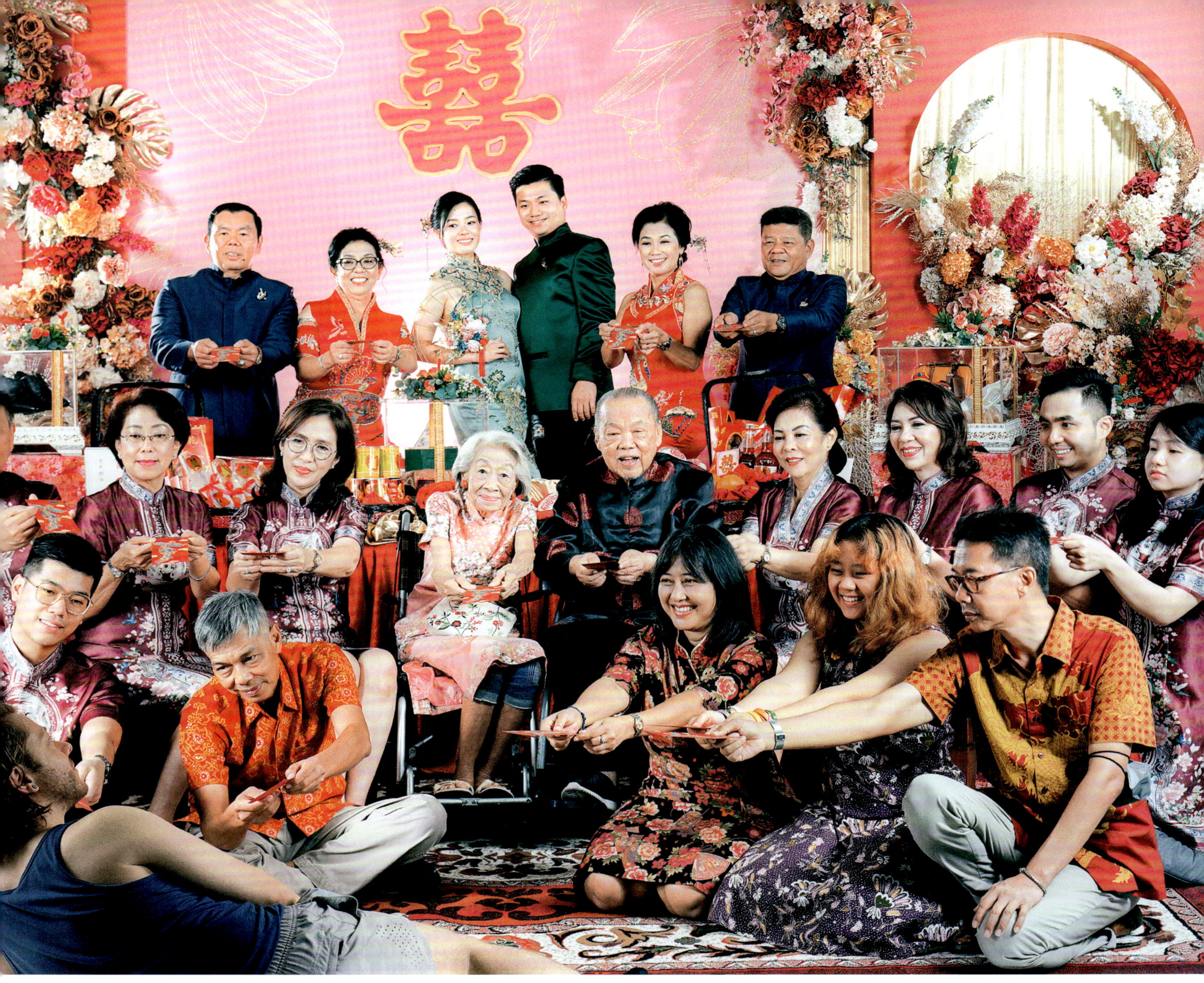

Red Envelope, 2023

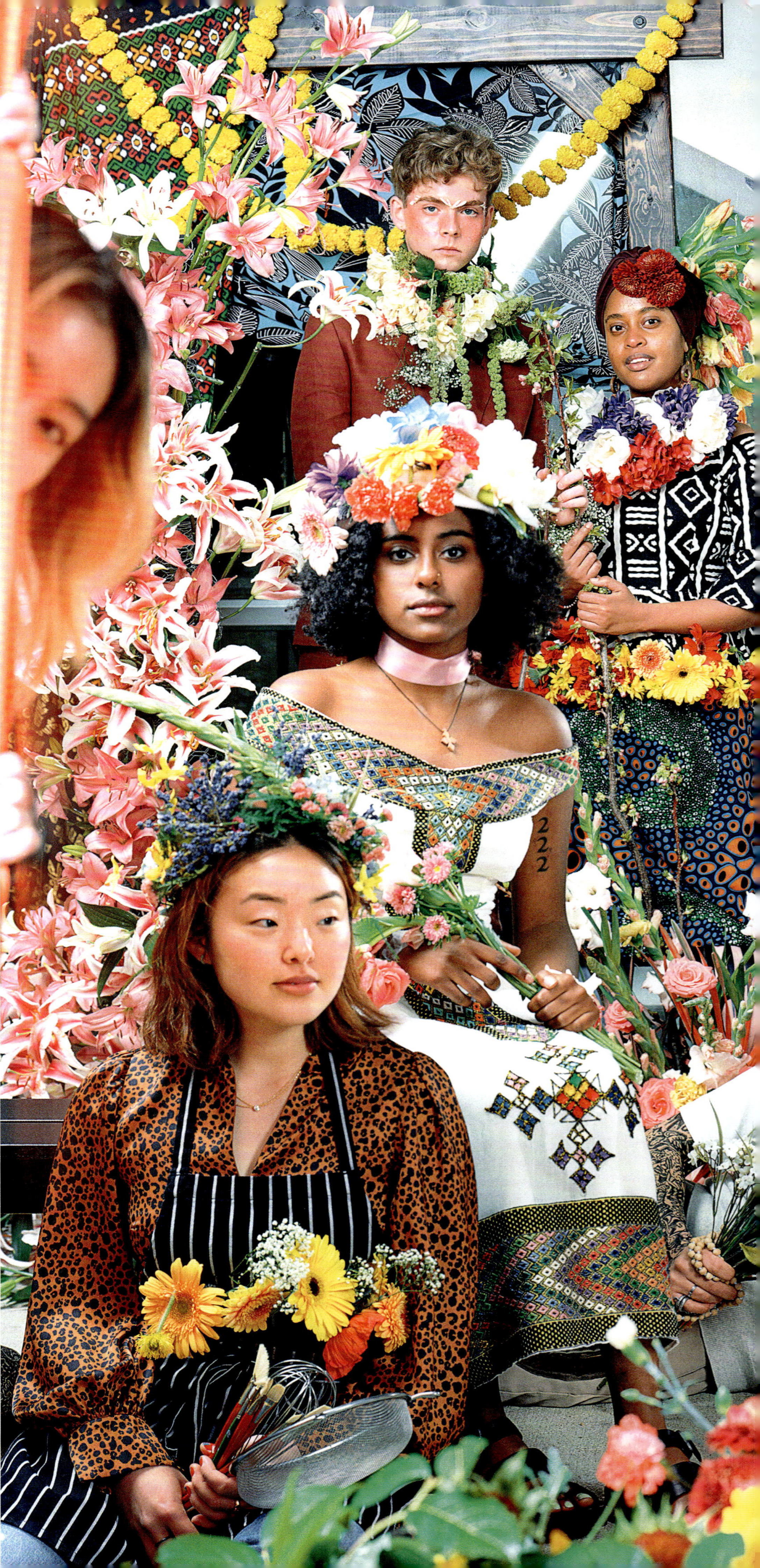

Perennial Blossom, 2022
All photographs courtesy
the artist

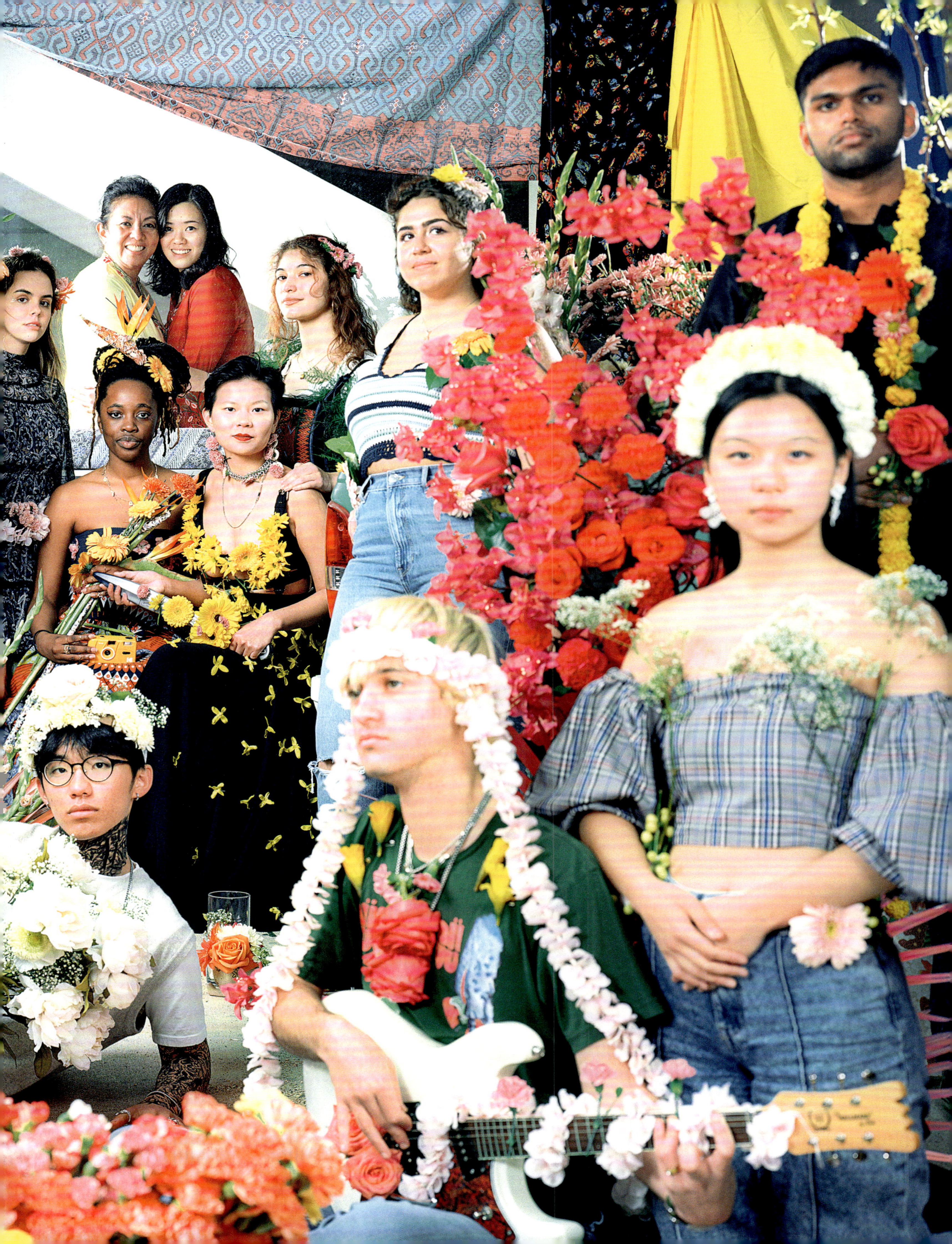

Arthur Ou
Viewfinder

Mimi Wong

Arthur Ou initially planned to become an engineer. Two years into his studies, he decided he wanted to be a photographer and moved across the United States, from California to New York. Still, he sees the two fields—the histories of technology and of photography—as being deeply intertwined. The camera as a device that enables and enhances our vision continues to fascinate the Taiwanese American artist. Currently, he teaches a course that explores the relationship between image making and science at Parsons School of Design, where he is an associate professor of photography.

Ou's latest project, *Viewfinder* (2020–ongoing), considers the act of seeing the world as a precursor to understanding our place within it. He depicts this experience vicariously through his subjects, who are between five and seven years old—an age when a young person starts to become more cognizant of where they are. Ou observed this developing consciousness in his own daughter Octavia, who was the first model he photographed for the series, back in 2020, largely out of convenience while New York was in lockdown. In the black-and-white image, his daughter's face is mostly obscured behind a pair of binoculars. The viewer cannot see what she's looking at. Instead, it's her gaze, directed somewhere outside of the frame, that holds our attention.

The stark white backdrop of the photograph further emphasizes her burgeoning subjectivity. Ou understands the locating of oneself—whether in the physical, relational, or cultural sense—is a necessary step in the formation of identity; he also notes that in a child this desire is even more complex. As the city began opening up, Ou expanded the pool to include local children from the neighborhood in Queens where his family resides. He told me recently, "I just had this thought of wanting to capture them in this simple gesture, trying to see beyond themselves."

What lies beyond may be as vast as the universe itself. Just prior to the pandemic, Ou traveled to a remote observatory in the Sacramento Mountains of New Mexico. Unique to the site is its offering of telescopes connected to a vast network allowing a user from any location to access and operate the equipment. Interestingly, what Ou felt compelled to record were not images of space but the telescopes themselves, tilted toward the sky, with their trailing tails of cables and wires, serving as an extension of our eyes, our vision.

Technology has granted us an incredible ability to see. Back in New York, Octavia balanced a tiny fragment of meteorite, barely a quarter of an inch wide, on the tip of her index finger. Ou snapped a macroscopic picture. In text written to accompany *Viewfinder*, he recalls that throughout the photoshoot, his daughter asked many questions about the original rock that fell from space. This leads him to remember a different set of origins, and he describes a portrait of his grandfather as a child in Taiwan wearing a Japanese-style school uniform, the large leaves of a banana tree creating a striking background. Both the tropical setting and the colonial forces that shaped his grandfather's life are apparent in the photograph. Ou doesn't talk much about his own life; perhaps he doesn't feel the need to. As he told his daughter, "I am in search of a view."

New Mexico Skies
(PlaneWave CDK), 2020

Mimi Wong is a writer based in Brooklyn.

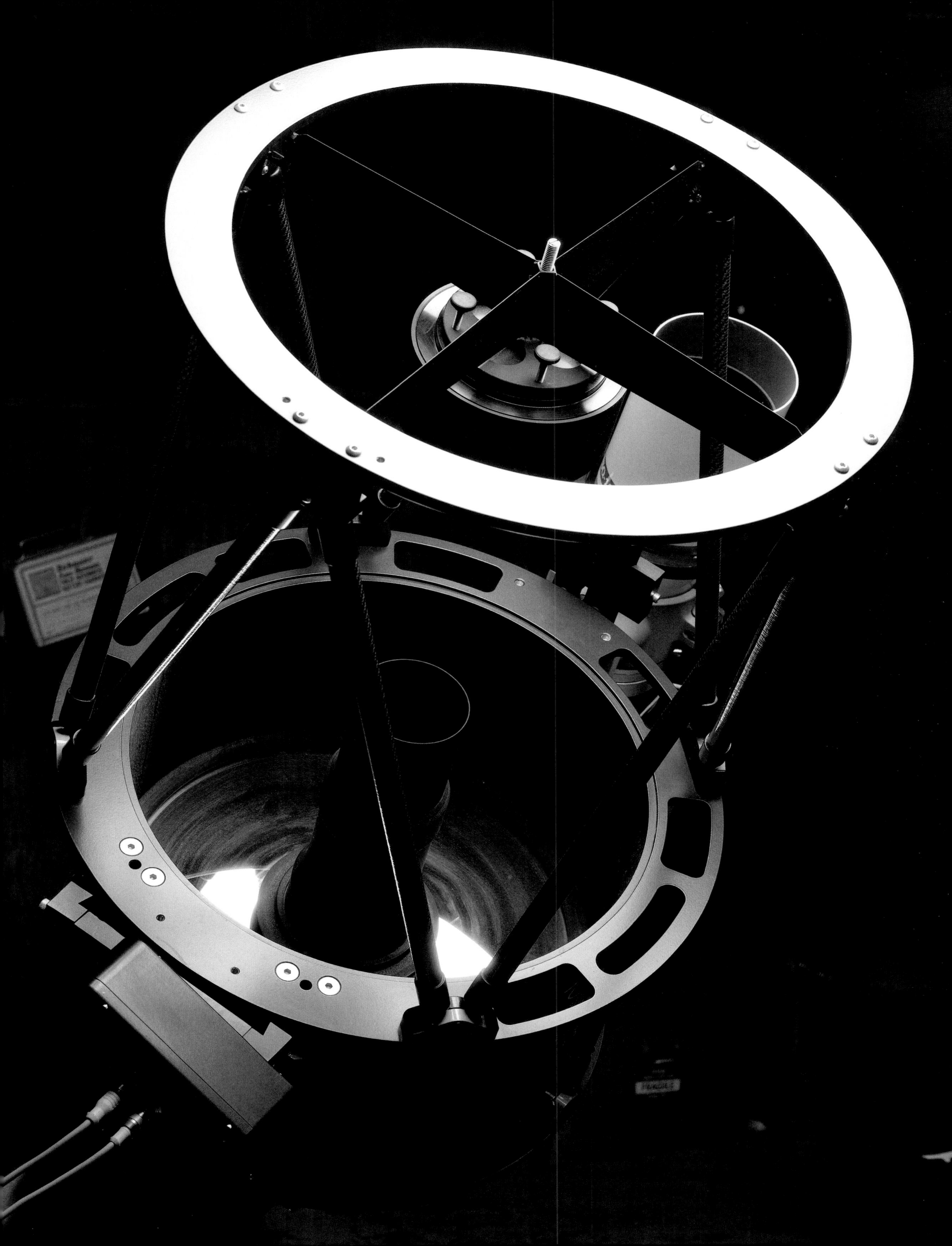

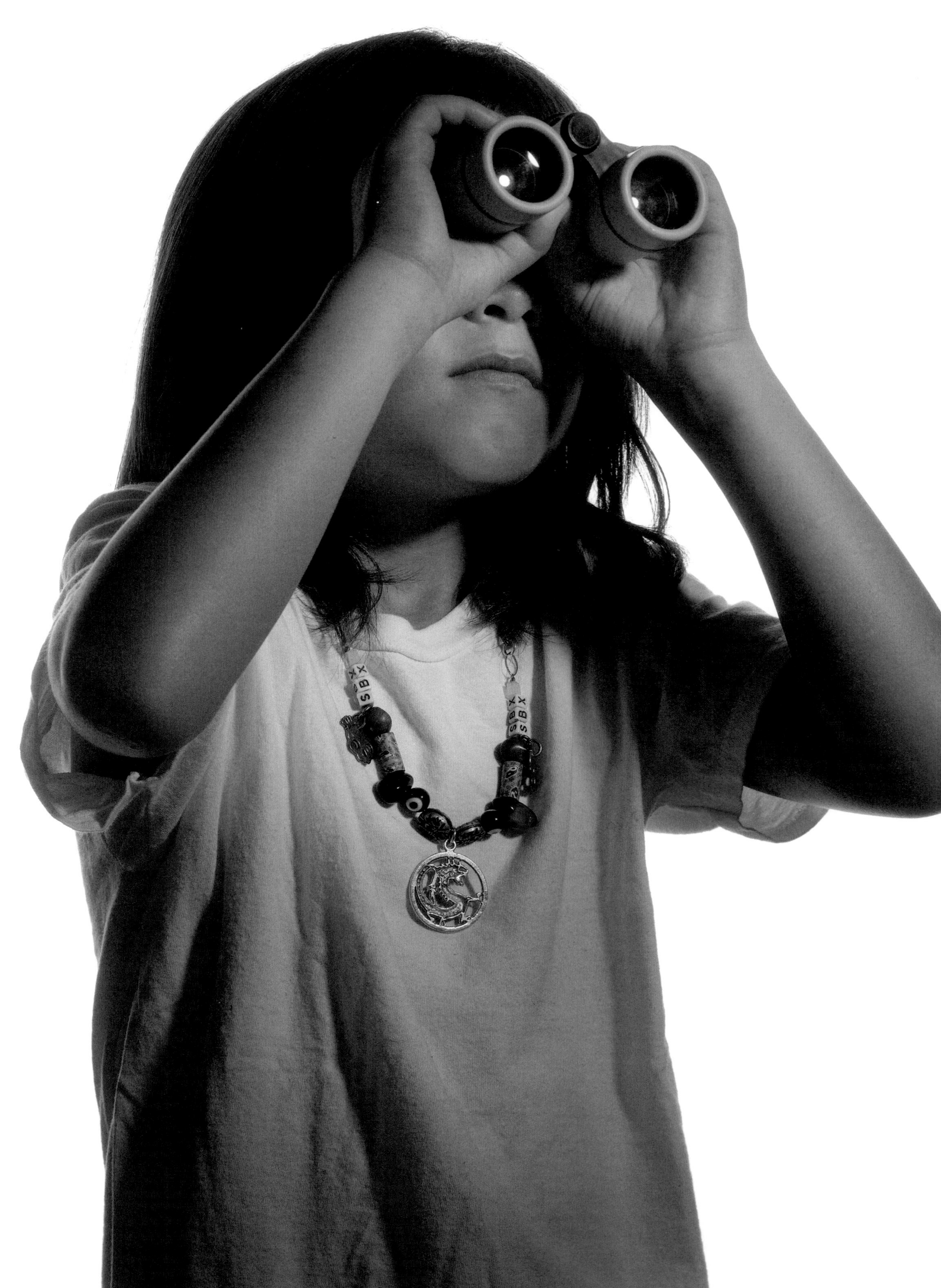

This page:
Untitled (Octavia with Meteor), 2020; opposite:
Viewfinder (Emmanuel),
2021

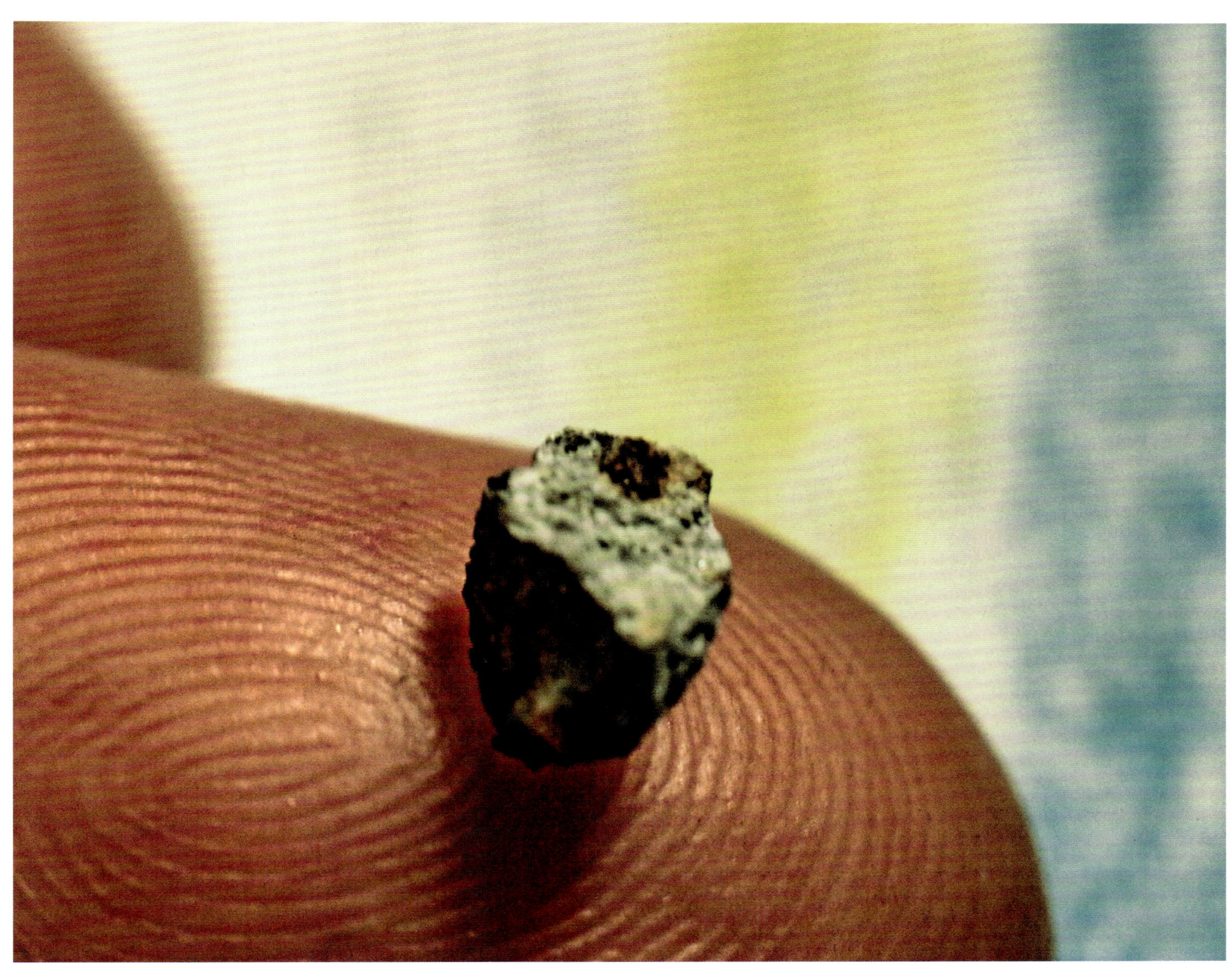

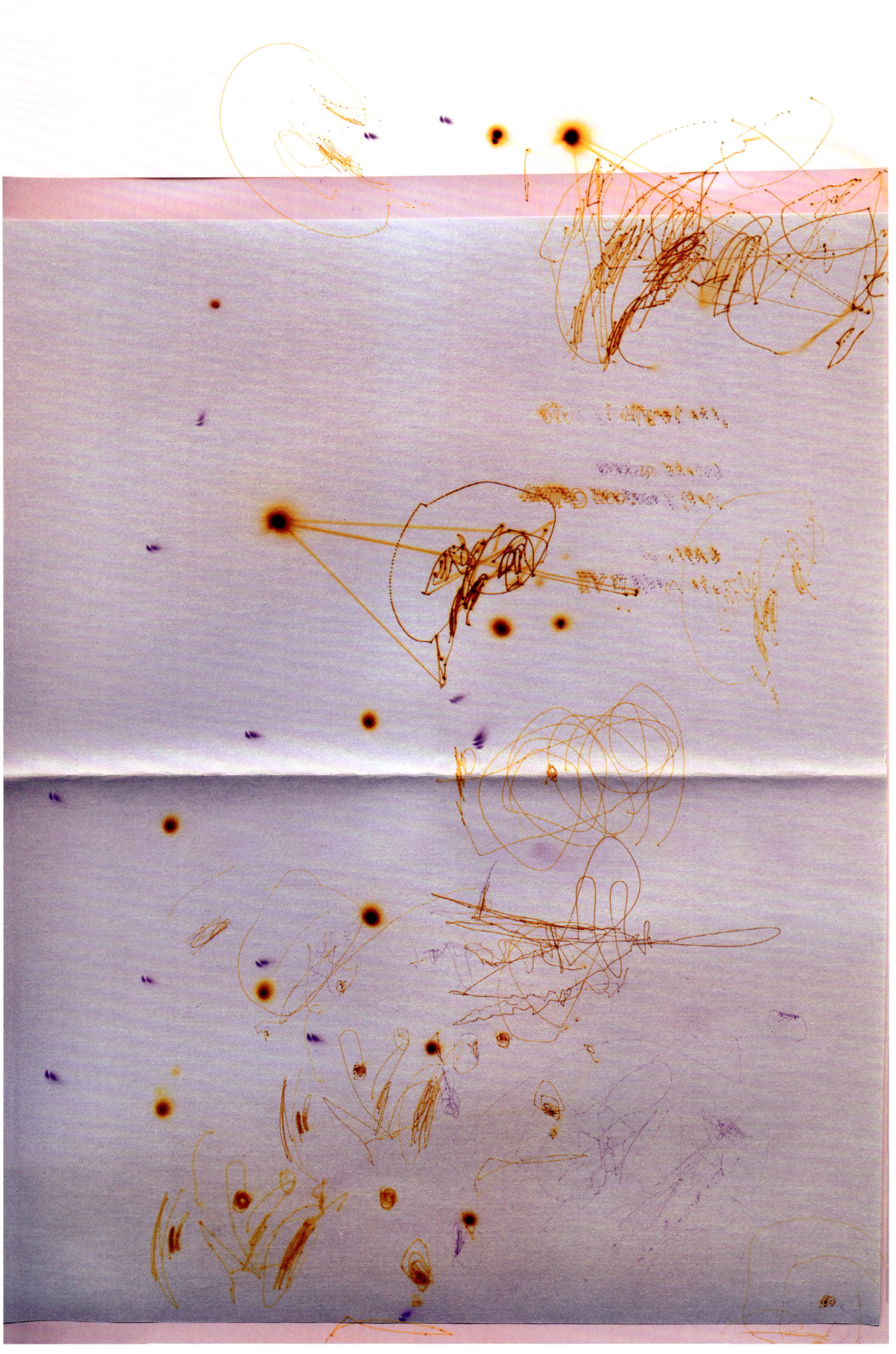

This page:
Untitled (Octavia Drawing), 2020; opposite:
Viewfinder (Mireille), 2021
All photographs courtesy
the artist and Eleni Koroneou
Gallery, Athens

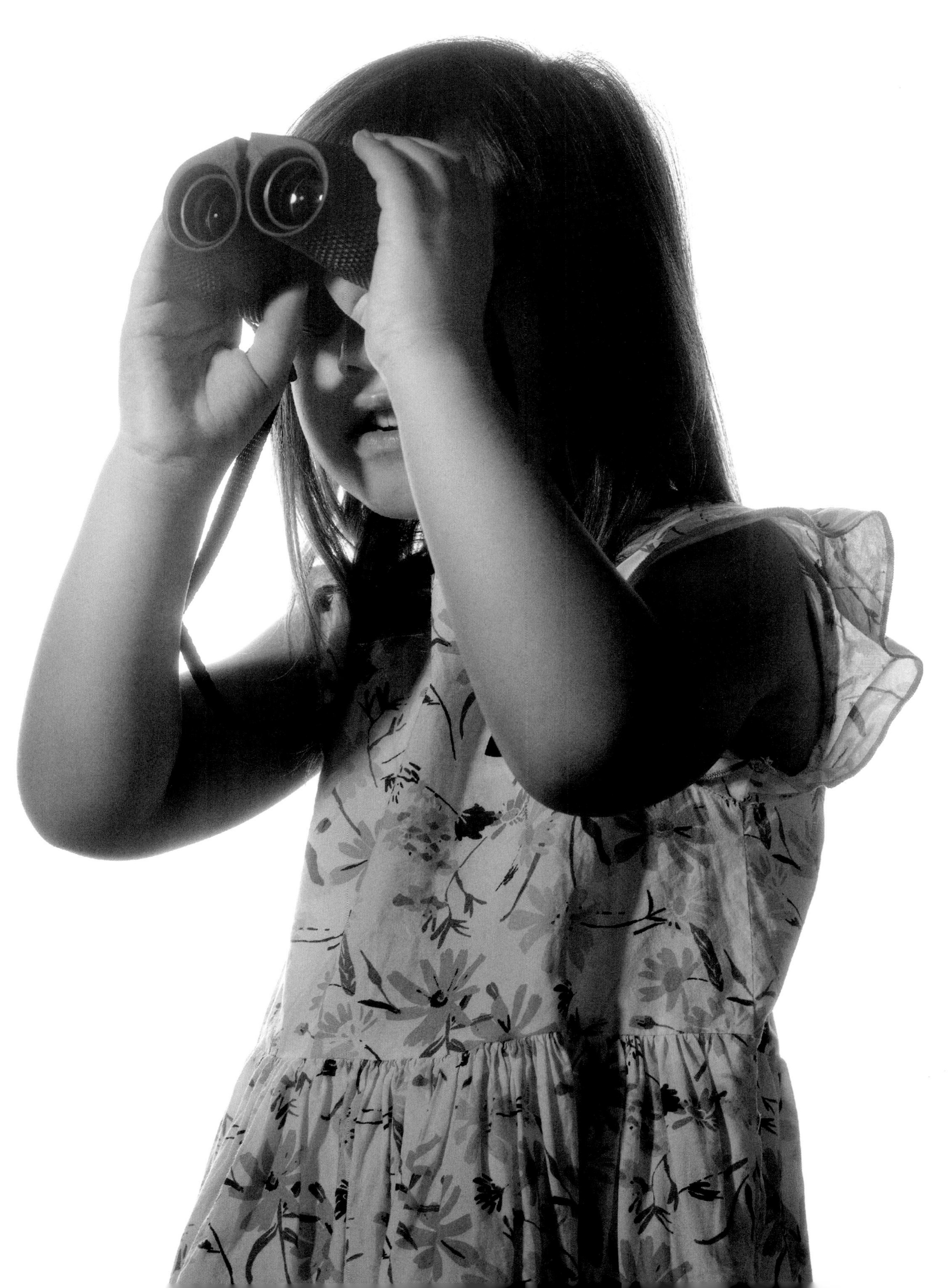

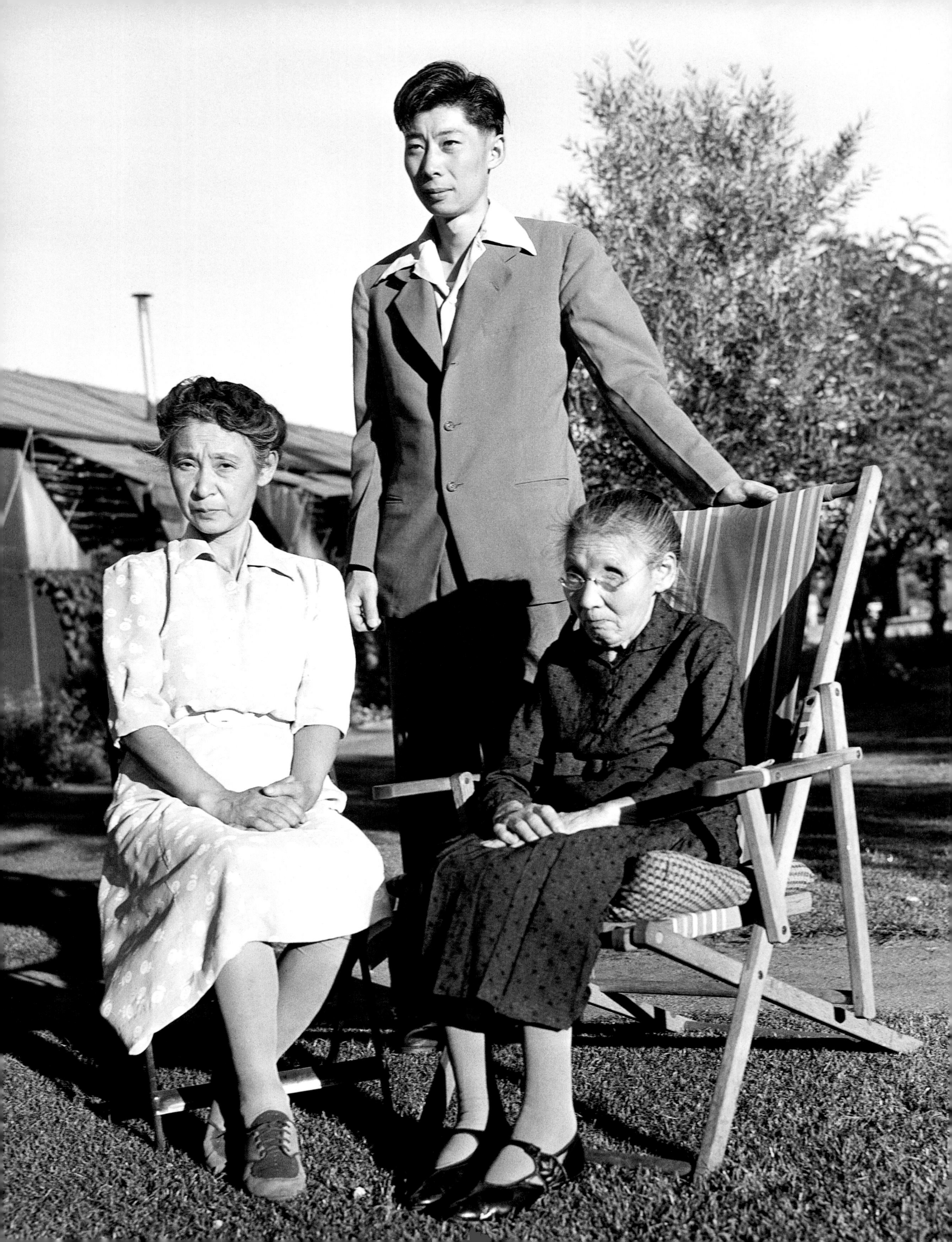

Toyo Miyatake

Manzanar Stories

While interned during the Second World War, Toyo Miyatake created—sometimes surreptitiously—a vivid record of life inside the infamous California prison camp.
Ken Chen

The week after Trump won the presidential election, I attended an Asian American community meeting in Manhattan where one of the attendees told me the following story. The day after the election, he ran into a senior partner at his work, jubilant about the results. Now, the older man said, we can finally round up the gays, the Muslims, and the immigrants. Shocked by this brazen declaration, my new acquaintance pointed out that he was gay himself, and the children of immigrants. When he returned to his office, he saw an email. It was not an apology. The partner wrote that *Korematsu v. United States*—the 1944 Supreme Court decision justifying the Japanese American prison camps—was still good law.

This senior partner wasn't alone. I remember waiting for a flight at an airport and watching Fox News pundits suggest that the prison camps provided a precedent for us to register and imprison Muslims. Then ICE started taking children who had traveled across the border and throwing them in Fort Sill in Oklahoma, which once imprisoned some seven hundred Japanese Americans. I thought the camps were ancient history, an Asian American friend bemoaned to me at a coffee shop. But they weren't.

In 1942, Toyo Miyatake left his studio in Los Angeles's Little Tokyo and brought his wife and four children to the Manzanar concentration camp in the central Californian desert. Cameras were prohibited, so Miyatake snuck in a lens and fashioned a wooden box into a body for his surreptitious camera. "As a photographer, I have a responsibility," he told his teenage son Archie. "I have to take all the pictures in Manzanar to keep a record of what's going on here."

An unusual candidate for incarcerated auto-ethnographer, Miyatake had been a well-known Pictorialist before the war: a friend of Edward Weston's, a collaborator of the cinematographer James Wong Howe, and winner of an award from the International Photography Exhibition in London. His métier consisted of poetic abstractions. His landscapes captured no humans, just the delicate shadows of bushes, falling like brushstrokes over snow-covered hills. The figures in his Little Tokyo cityscapes exist only as silhouettes. His dancers, gestures of shadow and motion. But there was another Miyatake: the much less expressionistic professional photographer who ran a commercial studio. He courted his wife by taking her picture, yet his most libidinous portrait shows Michio Ito, the charismatic performer who danced alongside Martha Graham and inspired W. B. Yeats's Noh theater experiments. In Miyatake's portrait from 1929, Ito seems capable of conveying modernist ferment through just a hairstyle and a glance. His hair hides his face in a center part, but even this obscured gaze communicates an erotic recalcitrance. He looks like he's arrived from the future,

What did Miyatake, driven by a mission to document an abhorrent experience, decide to preserve?

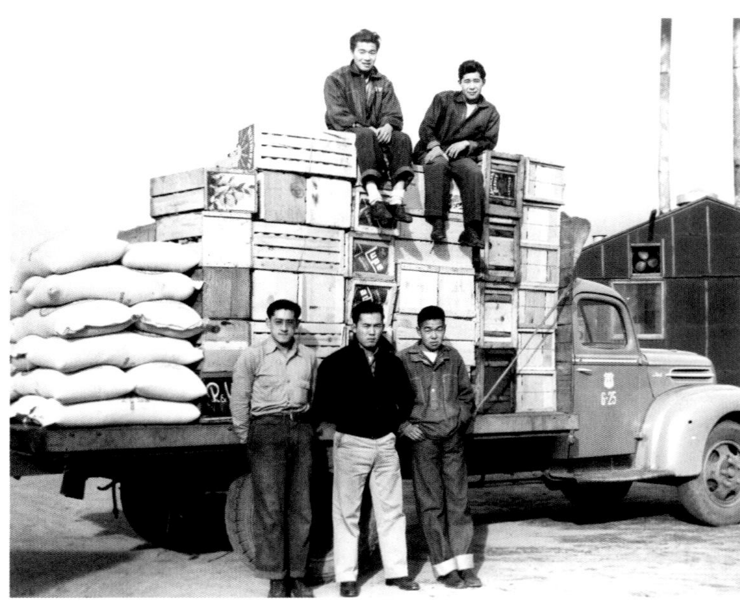

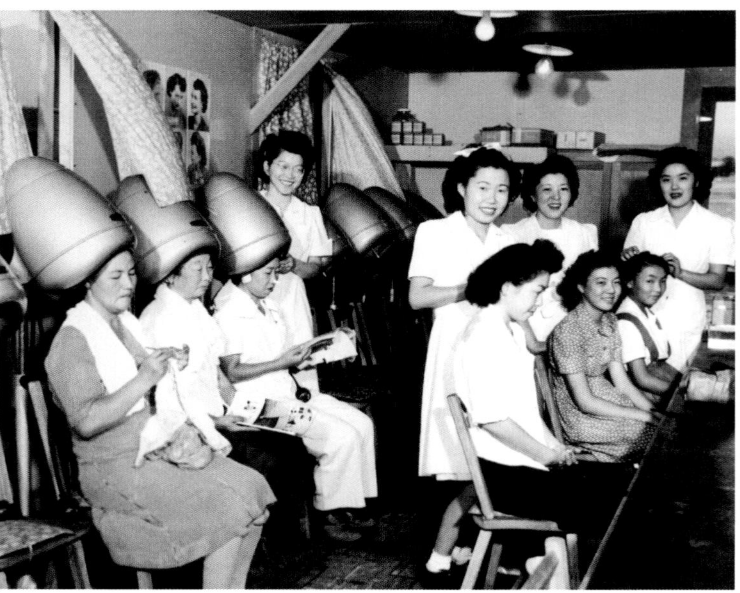

the way silent-film actors sometimes do—or at least from the grungy glam 1990s of the actor Leslie Cheung.

In 1942, Ito was deported to Japan as an enemy alien, and Miyatake banished to Manzanar, a dreamy aesthete and studio portraitist in a prison wasteland. When viewing the colonial archive, we often search for how oppressed people understood their own predicament. For life at Manzanar, we can simply look at Miyatake's photographs. What did this man, driven by an ethical mission to document an abhorrent experience, decide to preserve? A baseball batter readying for the pitch. Children cradling their dolls, borrowed from a toy loan center. Smiling majorettes twirling their batons in the air. When I've taught the literature of the Japanese American imprisonment, it is precisely these details that trip students up— the sense that daily life continues, even in a concentration camp. In *Farewell to Manzanar* (1973), Jeanne Wakatsuki Houston describes her brother's playing in a prison swing band. In *Citizen 13660* (1946), Miné Okubo writes that the prisoners at the Topaz camp in Utah "went wild with excitement" over a snowball fight. Why, my students essentially asked, wasn't everyone constantly miserable?

Obviously, we shouldn't undersell the camps' fundamental crappiness. These permitted types of recreation were ways of assimilating prisoners into American nationhood (baseball!). When Miyatake was at Manzanar, sewage tainted the drinking water with *E. coli*. Residents died in the sweltering 110-degree heat. Military police fired on a rioting crowd, killing two. "Manzanar was a devil's playground," said Fukiko Elisabeth Komatsu, imprisoned with her mother and siblings, "and the dust storms came through at 60-miles an hour to make our lives even more harsh and miserable." Nor did Miyatake live at the Tule Lake concentration camp, the prison for the radicals, which Konrad Aderer's documentary *Enemy Alien* (2011) calls the Guantánamo Bay of the Japanese American incarceration experience. There, prisoners were shackled in the camp stockade, shot at by battalions of tanks, or simply executed in broad daylight. We might describe these prisons using the work of the theorist Giorgio Agamben, who writes that during crises such as the Third Reich and, arguably, post-9/11 America, groups can become stripped of their legal status and reduced to what he calls "bare life." My students were essentially asking, "Why weren't the prisoners diminished into pure abjection?" The answer is that Agamben was wrong. The men locked up at Attica prison wrote poetry. People in refugee camps, which activists wryly call the most permanent form of architecture, still find ways to care for one another, make art, and live life. Miyatake photographed women getting their hair done.

"Although Miyatake lived in the hothouse environment of simmering anger, fear and suspicion that some Manzanar chroniclers have described," the author Nancy Matsumoto writes, viewers may be "disappointed," because "his photographs bear no signs of violence or anger." The enigma of his images is their mundanity, which we can better understand if we compare them to those of Manzanar taken by two of America's most famous photographers, Ansel Adams and Dorothea Lange. A landscape photographer uninterested in portraiture or politics, Adams wanted to show that the prisoners weren't terrorists but smiling schoolgirls, Norman Rockwell–esque nuclear families, and proud men in uniform. What did Adams omit? Any cultural difference, as well as the barbed-wire fences and guard towers.

Dorothea Lange called Adams's efforts "shameful." Her photographs, which were censored and impounded by the military until 2006, depict Manzanar as a stark, perpetually dusty prison. As in her migrant portraits, she displays a novelistic ability to capture her subject's gaze, the solemn look or glance cast slightly askew, insinuating some private turmoil. While Lange's images are generally seen as better than Adams's, both had one thing in common. They took photographs of their own projections. Adams saw the prisoners as model Americans, Lange as people

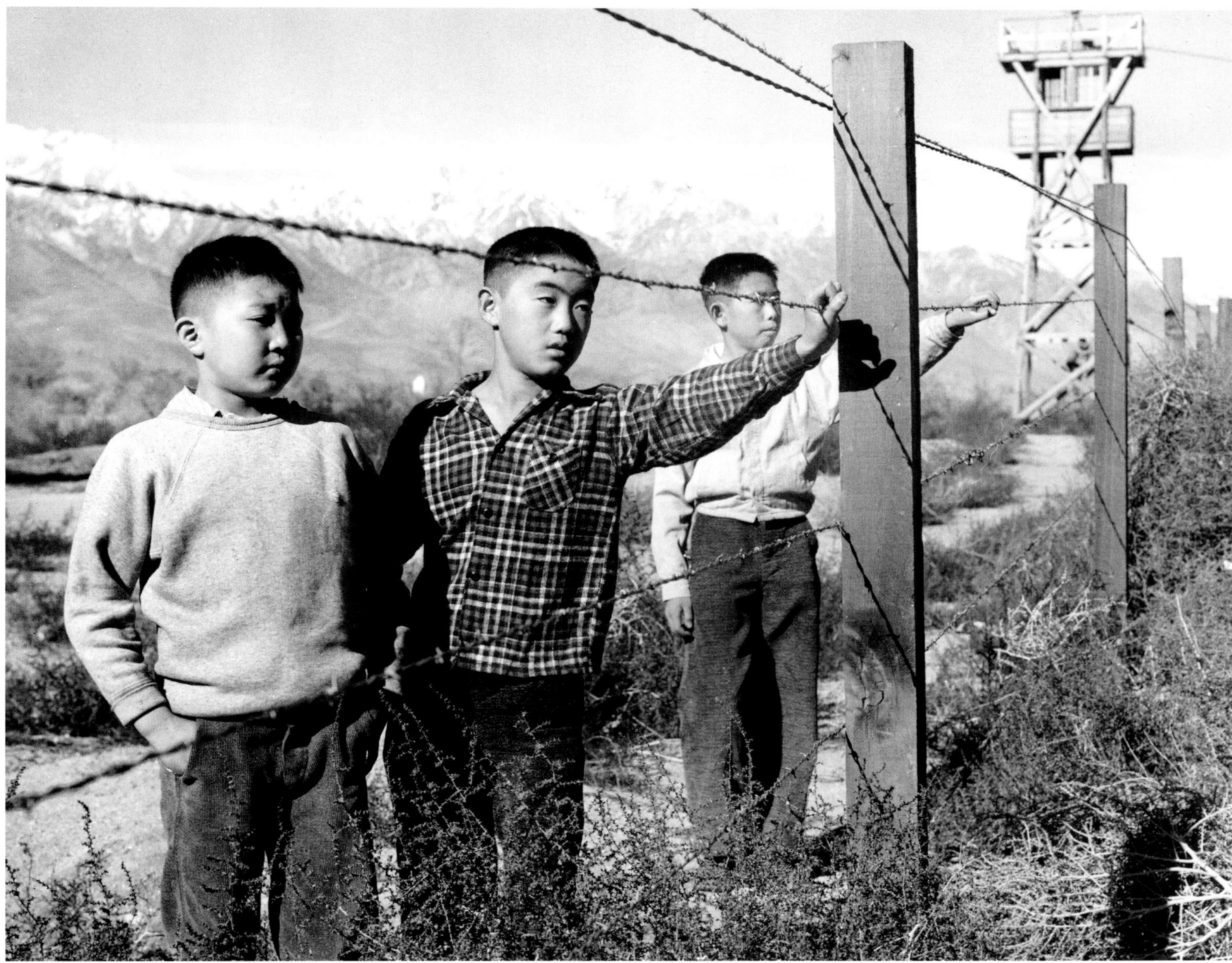

experiencing injustice. Miyatake did not understand the Japanese Americans as political idealizations—and that is exactly what perplexes us about his work. He saw little need to glorify, humanize, or even individualize the prisoners. For he was one of them.

One Miyatake photograph shows a crowd facing the monument at the center of the Manzanar cemetery. The obelisk fills the left third of the image, a white geometry, its paleness continued by the flecked outline of the Sierra Nevadas. Aside from a girl looking toward the camera, we cannot see any of the mourners' faces. Their bodies form a black mass barely recognizable as people. They turn away from us. They will not tell us what they know.

Avoiding the poles of didacticism and aesthetics, Miyatake documented outside such binaries. "Not yes or no, it could be maybe," the artist Hirokazu Kosaka says in the 2002 documentary *Toyo Miyatake: Infinite Shades of Gray*. "It's not white or black but infinitesimals of gray. That's what Miyatake was trying to create." Some of his images lack any people, depicting Manzanar as a barren environment. Barracks tile and recede to the background, but instead of a horizon opening to a broader world, the foreground is encased by Mount Williamson. Not unlike in Hokusai's prints of Mount Fuji, the peak is a spectral crystal, a gargantuan mass always visible but never foregrounded, the inescapable reality of imprisonment banished to the unconscious.

It is not necessarily that Miyatake preserved some authentic truth. Another photographer who once worked at his studio, Jack Iwata, composed similarly quotidian photographs of daily life

in these prison camps, but his images occasionally suggest more emotional range, both stark drama (American soldiers holding bayonets as cars enter Manzanar, black smoke rising up in plumes from a fire at the Tule Lake camp) and joy (a woman wearing a crown declaring her the Queen of Manzanar). Seen beside them, what emerges in Miyatake's photographs is a meticulous reticence, a refusal of the evocative flourishes he once adopted as a Pictorialist. He became the diarist of a society, one who, whether because of personal temperament or camp surveillance, did not photograph the violence of the prison. Instead, he documented weddings, graduations, newborns entering the world in a prison. Both he and the photographer Corky Lee were forced by Pacific wars and spatial segregation into becoming community archivists, but they traveled in opposite directions. Lee had a flair for adventurism and famously captured Chinatown protestors brawling with cops. Miyatake spent the Manzanar riot in his barrack. Lee was a radical who gradually adopted expressive and inventive forms of mise-en-scène, but Miyatake left behind his lavish romanticism and the formal poses of his portraits. Unlike Lange's brooding depiction of ruminating prisoners, what is most mysterious about Miyatake's photographs is that we do not know how to make them available for our own emotional use.

Unlike Lee, Miyatake rarely took photographs that overly implied a political message, but there are exceptions. In a photograph for the 1944–45 Manzanar yearbook, a hand holds up pliers, positioned as if to sever the barbed wire slicing the background.

His most famous photograph, *Three Boys Behind Barbed Wire* (1944),
shows three boys considering the steel fencing that diagonally
intersects the frame. A guard tower stands behind them. Unlike
Miyatake's more quotidian portraits, this image vibrates with
implied psychology and the sense that these imprisoned children
also serve as symbols of some sort. There is a less famous version
of this photograph in which only one of the boys touches the wire.
He bends back slightly, his shoulder tucked back awkwardly, and
connects a single finger to the wire, as if feeling for the prick of the
barbs. In the more well-known image, two of the boys raise their
hands and almost lean on the wire, like dancers lined up on a ballet
barre. They are testing the boundary.

While it is tempting to reduce Miyatake's photographs
to documentation, *Three Boys Behind Barbed Wire* was more
constructed than it appears, the scholar Jasmine Alinder writes:
the boys actually stood outside the camp and looked in. Many
prisoners found the incarceration experience too terrible to
talk about, so perhaps we can read the photographs as not only
describing the implied barbarism of locking up children but
representing their future selves wondering how to probe the
repressed past. Akemi Ookas, the daughter of one of the boys,
reconvened the three subjects, now in their eighties, for the
2017 documentary *Three Boys Manzanar*, a project not unlike
Lee's 2014 restaging of Andrew J. Russell's 1869 golden spike
photograph—taken in Utah to commemorate the completion of
the transcontinental railway—to include descendants of Chinese
rail workers.

If the boys stood outside looking in, this meant Miyatake
positioned himself inside the prison. When the war ended and
the camps opened, some, rather counterintuitively, did not want
to leave. They may have had nowhere to go. The push toward
incarceration had been driven by corporate agribusinesses, which
seized more than a quarter of a million acres of Japanese American
farms. Leaving meant relinquishing the community of the prison
camps for the very racist world that had imprisoned them. Consider
a man named Joe Takeda, who returned from the Gila River prison
to his San Jose pear orchard, where assailants poured gasoline
on his home and shot at his car. Miyatake did not leave immediately.
He stayed and documented those who lingered. Ralph Merritt,
Manzanar's director, warned the now-free residents against
"crowding into the seven southern counties of California" and
creating "another Japanese problem." Miyatake did the opposite.
He spent the remainder of his life photographing Little Tokyo.
With both the Pictorialist movement and his fine arts career having
molted away, he trained his camera on the weddings, families,
births, and deaths of those who lived there. "So, the ancestors
are looking down. / The poet, and/or his poem, is looking up,"
writes the poet Brandon Shimoda, whose family members were
imprisoned in Utah, Montana, and Wyoming. "We are in between."

*High school students on
school grounds, Eastern
Sierras and barracks in
background*, ca. 1942–45
All photographs courtesy
Toyo Miyatake Studio

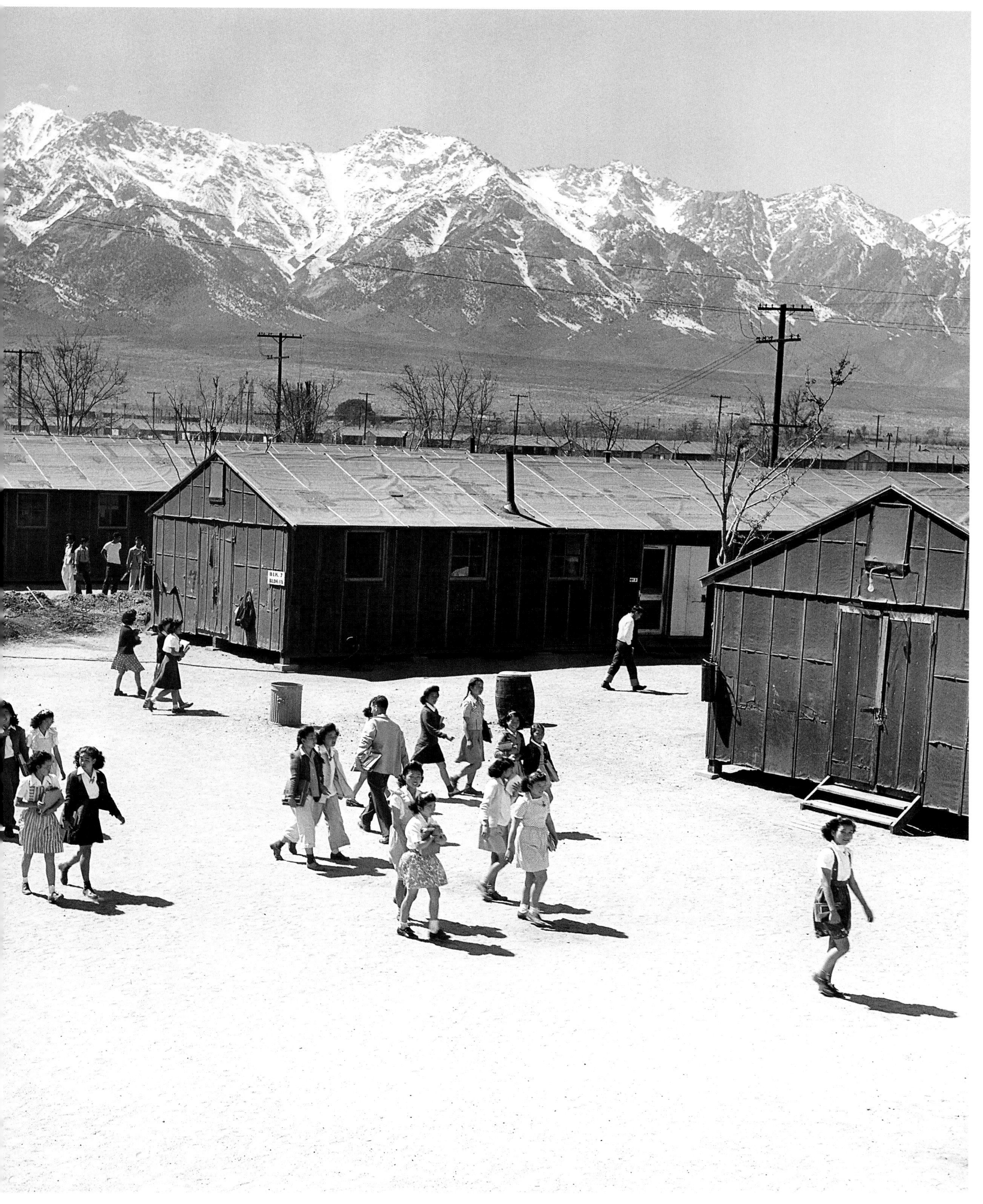

Bruce Yonemoto
North, South, East, West

Amy Sadao

Over the course of researching a project meant to be a fictional addendum to early popular photography of the mid-nineteenth century, Bruce Yonemoto learned that Chinese men had fought and died in the American Civil War. This discovery surrounds a series of portraits, *North South East West* (2007), depicting Asian men uniformed as Northern and Southern troops wielding period-style weapons, set amid portrait-studio standards: a balustrade, a velvet curtain, a vividly patterned floor.

Having spent years around video and film production, Yonemoto was able to access one of Hollywood's oldest wardrobe-supply houses, Western Costume, whose collection includes costumes used in *Gone with the Wind* and *The Birth of a Nation*, D. W. Griffith's 1915 pro-Confederacy film. In *North South East West*, Yonemoto connects Griffith's evocation of the Ku Klux Klan to contemporary forms of white-supremacist organizing, which have grown in recent years.

Yonemoto's soldiers vary in their age, ethnicity, and hairstyle; he appears to have directed his models' expressions as carefully as he selected their garments, postures, and backgrounds. "Period signifiers such as people's clothing and grooming may change with time, but the subject's face remains as the mirror of the soul," he told me. "*Kao ga hiroi* is a Japanese expression that literally means 'face is broad,' or that the person's stature in society has made their face widely recognized and admired. As a cultural phenomenon, *kao ga hiroi* may be construed as the cult of celebrity, but in my mind underscores Walter Benjamin's concept of photographic portraiture as the last refuge of cult value, the face as representation of self."

Yonemoto has frequently drawn upon cinematic and art-historical references in works such as *Before I Close My Eyes* (2010), which involves men in military costume watching footage from the Vietnam War, and *Beyond South: Vietnam (Caravaggio)* (2010), for which he cast Asian models to reenact Caravaggio paintings. *North South East West*, with its layers of queer eroticism, rewrites deeply held and endlessly repeated cultural fictions that insist there were only ever two genders, that there were only ever two races, and that there is hierarchy to how we desire.

North South East West unspools parallel lines of yearning and memorialization, as the young Asian figures challenge lineages of wartime iconography, of imaging masculine beauty, and of depicting race with only Black or white bodies. The series shows us homoerotics, youth, and imminent death—and deploys conventions of nineteenth-century cartes de visite into our moment. Yonemoto's images echo cinematic depictions of home-front-bound family members, lovers, and friends (he remembers the popularity of Ken Burns's 1990 Civil War television documentary series). The act of photography can be preparation for war—the creation of a portrait to be cherished by those who love doomed heroes.

All photographs from the series *North South East West (NSEW)*, 2007
Courtesy the artist

Amy Sadao is a curator based in Philadelphia. She was a cocurator of the FotoFest Biennial *If I Had a Hammer* in 2022.

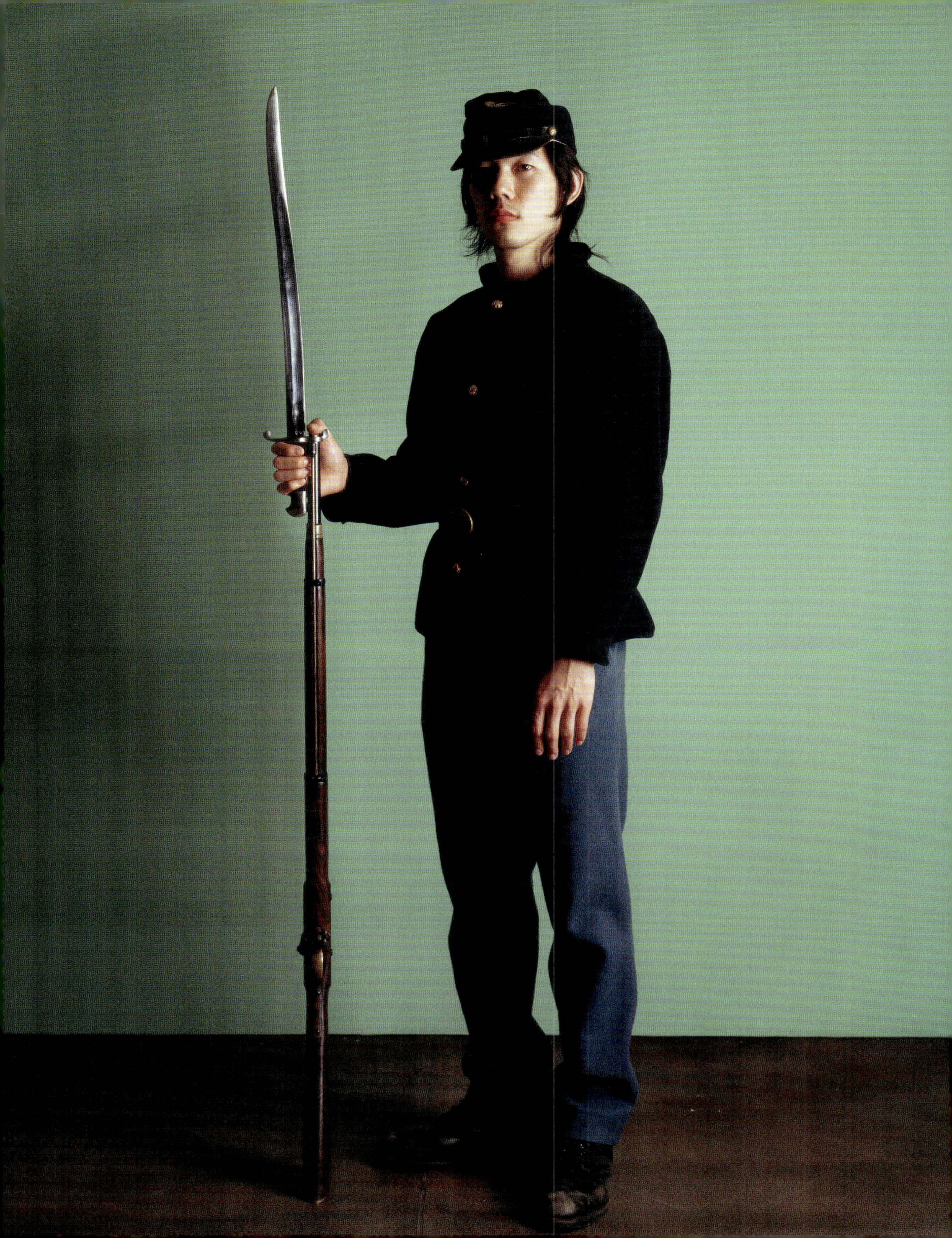

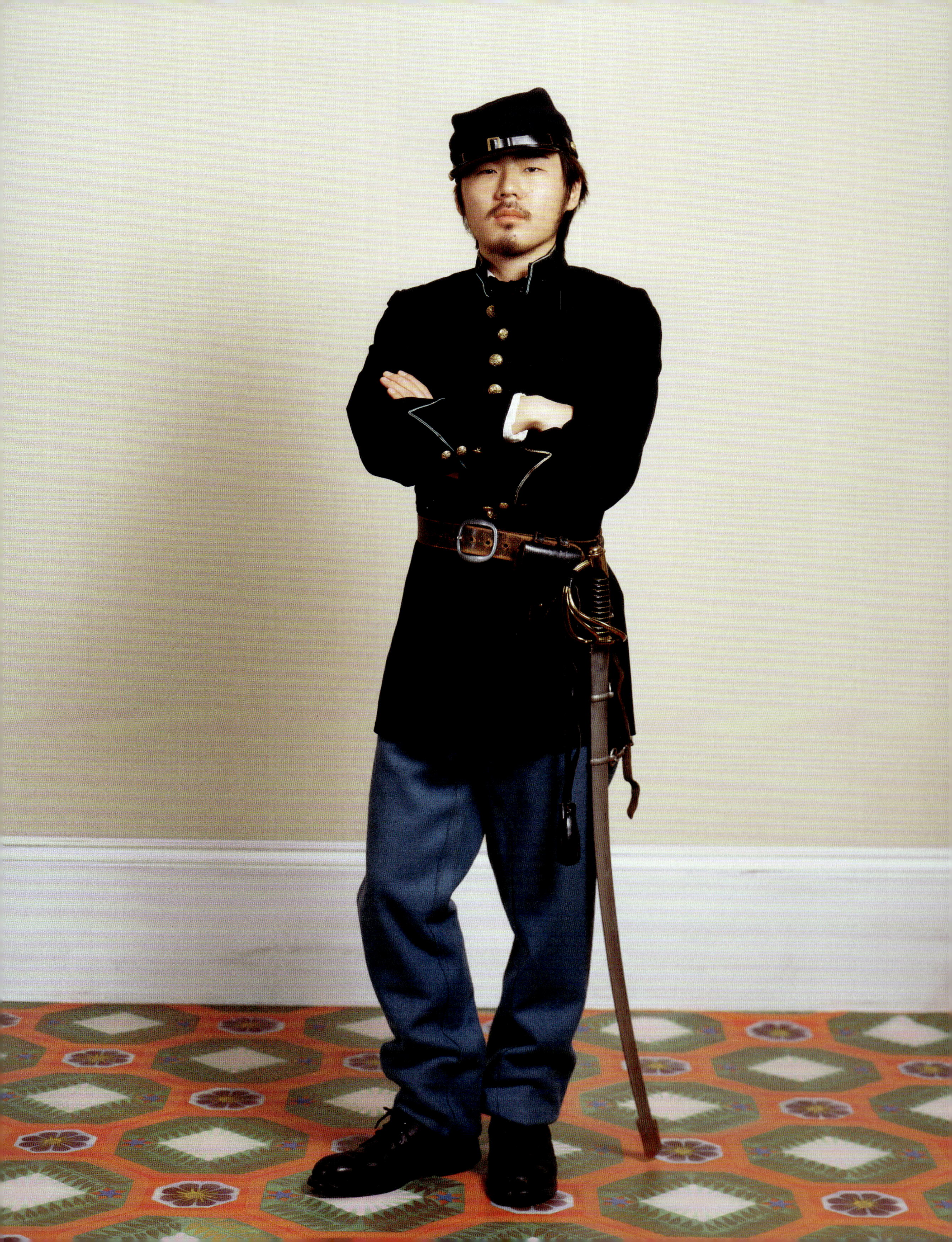

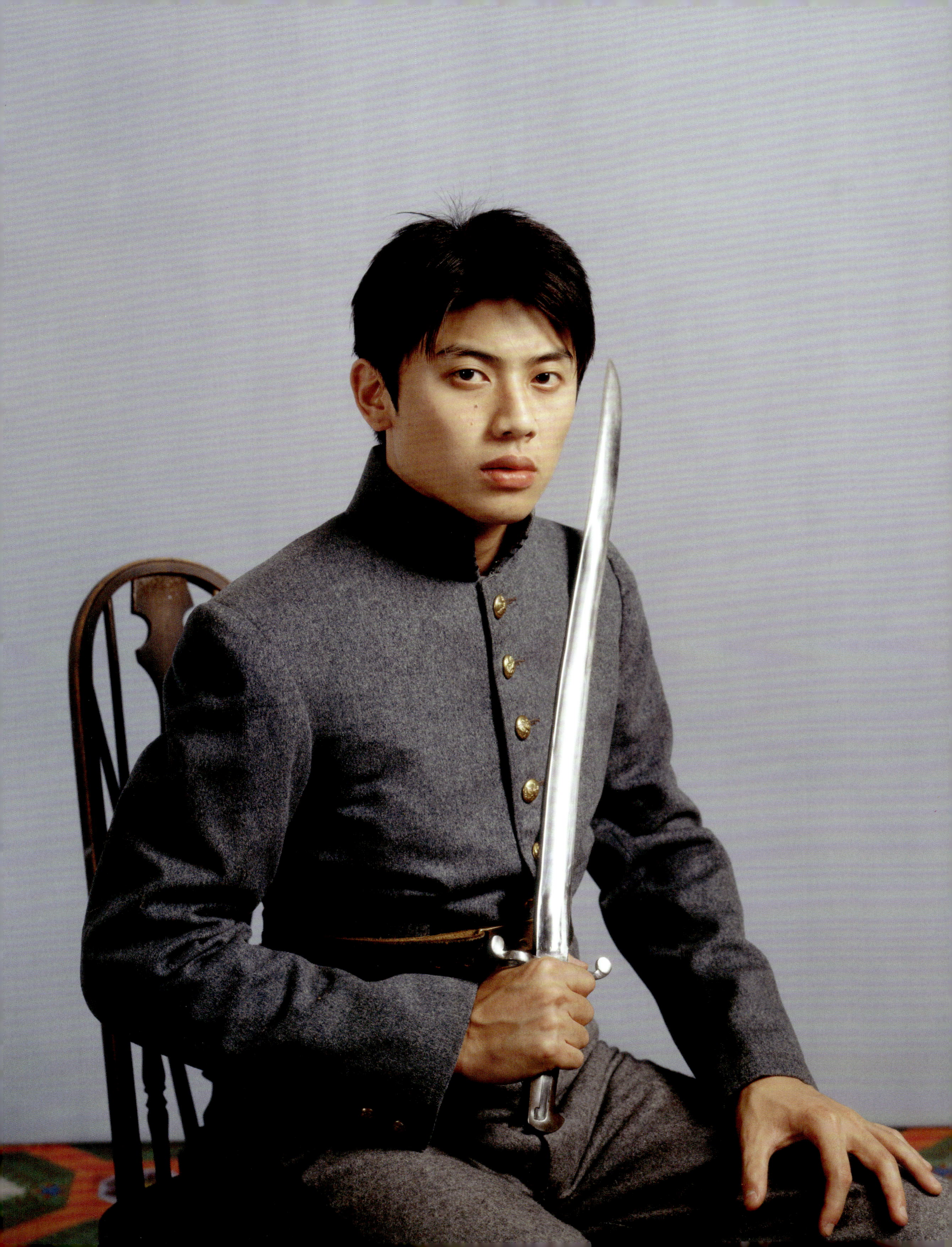

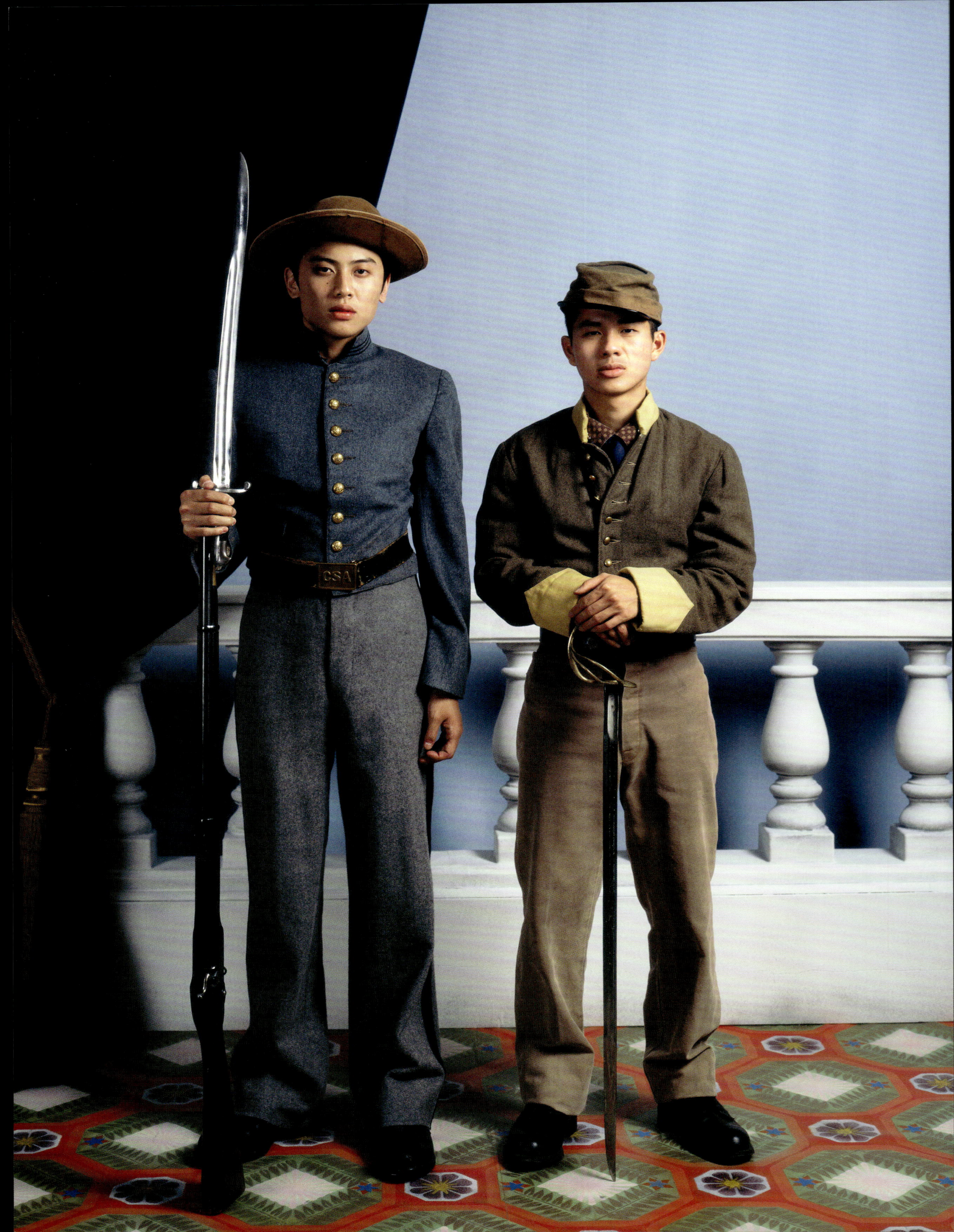

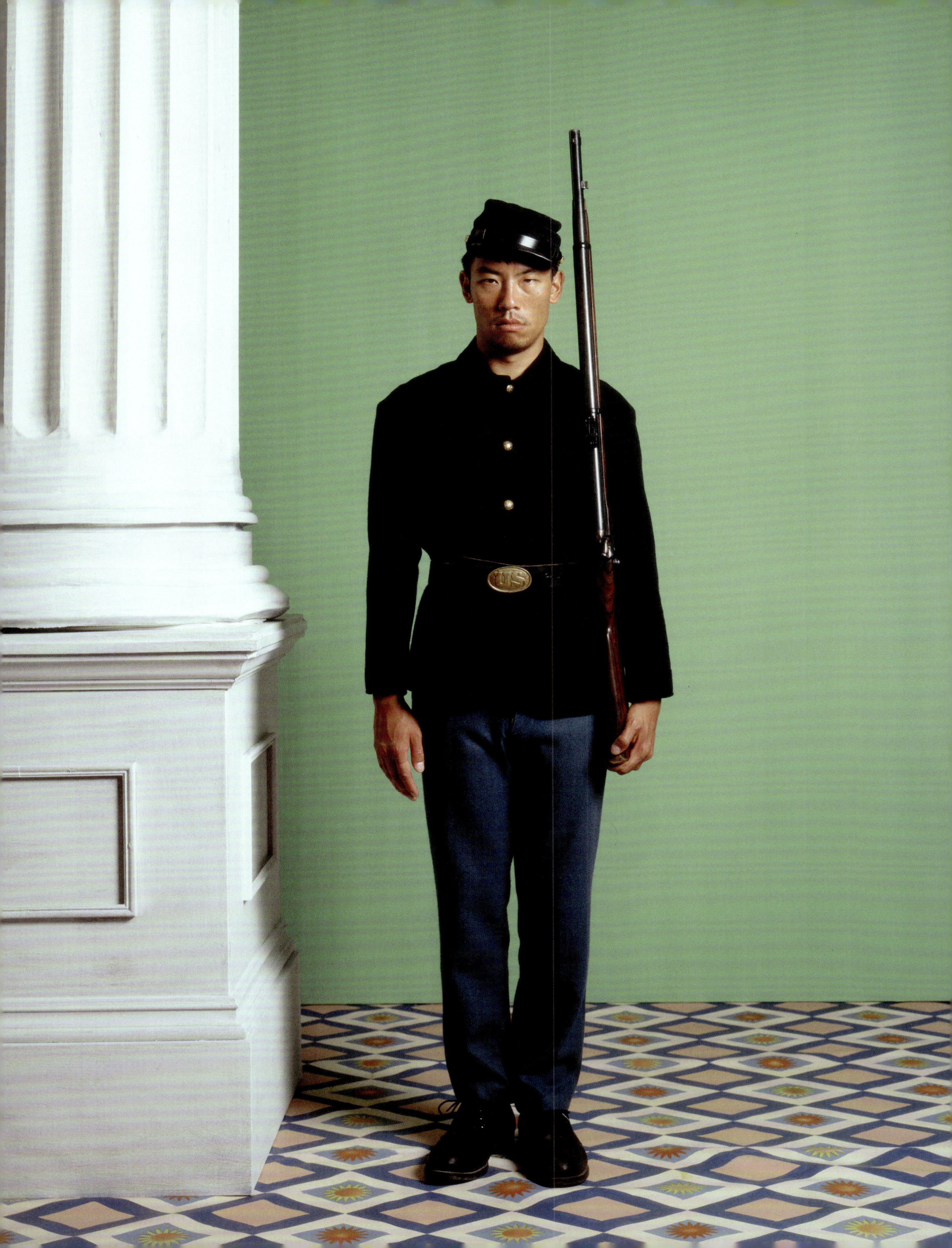

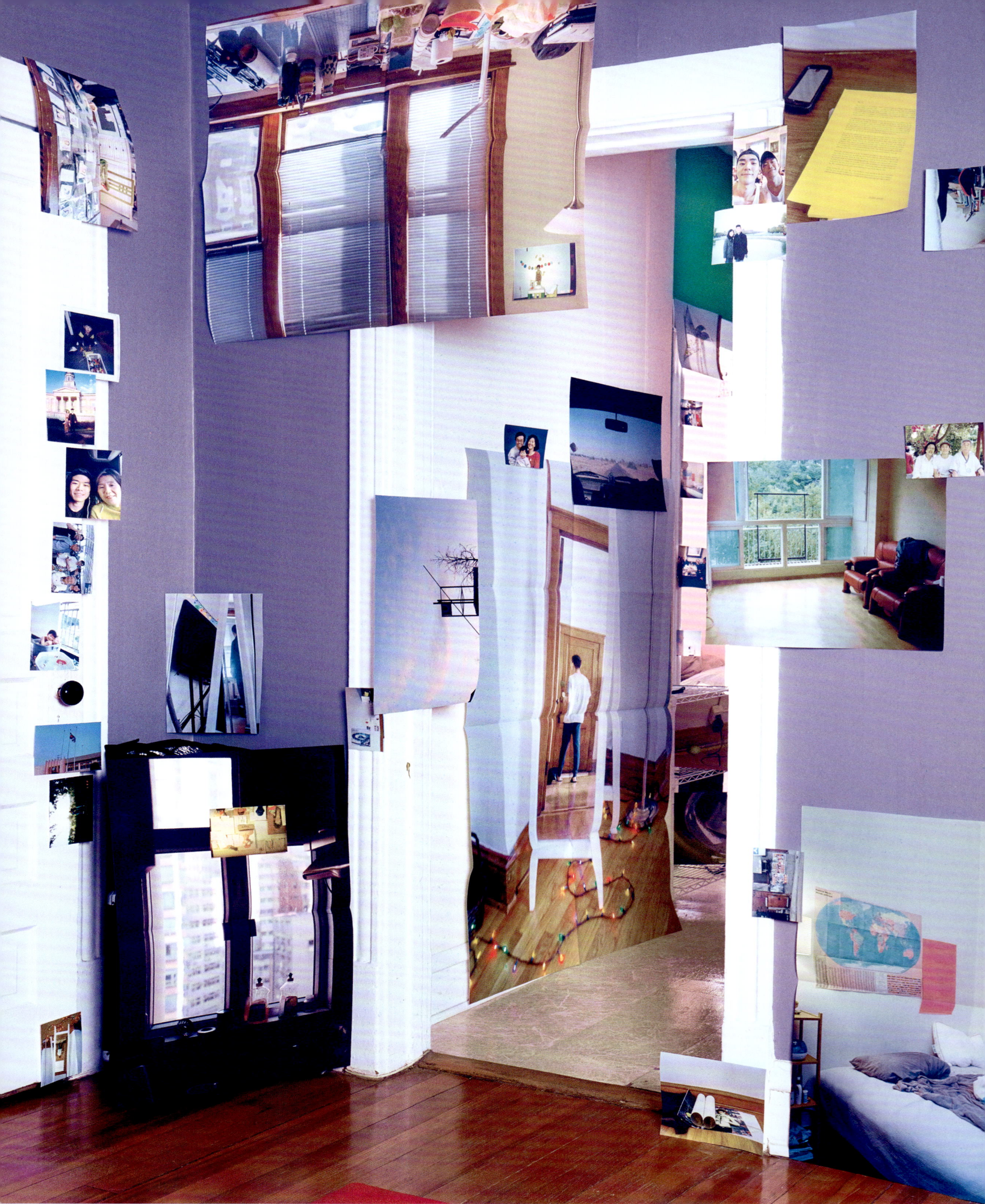

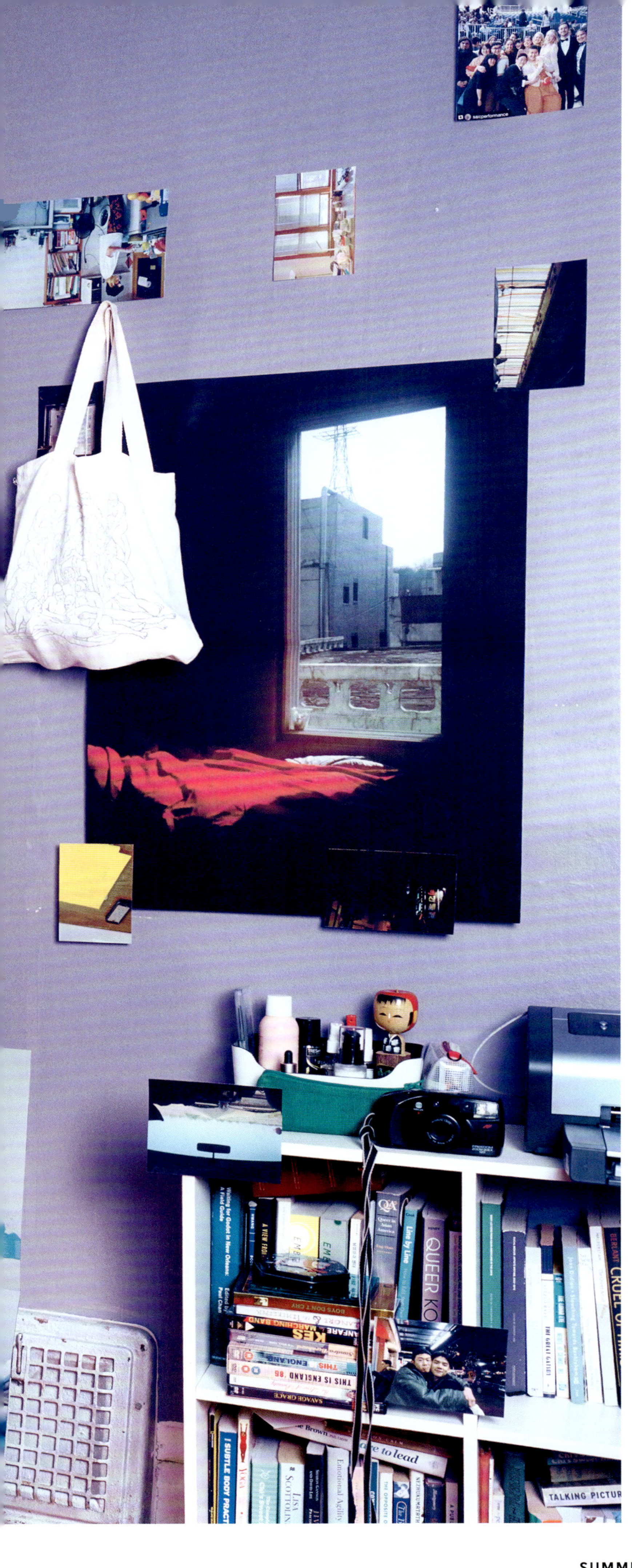

Guanyu Xu
Resident Aliens

Xuan Juliana Wang

In 2018, when he was twenty-six years old, Guanyu Xu returned to China for two weeks to stage his series *Temporarily Censored Home* (2018–19) in secret, while his parents were at work. He transformed their traditional Beijing apartment using hundreds of images from his new, thrilling life as an artist and out gay man in Chicago, along with fashion magazine pages and stills from movies he loves. Xu photographed his installations, then took everything down before his parents returned home. The resulting series reveals unexpected vantages of and contradicting perspectives on the person his parents don't fully know.

Then the pandemic began. Months passed, years. He was able to observe America more closely while viewing China from afar. His father retired. Xu graduated and got an academic job. Four years later, he still hasn't been able to return to China. Now, even his childhood home seems to have moved on. "It's as if my memories of the actual place have been replaced with my staged photographs," Xu recently told me. "It's becoming hard to remember what the home I grew up in actually looked like."

His latest series, *Resident Aliens* (2023), uses the same collage elements and performance aspect to immerse the viewer in the homes of individuals and couples with varying visa statuses in the United States. Most of the participants in *Resident Aliens* were found on social media: a few friends, one refugee, and many who had been international students like Xu. Some hold visas that require them to marry, or forbid them to work, or require them to study, or forbid them to leave. Their conditional status in this country makes them vulnerable to exploitation. United States Citizenship and Immigration Services demands from them documents and ever-increasing application fees. The decision they wait for is ultimately based on arbitrary matters beyond their control.

Xu's re-creation of each subject's history through his process of photography and installation is an emotional exercise imbued with care. "In a sense, I am a foreign agent, acting upon a verbal agreement, and I am invading their space. It is an exchange of power," Xu says. "But my subjects and I are equals. I understand what it takes for them to open up their homes for me, to go through their belongings to find artifacts, and to ask friends and family to send me childhood photos."

The process requires two sessions. In the first, Xu arrives to photograph the subjects, their environment, and their possessions. In the second, he returns with variously sized prints of his photographs and activates the surfaces of the rooms, temporarily transforming the subjects' home into a collaged form of portraiture. The altered living environments are photographed. Then he takes everything down. What we don't observe is the participants seeing their plastered-over homes divulging their identities all at once. Xu always asks if they want to keep the documentation he has made of their current life. Some want to keep all of it. Some want nothing.

Xu's work spotlights the way we experience time and memory, offering a tantalizing vision of choice and change. In one photograph, a toy skyline on a bookshelf seems to transport the entire room back across oceans, into city streets the participant might have known by heart, reflecting the choices made, the price paid in order to stay in this "free" country. "Doorways can signify opportunity," Xu says, "but ironically, a photo of a doorway is just a flat surface, and you can no longer walk through it."

Each image becomes a deeply personal journey, each detail revealing perspectives gained, lost, or forgotten—as in languages, relationships, passports, and identities. With these pictures, one can't help but wonder: What happened to these would-be Americans? When Xu reached out to his subjects for the second session, he found that many of them had already left these rooms. They'd relocated to different cities or returned to their native countries. Others continued their immigrant stories in other countries, on other continents, moving their lives beyond the confines of Xu's photographs, of their own free will.

Xuan Juliana Wang is the author of the short-story collection *Home Remedies* (2019).

Previous spread: *SL-06172015-02112022*, 2022; this spread: *DJ-08182018-01172022*, 2022

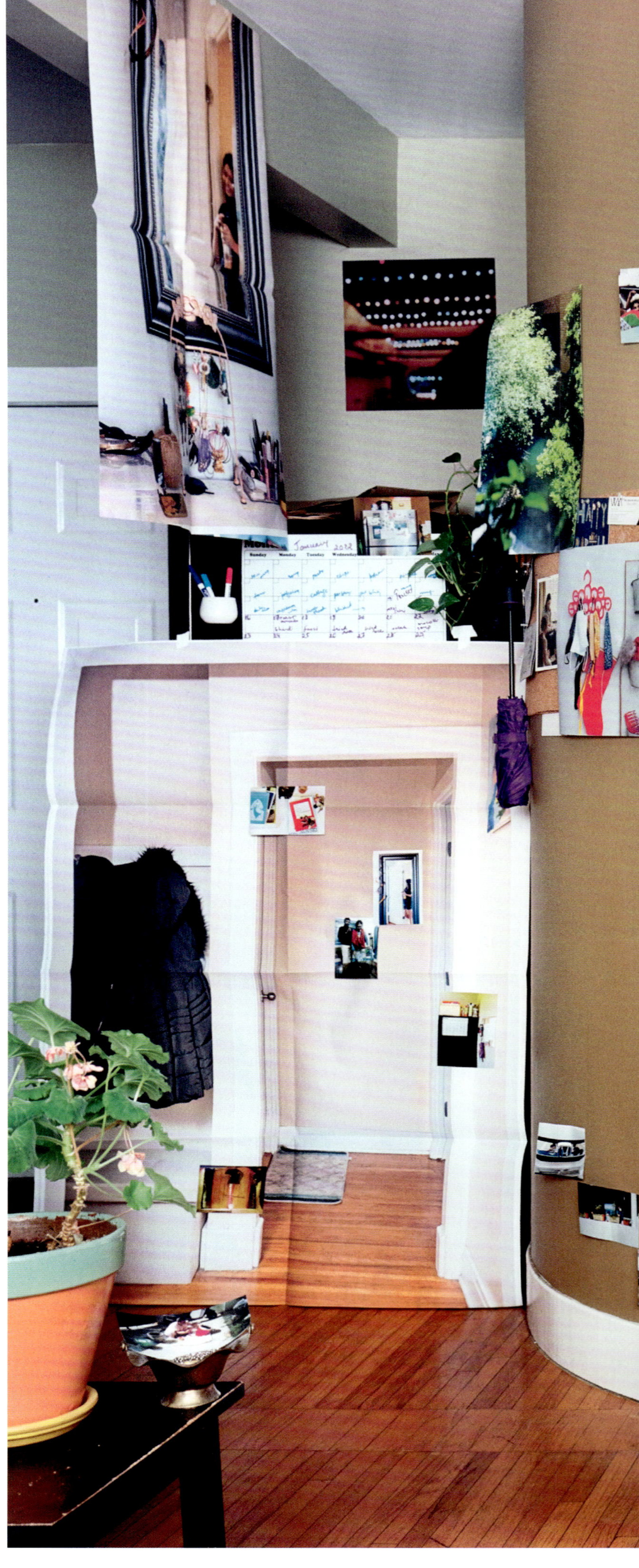

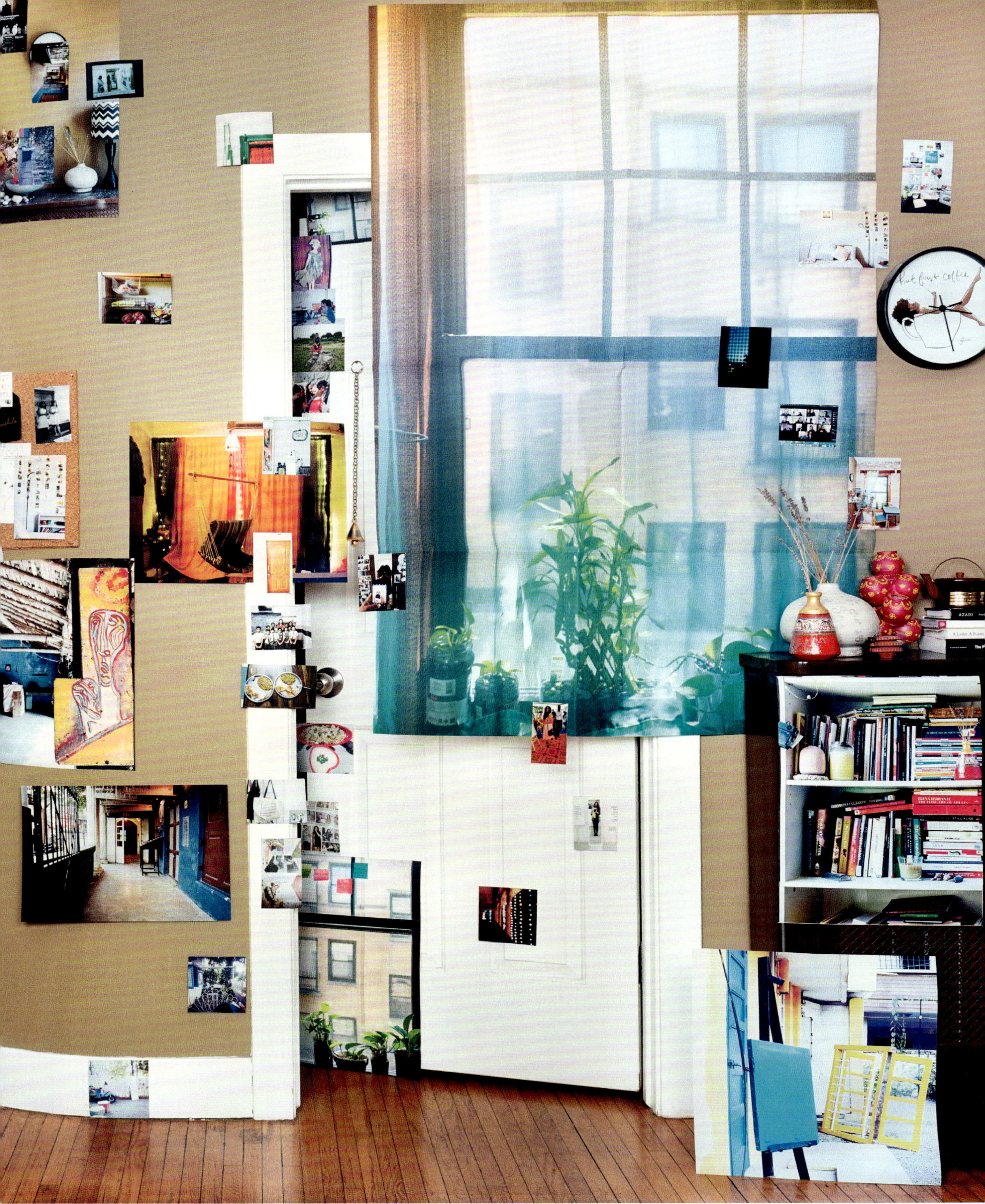

AK-08102008-05032021,
2021

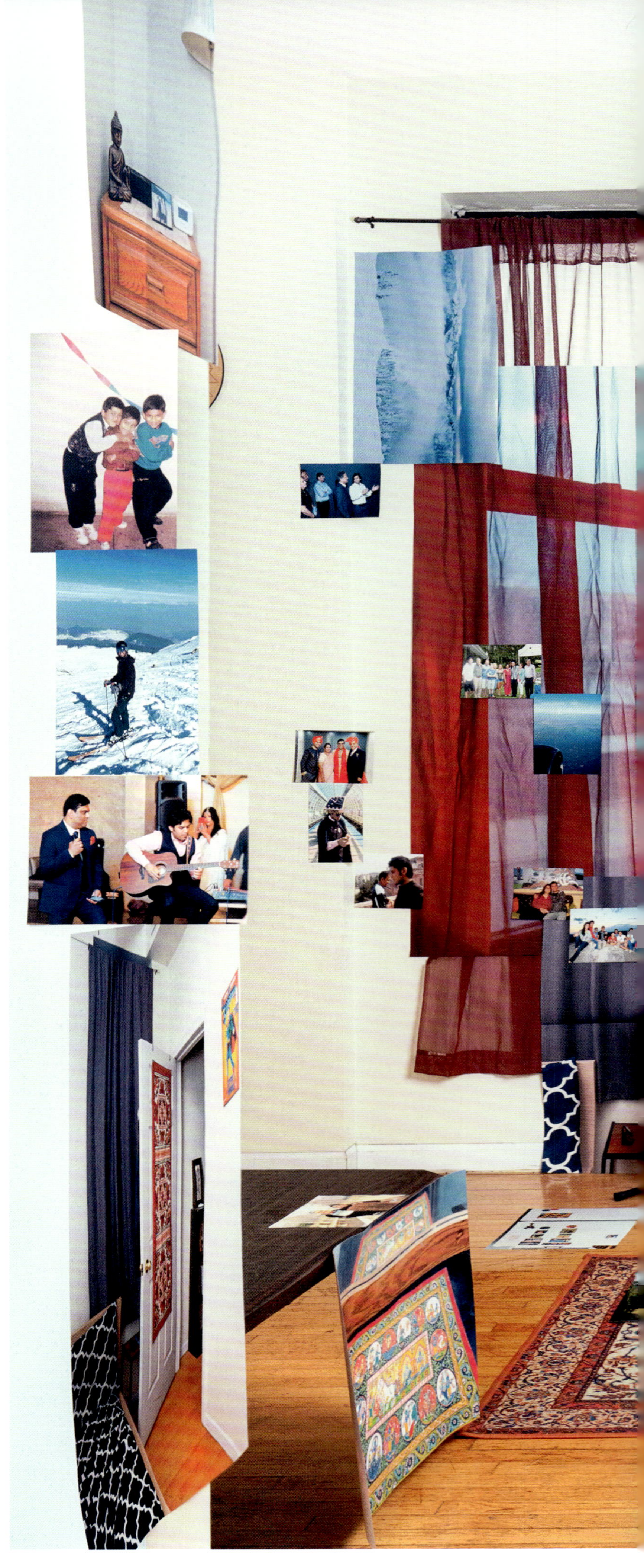

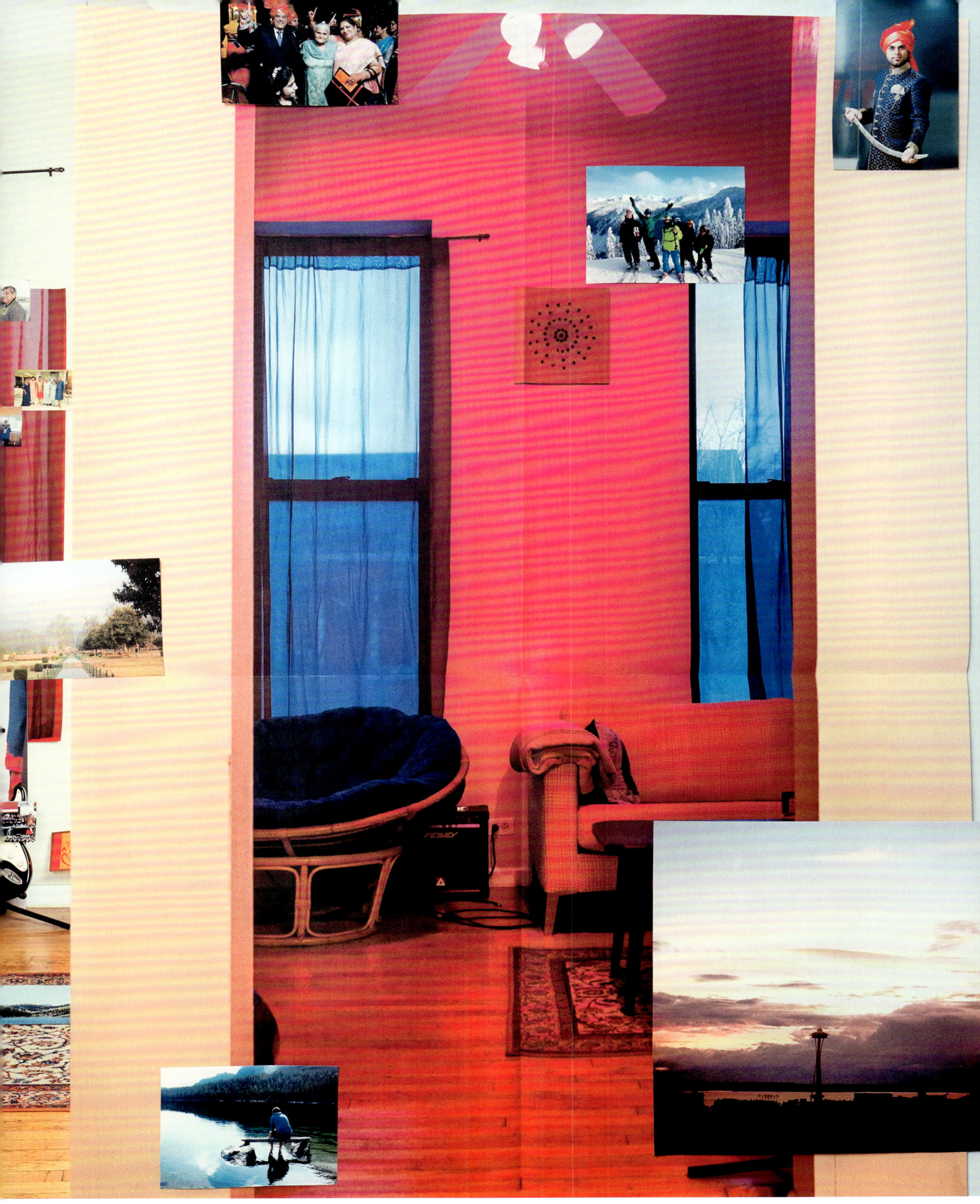

LP-08292016-04112021,
2021
All photographs courtesy
the artist; Galerie du Monde,
Hong Kong; Gaotai Gallery,
Urumqi, China; and Yancey
Richardson, New York

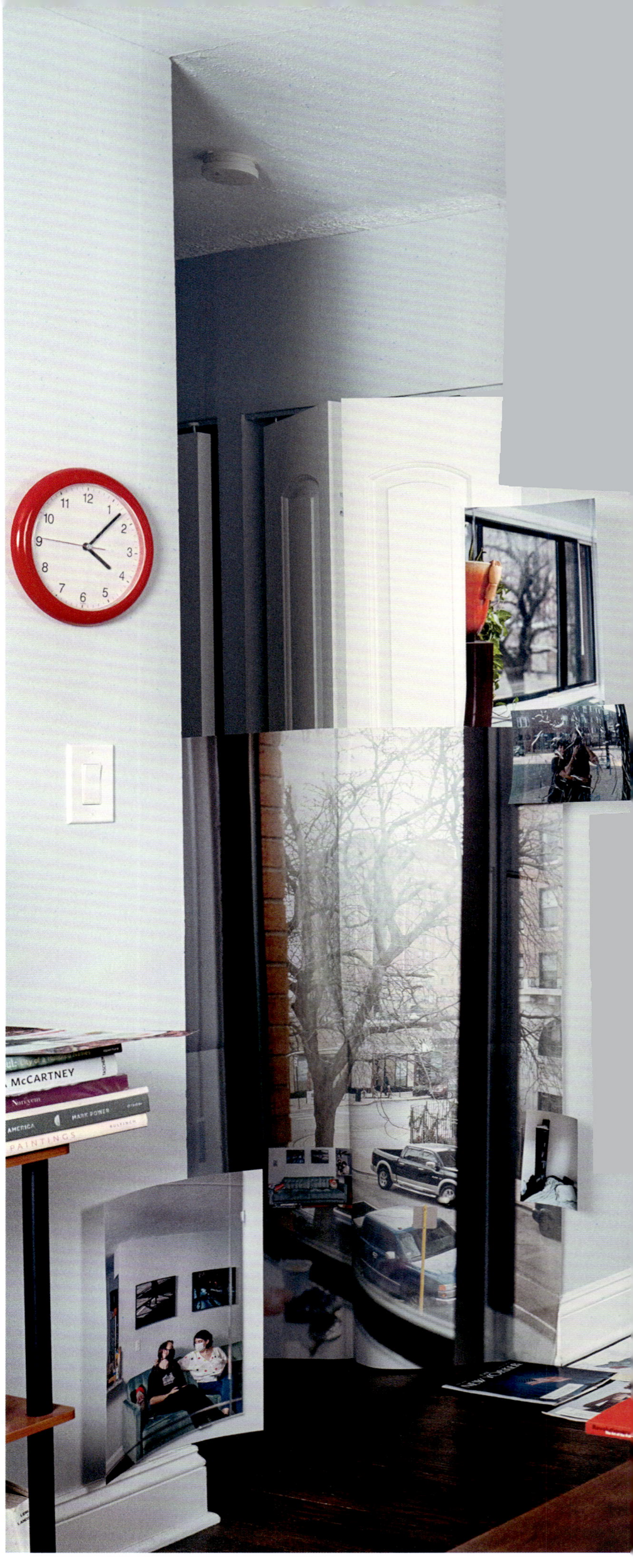

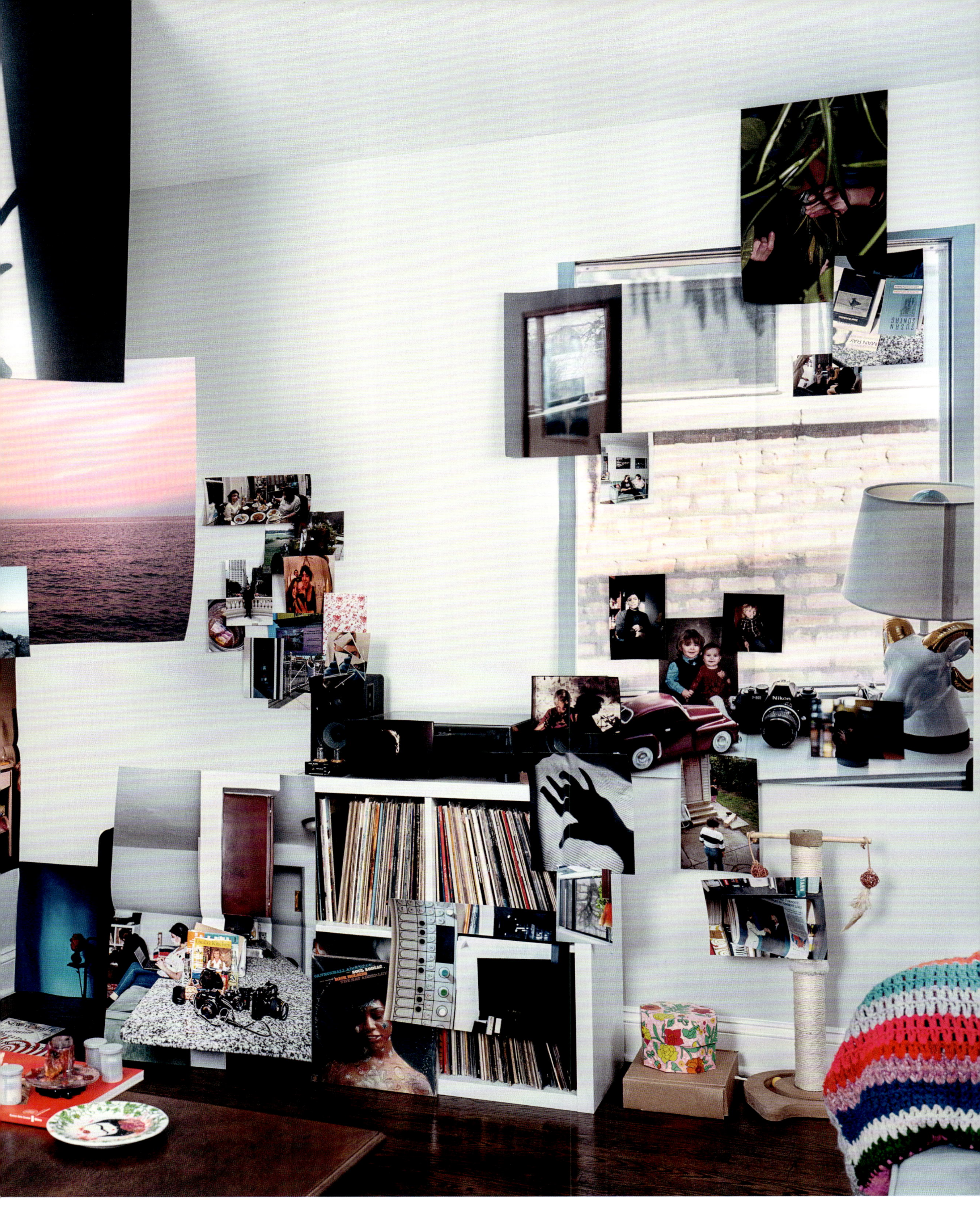

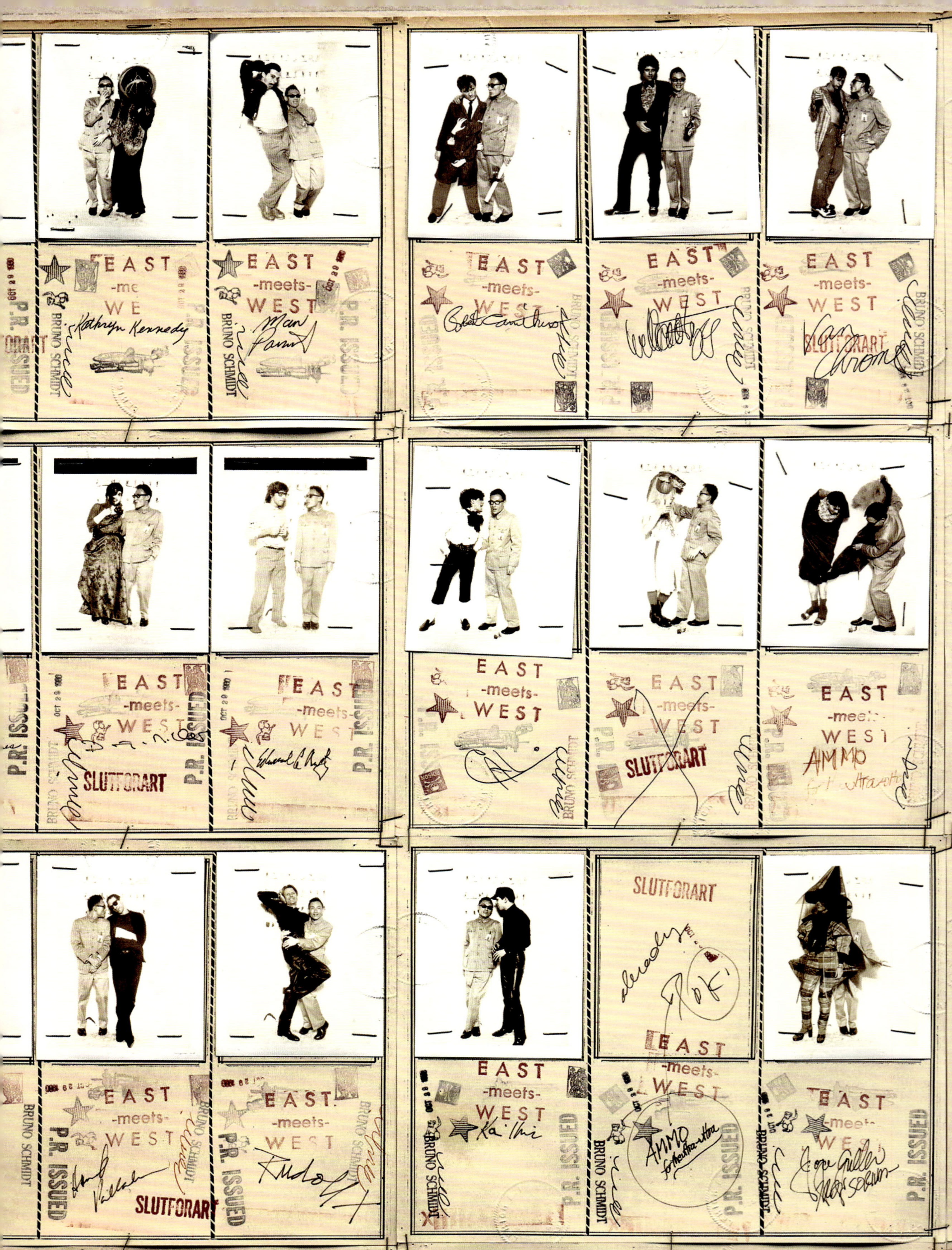

In the 1980s, Tseng Kwong Chi made a name for himself in New York's downtown circuit with his distinctive Mao suit. He lived a form of performance, embodied the role of a Chinese dignitary—and turned his nocturnal life into art.

The Downtown Diplomat
Simon Wu

East Meets West,
(Danceteria, New York)
(detail), 1980

On an early 1980s episode of a Manhattan public-access television show, a slim man wearing sunglasses and a Mao suit walks onto the screen. He is about to treat viewers to a performance. "This is Kwong Chi, ladies and gentlemen," says Kestutis Nakas, a Lithuanian American theater artist and the host of the program. "He's been doing this kind of thing all over town." Tseng Kwong Chi holds a cable release for a camera in his hand. The two shuffle into place, preparing to have their picture taken. The broadcast skips to them looking down at a Polaroid. Nakas points to a name badge on Tseng's chest: "I see that you're a visitor here." "Uh-huh," Tseng says, "I'm a permanent visitor here." The badge on his chest was part of his character, a pretend Chinese dignitary, except that if you looked closely, it read "SLUTFORART." Tseng's appearance on the show, called *Your Program of Programs*, is the only video recording of one of the performances behind the artist's Polaroid panel works, for which he would set up a camera at a location, usually a party, take self-portraits with everyone who arrived, then display them in a grid.

Tseng—performative conceptual photographer, documentarian of East Village life, "permanent visitor"—made his appearance on Nakas's show just a few years after moving to New York. By this time, he'd already made a name for himself in the downtown nightlife circuit with his distinctive Mao suit, a sartorial signature he'd arrived at almost by accident. Months after landing in New York, Tseng's parents treated him and his sister, the dancer Muna Tseng, to dinner at Windows on the World, the restaurant at the top of the former World Trade Center. Tseng wore the only suit he

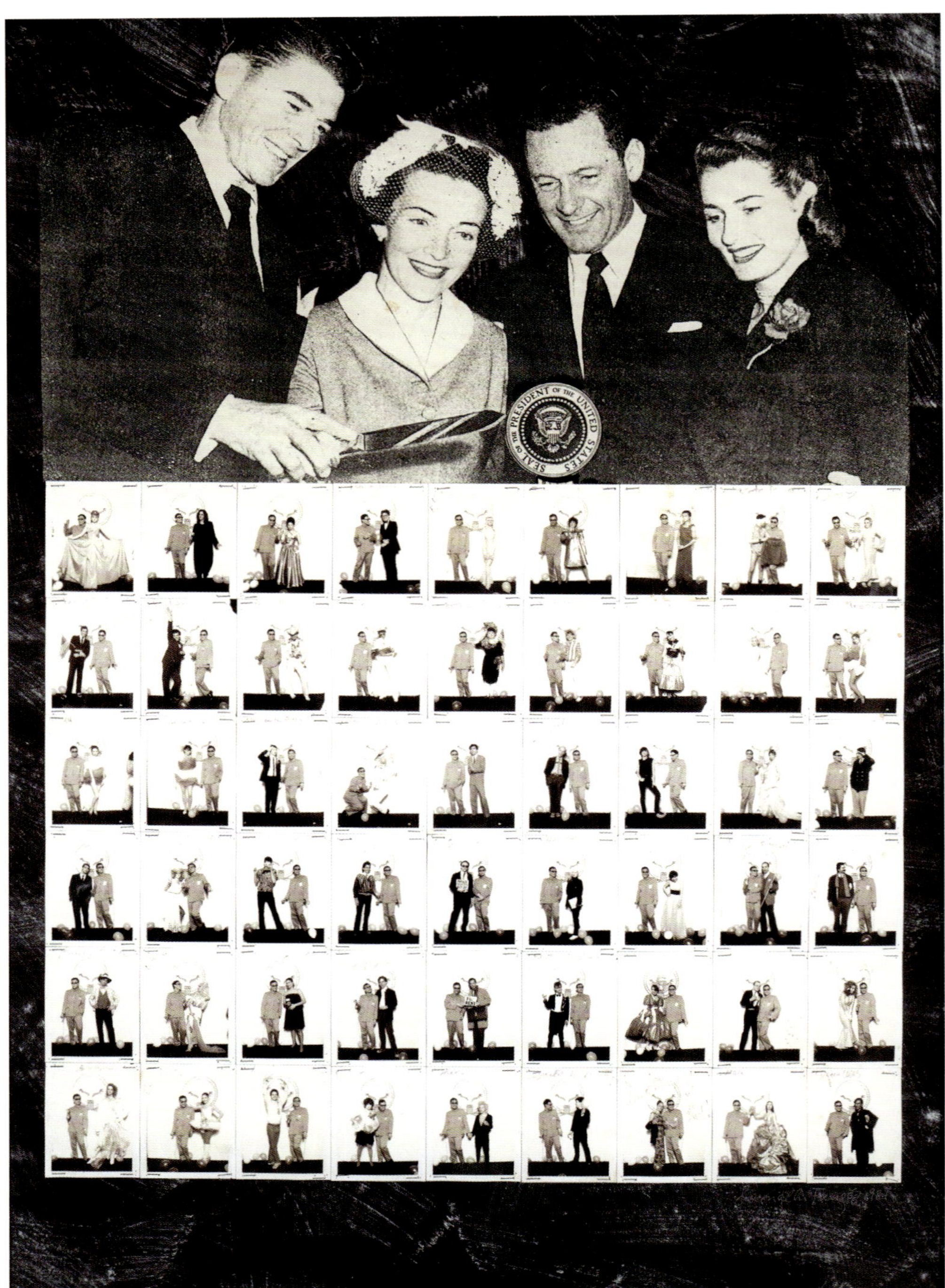

had: a gray Mao suit that he had purchased at a Chinese boutique in Montreal. The store's owner had bought an entire warehouse of the suits, betting that they might be the next big fashion trend in Canada (they weren't). Tseng's parents were mortified, but the maître d' mistook him for an ambassador and gave them the best table in the house. The suit would likewise help give Tseng entrée into New York's downtown art world.

In a recently unearthed interview from 1987, Tseng describes the origin of his taking Polaroids. "The whole reason I started that was because I didn't know very many people in New York, because it was just when I came to New York. And that was one way for me to meet as many people as possible in a party context, as well as a way for me to be noticed by other people." He would soon make similar collaborative images around the city—on the Staten Island Ferry, in the Harlem ballroom scene, at the Jacob Riis Park beach in Queens. In existing scholarship, the photographs are usually considered in isolation, the panel assemblies themselves a kind of afterthought, but these are significant as artworks in their own right, connecting Tseng's interest in "tourism" and the body, his prolific documentary photography, and his

vibrant nocturnal life into constellations that foreshadow today's Instagram grids.

When I met Muna Tseng at her Christopher Street apartment last winter, she mentioned that her brother was a Virgo—a sign notorious for organizational acumen—which may partly explain his interest in the grid. But seeing these works in person, amid binders of negatives and outtakes, I started to understand them differently, as a wilder, unrulier way of making a party's archive. Muna's apartment is also where Tseng's estate is housed; with part-time help, she negotiates her active dance practice with the assiduous management of the estate, a balance palpable in the space's artful clutter. Boxes of photographs are stacked in a soft Tetris-like grid behind mirrored closets. As she pulled out binder after binder, I was aware that outside, a Sweetgreen and a Honeygrow, new health-conscious food chains, had opened, signs of how much the city has changed in recent years, yet inside, records of old New York lived on through the diligent care of loved ones.

Born Joseph Tseng in 1950, Tseng grew up in Hong Kong and Vancouver and left home at sixteen after coming out to his father (in a basement, following a fist fight). He studied photography in

Paris, then moved to New York in 1978, into an East Village apartment that Muna found for him—just down the block from her own place. On a spring day a year later, outside of his apartment, he met a boy with round glasses and curly hair. First (maybe) lovers, then friends, the artist Keith Haring and Tseng became inseparable. They were mainstays of the nighttime swirl of artists and celebrities in the 1980s East Village scene—Madonna, Kenny Scharf, Ann Magnuson, John Sex, Bill T. Jones, Cindy Sherman, and so on.

Tseng is perhaps best known for his *East Meets West* series (1979–89), in which he dressed as a Chinese tourist in front of American and international monuments such as the Statue of Liberty, the Hollywood sign, Disneyland, and the London Bridge. But he was also a prolific documentarian, leaving behind an archive of more than twenty thousand photographs of Haring's work, as his "official" photographer; portraits of artists, including Julian Schnabel, Jean-Michel Basquiat, and Andy Warhol; and hundreds of snapshots from nights out and about in the city. Tseng and Haring made art for a raucous ten years, from 1979 to 1989—the length of Homer's *Odyssey*, as Muna noted in a 2021 interview—before Tseng died in 1990, from AIDS, at home in New York, less than a month after Haring.

First Invitational: Club 57, Mudd Club, New York (1980) was Tseng's first panel piece, made for the opening of an exhibition that Haring curated at Club 57. To create it, Tseng set up an impromptu photo booth at the party's entrance and over the course of the night composed a grid, Polaroid by Polaroid, measuring forty-five by forty-three and a half inches. As each guest walked through the door, a new image was made and added. The piece tracks the passage of time over the course of the party and also serves as a roll call of guests, an incomplete archive of a night, until the panel ran out of space—maybe just in time for the party to get going and Tseng to join in. (One unidentified partygoer inscribed their photograph "Confused, Baffled, Easily Stimulated.")

The panels are also a catalog of body postures. "I got interested in body language. Body language of New Yorkers in nightclubs

Tseng and Keith Haring were mainstays of the nighttime swirl of artists and celebrities in the East Village scene—Madonna, Bill T. Jones, and Cindy Sherman.

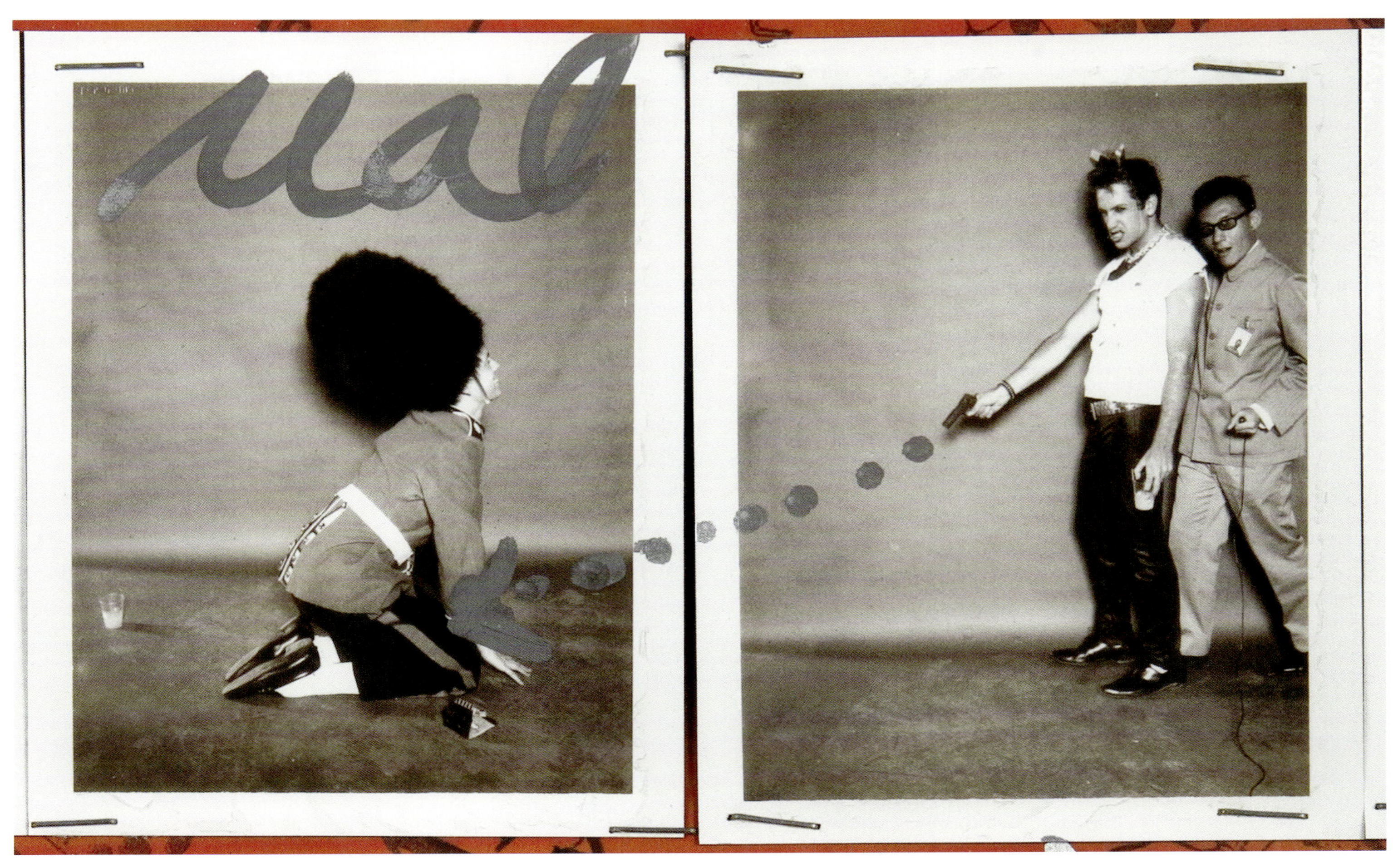

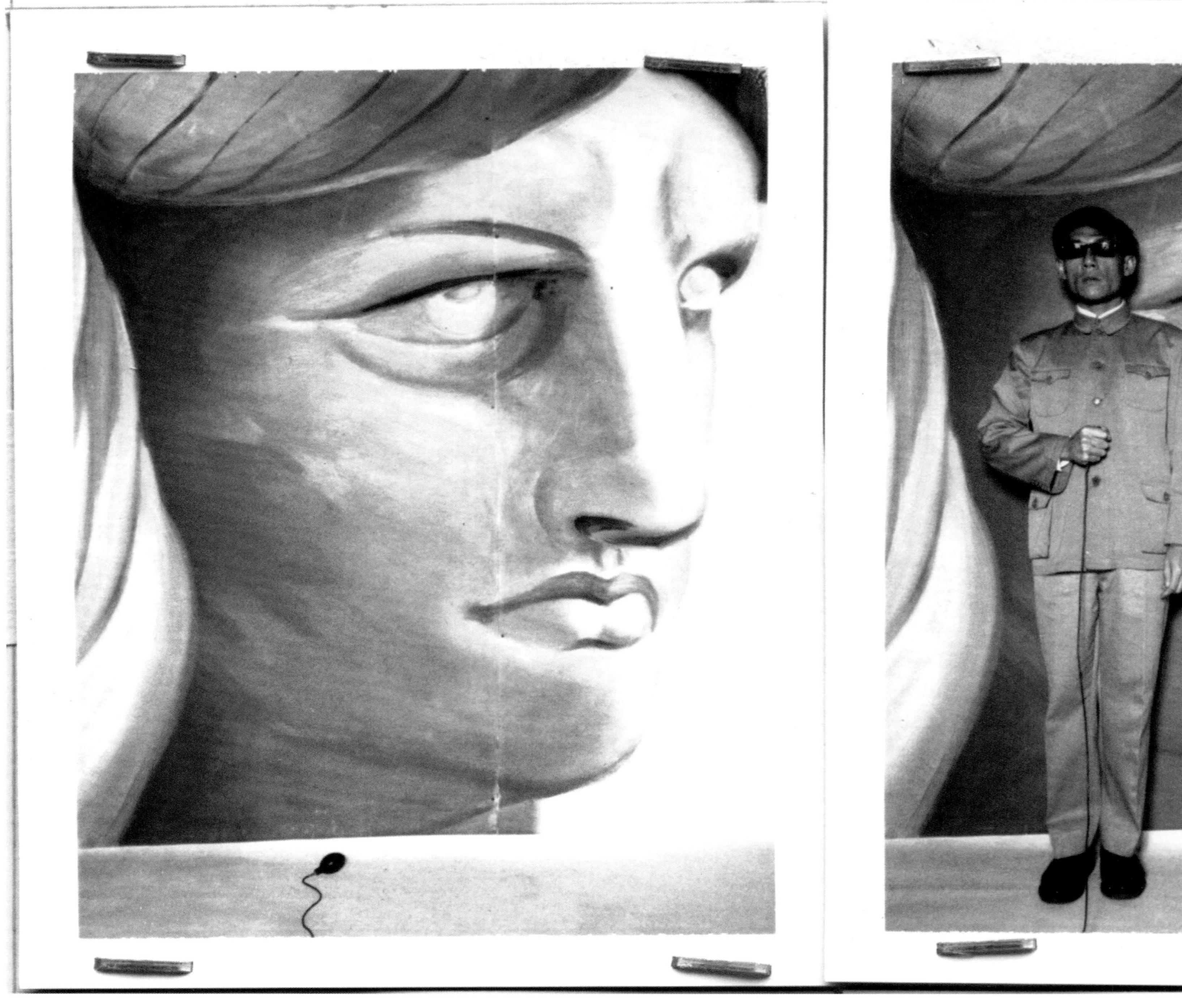

Keith Haring's 3rd Annual Party of Life, Palladium, (New York), May 21 (detail), 1986

and different situations," he says on the episode of *Your Program of Programs*. "And, well, Keith asked me to do this thing at Club 57, so I thought, Well, I'll study the body language of all the people in Club 57. And they were all twisted." A bent knee, a cocked hip, a shy smile, a confident glower; the panels are studies in what we might call a club contrapposto. If in the 1960s Minimalists were experimenting with the logic of the grid, Tseng's unintentional rejoinder in the '80s was to fill that austere grid with the pliable tissue of social relationships. Their panel-like form also resembles the loose behind-the-scenes feeling of a contact sheet—as if each were a rehearsal of the same picture. In another party panel, which Tseng would make the next year for a royal-wedding-themed party at the Underground, some of his friends seemed to acknowledge the medium of the grid, playfully posing like a BDSM dog across two frames. Tseng also liked the idea that the Polaroids— as a light-sensitive medium—would document the initial flare and the gradual fade of a new relationship. "Every relationship you have with other people, it never stays fresh," he once said. "You know, some people just fade away from your life and you never see them

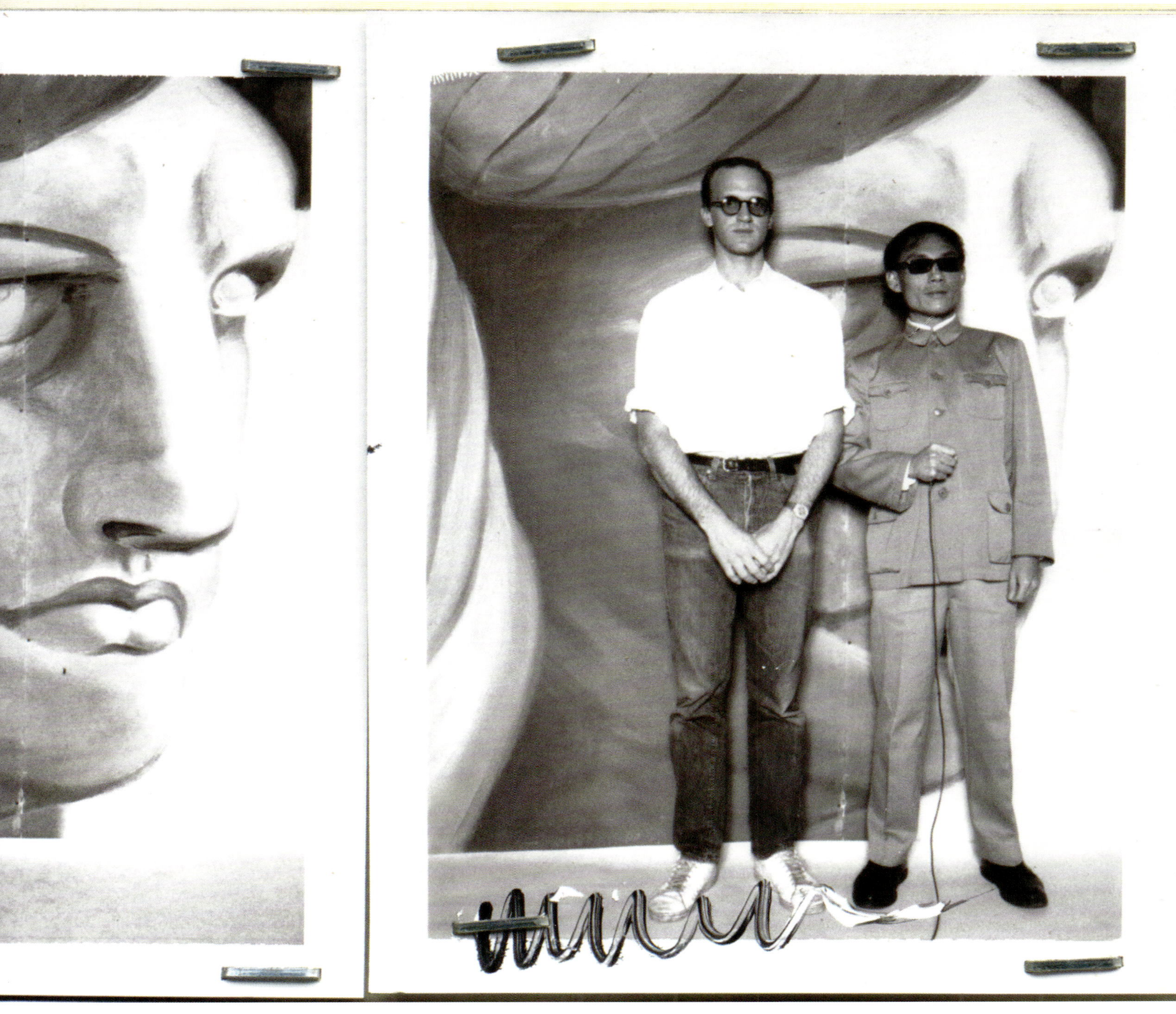

again"—an idea that introduced an element of decomposition to the otherwise stalwart minimalist grid.

Tseng referred to the making of his Polaroid panels explicitly as a performance—even if today it might just seem like a human photo booth—and a performance connected to identity-based subject matter. In the 1987 interview, he describes the panels as an extension of the play on tourism seen in his other projects. "It's an exchange, yeah, it's an exchange of . . . it's kind of like an exchange of confidence," he said. "Instead of shaking hands, instead of just shaking hands and saying 'How are you?' I invite them for one Polaroid. Which I keep. [Laughs]." The "touristic" element of his nightlife photographs feels even more apparent when we look at the panel that he made on the occasion of a party with an "East Meets West" theme at the nightclub Danceteria. It is unique among the Polaroid panels because the photographs have been arranged to resemble a passport book, with sets of three images sitting above a space with signatures and stamps that read: "EAST -meets- WEST," "SLUTFORART," and "P.R. ISSUED."

The East-meets-West dynamic is also enacted, perhaps unintentionally, across the fashions featured in the Polaroids. Tseng stands in for the East as he takes pictures with the mostly non-Asian partygoers, who represent the West. Tseng's Mao suit remains a constant, while the partygoers' clothes change. In 1980, he would crash the Met Gala in the same suit, taking pictures next to the city's socialites, who wore orientalized costumes for the opening of *The Manchu Dragon*, an exhibition (organized by Diana Vreeland) of Chinese costume from the Qing dynasty. Tseng would later delineate a difference between Eastern and Western philosophies of fashion in the 1987 interview. "You know, because fashion is a very western statement," he explains. "It's a very western concept that you change your clothes every day, instead of wearing the same clothes all the time." Discussing a planned but unrealized sequel to his *East Meets West* series, he envisioned traveling to mainland China and dressing as an Americanized Chinese tourist—which, to him, meant getting a perm and wearing designer jeans, Ferrari sunglasses, and an Armani suit. "I would like to grow my hair a little bit longer and have a permanent, like so many westernized Chinese

Although Tseng predates the flourishing of identity politics in the 1990s, his work resonates today because of its provocative engagement with stereotype.

do, and um, you know, wear designer sunglasses. And I would keep changing clothes—which is a statement in itself."

As Ronald Reagan took office and the culture wars ignited, Tseng, in two 1981 panels, addressed these political divisions within his photographs. The first, made on the occasion of a party at the Mudd Club—ironically, celebrating the president's inauguration—sets his usual Polaroid grid against a black-and-white photograph of the Reagans menacingly holding a knife next to the seal of the presidency. In the second, which would grow into its own project called *Moral Majority* (1981), he took pictures with a very different kind of "party"—members of the Moral Majority, a conservative political group founded in 1979 by the religious leader Jerry Falwell. Posing as a photojournalist on an assignment in DC, Tseng switched his signature Mao suit for a seersucker one to set the men at ease, and documented the insertion of his "tourism" into an antigay, antifeminist, and anti-immigrant milieu. Tseng's body is the through line across these projects. "I'm always in the photograph because it all has to do with tourist snapshots," he explained. "It's a reaffirmation by a tourist—by someone, you know, who has gone somewhere, and it's like proof I was there."

Although Tseng predates the flourishing of identity politics in the 1990s, his work resonates today because of its provocative engagement with stereotype. Tseng at the time had never stepped

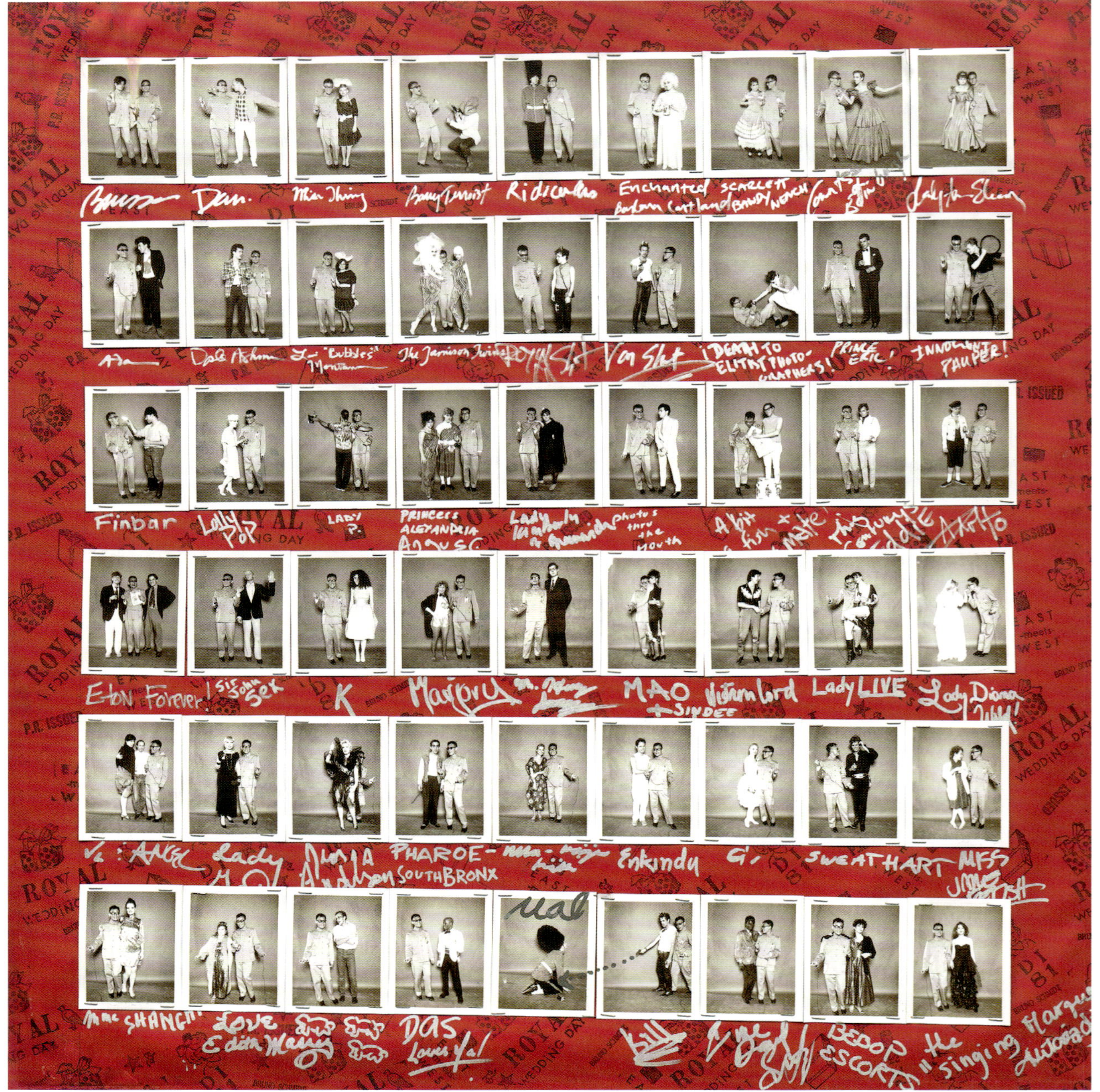

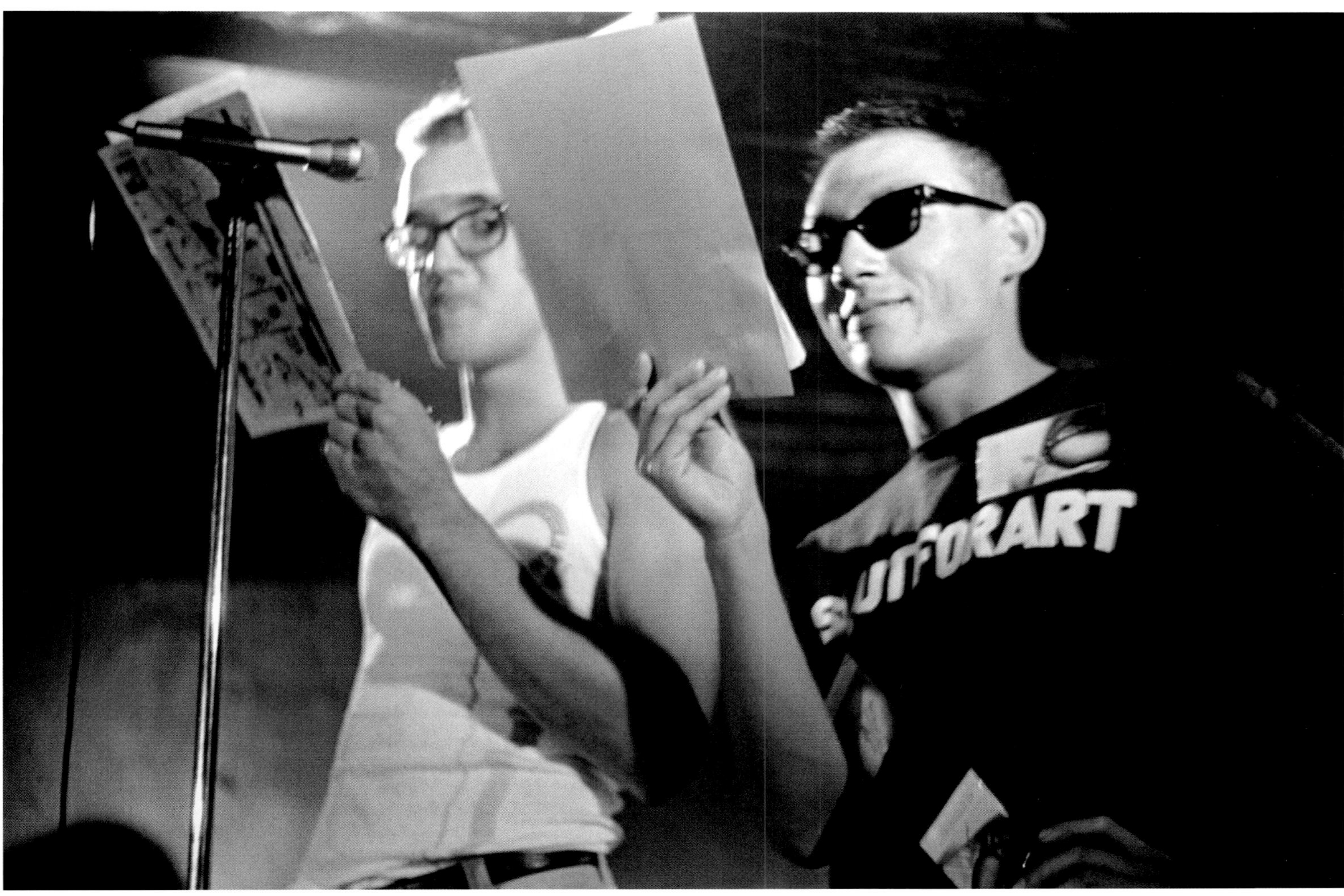

foot in mainland China, yet the Mao suit seemed to manifest what everyone else saw in him: the Chinaman. "He was dealing with identity politics," Muna remarked in a recent *Zolima CityMag* interview. "Even though he did not ever say 'I'm a Chinese artist' or 'I'm a Chinese-American artist' or 'I'm a Chinese-Canadian artist.' He just said, 'I'm an artist.' He did not want to be ghettoised. And I think that comes from the fact that our parents were outward-looking. He would say, 'This is my art. I dress as a Chinese citizen, but I'm in the world.'" This tension between what others saw of him and what he thought of himself would become the playful, and painful, afterimage of his art.

The legacy of Tseng's intentional self-orientalization remains complicated. The Mao suit granted him access to various worlds of white power. A forthright admission of his otherness somehow inoculated him from any threatening impulses, as if saying: *My allegiance is to China, rest assured; your America remains untouched.* Tseng decided to be overtly Asian, exacerbating stereotypical qualities to preempt the punch line. There was no need to go back to where he came from, because he had never left; there was no presumption of being American. The costume was a deadpan tautology: Asian = Asian. The exact hurt of being flattened in this way is being associated with all of the word's stereotypes—emasculated, bucktoothed, effeminate, sexually inviolable, fetishized—and exacts an emotional cost that is lost to history. Did Tseng avoid other Asian people because of it? How many Asian friends did he have or lose? There are only two or three Polaroids in which he appears with another Asian person—in one he's with Benjamin Liu, Andy Warhol's studio assistant, and in another he's with his sister. "It is not easy being a Chinese tourist," Tseng told *Inside Magazine* in 1989. "Should I tell them the truth, that I am actually a New York conceptual performance artist/photographer carrying on my lifetime art project of the East meeting the West?"

Perhaps as he intended, today it is rare to see photographs of Tseng *without* the Mao suit, his own self and his performance of being the "other" possibly having merged. I searched for photographs of him without the suit on, the suit that began to seem like both a superpower and a prison of his own making. I wanted to know if there was a version of him that existed outside of the performance.

Of course, there are images of him without the suit. Some great ones. They just don't get the same attention. In a particularly nice one, he's reading a poem onstage next to Haring at Club 57. In another, he's at dinner, in a black suit and blazer. Seeing pictures of him without his Mao suit, I felt relief. I felt, involuntarily, that he was like me, and I wanted to know that in the future my image would not also be limited to a caricature of my race. He was human. Even if Tseng had done it on purpose, I couldn't help but mourn a version of his practice that was not predicated on an imposed otherness. Honoring the grit of a generation of pioneering Asian American artists while deconstructing the conditions that produced that hardship to begin with remains a challenge of the present. Yet these are problems of the archive, not of a life. "When Tseng and I landed in New York to become artists, we did not see ourselves as not belonging," Muna states in *Boundless Minds and Moving Bodies in 80s New York*, the 2022 book about the siblings' collaborations with Keith Haring. "We saw it as: 'Okay, we've gotta make it here. We gotta be somebody in this world.'"

Simon Wu is a New York–based writer and curator. His first book, *Dancing on My Own*, will be published in 2024.

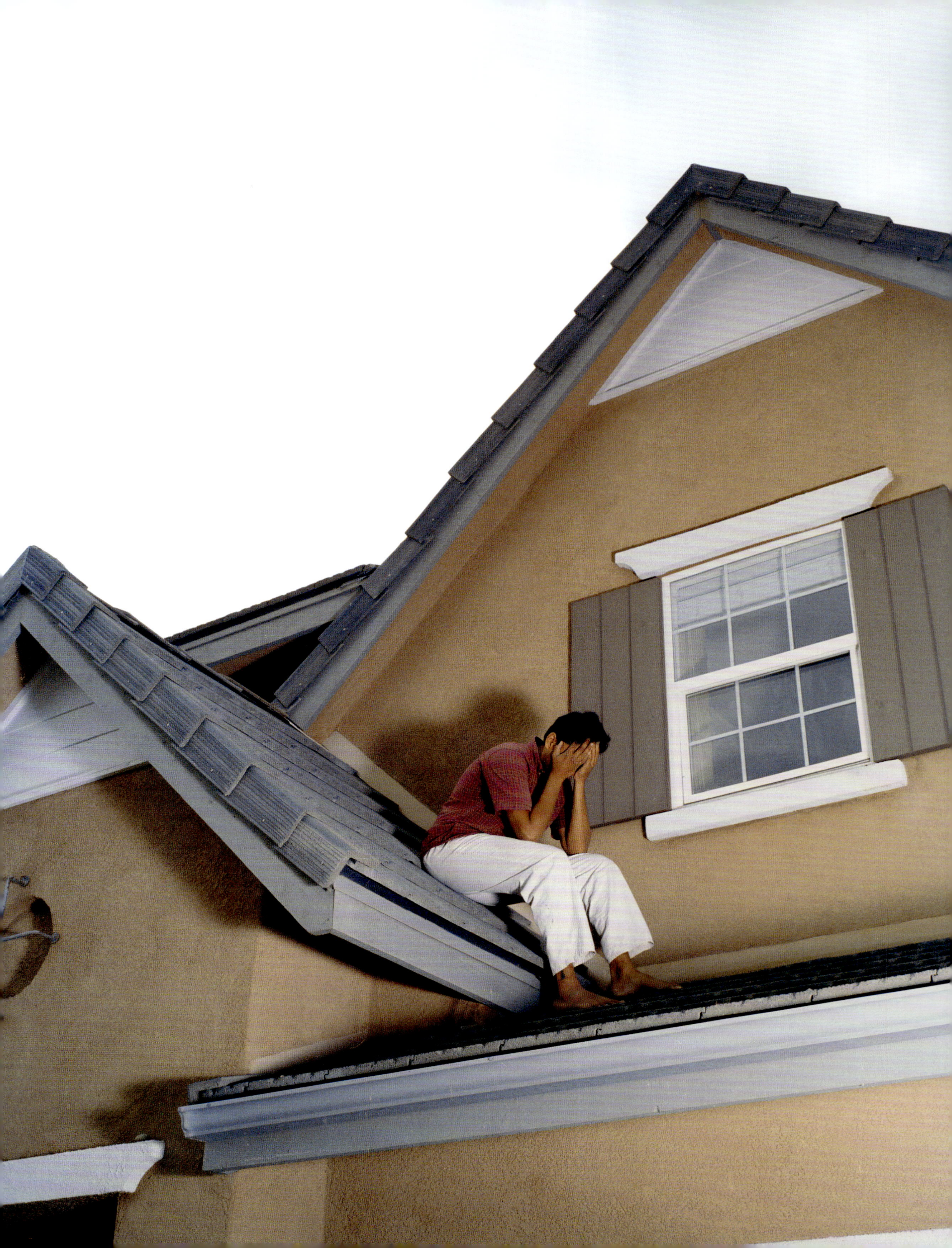

How can art made in domestic spaces push back against expectations of assimilation?

The Possibility of Home

Xueli Wang

A panel of solid black is interrupted by fragments of human form: an elderly woman stepping halfway into the frame, her expression animated by something in the dark. Down by her side, a sliver of a child's face peeks out with one curious eye. In front of them, a floral-patterned bandana levitates in midair, as though to suggest the presence of some phantom we can't see. *In Passing*, taken in 1969 in San Francisco's Chinatown, reflects the intuitive gaze of a longtime local. It is a mode of looking that is at once attuned to the intricate sociality of one's own community and unconcerned with accommodating the needs of an outside viewer, registering instead rich stretches of ordinary life as darkness.

The artist, Irene Poon, spent many years photographing the neighborhood of her youth, weaving dreamy images out of the fleeting faces and encounters of everyday life. As her contemporaries Charles Wong and Benjamen Chinn had begun to do a decade earlier, and previous generations of Chinatown photographers,

Miraj Patel, *Tears Through the Glitter*, 2020
Courtesy the artist

Poon's most striking compositions feature dense black areas that shroud and fragment her subjects, like blind spots made visible.

such as Mary Tape, had done as early as the nineteenth century, Poon used her camera to replace the distant, exoticizing gaze of the tourist with that of an intimate insider caught up in the same quotidian rhythms as her subjects. But her work also goes further: Poon's most striking compositions feature dense black areas that shroud and fragment her subjects, like blind spots made visible.

In *Memories of the Universal Café* (1965), a forearm hovers, disembodied, over a table of food. In *Fire Crackers Await* (1969), a woman in apron and slippers floats in negative space at the bottom of a staircase. Often, the enveloping blackness shows up as background while figures linger at thresholds—doorways, balconies, windows—a recurring motif, marking the unseen interiors from which they emerge and into which they can retreat. Poon usually lets in just enough details to suggest that the negative spaces aren't empty but rather full of presences we can't see. Curiously, Poon honed this aesthetic of visible invisibility just as the political awakening of the Asian American movement swept through the campuses of the Bay Area and beyond, including Poon's own alma mater of San Francisco State College.

What does it mean at this historic moment to turn one's camera toward the banal details of ordinary life, to center the familial figures of children and grandparents, and, what's more, to cast them on the edge of spatial indeterminacy, to allow them to go dark? If the Asian American movement sought to forge a clear political identity for Asians in the United States— as multiethnic, oppositional, anti-assimilative—then Poon's work opens onto the obverse: the messy, exploratory, unfinished private spaces and relations that sustain such acts of public self-definition. If Asian America is built on generations of activism,

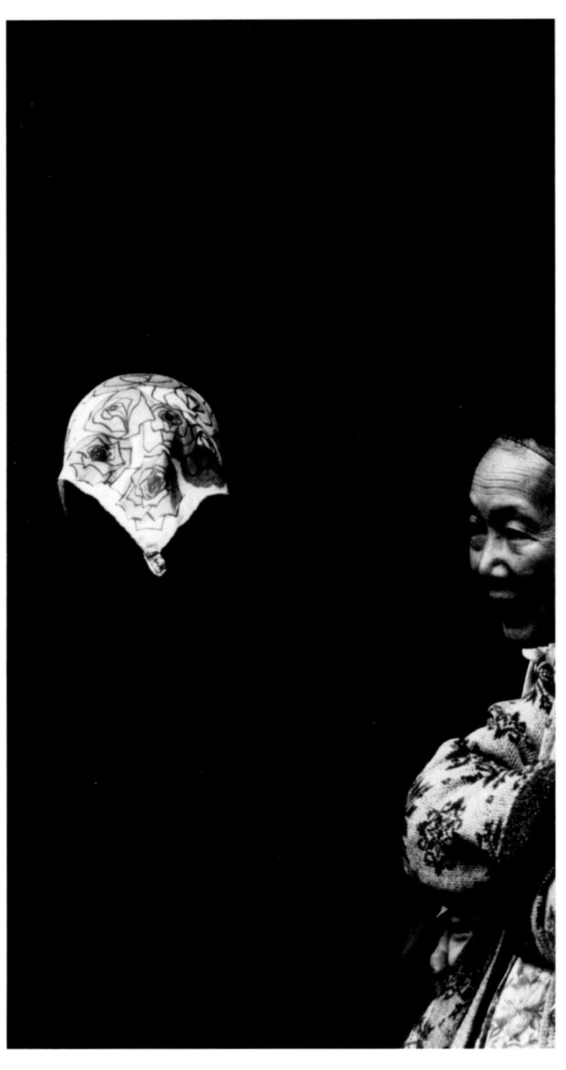

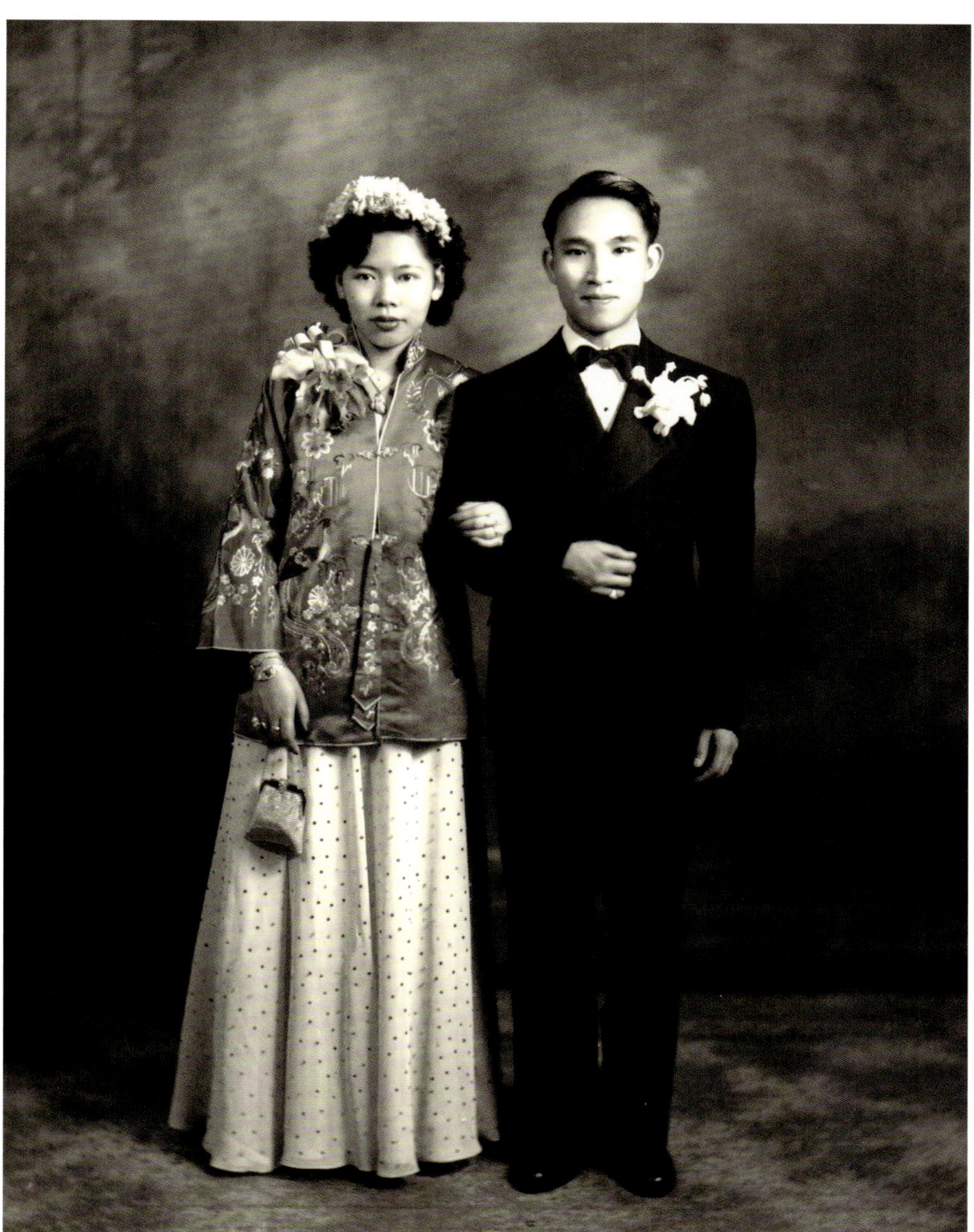

Poon's shrouded compositions remind us that it is also built on generations of what the performance scholar Summer Kim Lee calls "staying in."

Staying in, writes Lee, "critiques the compulsory sociability and relatability demanded of minoritarian subjects to go out, come out, and be out." To stay in isn't to cut off relations with others but only to refuse to be *relatable*—that is, to act in ways that conform to the standards and values of an outside public. For Asian Americans, to stay in means to slip out of our assigned roles within a visibility predicated on binaries of injury and protest, trauma and resilience— as entrenched as ever in our era of anti-Asian hate. Staying in opens up other registers of sociality: of rest, pleasure, play. It encapsulates the banal, domestic, familial spaces and relations that make up the substance of our lives but leave little trace in history.

As one of the few places to register this history of "staying in," Asian American photography before and since Poon has found inventive ways to engage with such interior spaces and relations, often against the demands of public visibility, sociability, even legality. Take, for example, the phenomenon of the composite family portrait, which emerged in the early twentieth century to create what the art historian Thy Phu calls a "counterarchive" of familial intimacy in the era of Chinese exclusion. In the 1920s and '30s, a time when Asians were effectively banned from entering the United States, Chinese American photography studios used collage techniques to piece together portraits taken thousands of miles apart, visually reuniting family members separated, sometimes for a lifetime, by racist immigration policies.

May's Photo Studio, which was opened in 1923 in San Francisco's Chinatown by the husband and wife Leo Chan Lee and Isabelle May Lee, made such portraits for those in their community. One example shows a family of six posing against the backdrop of an ornate interior. The wife and husband sit at the center, on either side of a table, a set of teacups between them, as though they will momentarily turn toward each other to take a sip. But the illusion of togetherness is broken by the flatness and unnatural glow of the husband, the only one in Western attire. A closer examination reveals the rough outline that snakes along his head and shoulders like stitches, a sign that he has been cropped from another photo, a place an ocean away. At a moment when studio portraiture had become a government tool to track Asian bodies via the introduction of photograph identification documents, Chinese American studios found a different use for photography: to weave together dream interiors of familial wholeness and imagine a utopian space without borders.

Ricardo Ocreto Alvarado provides another vision of "staying in" through his photographs of house parties in the

Alvarado provides another vision of "staying in" through his photographs of house parties in the 1940s and '50s.

1940s and '50s. Alvarado, who had no formal photography training and worked as an army hospital cook by day, brought his Speed Graphic camera to countless gatherings of friends, family, and relatives within San Francisco's growing Filipino American community. Taken in an era when segregation kept people of color out of many restaurants, clubs, and other mainstream social settings, Alvarado's photographs center the private home as a precious site for nourishing an otherwise impossible social world.

In one photograph, a sparsely furnished room is offset by its buoyant inhabitants spilling out from the top of the frame. Handsomely dressed parents, children, and relatives gather in loose rows as though for a group shot, but only half look at the camera; the others are engrossed in their own micro-dramas— eating, crying, daydreaming—creating a rich tapestry of crisscrossed gazes. Near the center of the group, the beaming host turns away from the camera to offer up a heaping plate of *lechón* (roast pig) to her guests, further derailing any attempt at a standard pose.

Alvarado's interior scenes often include other minority friends and coworkers, from the same area in San Francisco, whose communities overlapped and merged with Alvarado's own. A live band of Filipino, Black, and Latino musicians play at a house party; interracial couples dance, hands loosely interlaced, in a living room draped with streamers. These figures, open and carefree before the camera, owe their casual radiance perhaps to a sense

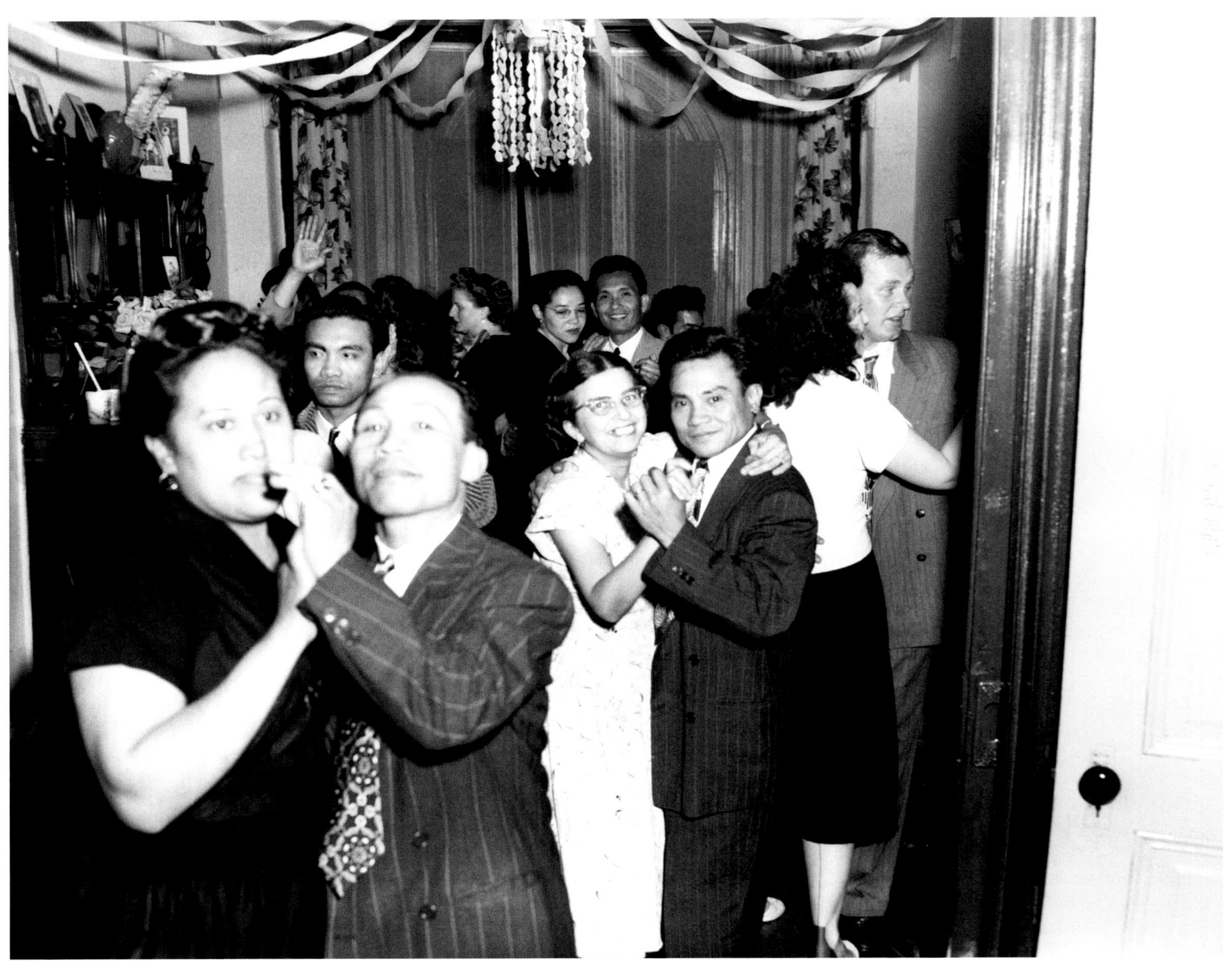

of safety in the presence of the photographer. Like Poon, Alvarado inhabited the spaces he photographed, resulting in images that tend not toward public display but shared interiority, the pleasure of enclosure, the relief of "staying in."

Like their fleeting subjects, photographs of Asian American interior life—real and imagined—occupy a tenuous place in American art history. Both the work of Alvarado and May's Photo Studio were buried away for decades and rediscovered only by chance. Alvarado's daughter stumbled upon some three thousand negatives in the basement of their home after her father's death in 1976. A young art student on a walk encountered and rescued from a Chinatown dumpster the archive of May's Photo Studio in 1978, after its owners had passed away. Still, home spaces, familial relations, the vast terrains of quotidian time: these remain abiding interests in Asian American photography. In recent years, a younger generation of artists has waded into the interior world of "staying in," finding new strategies to contemplate the secret histories it enfolds, the legibility it withholds.

Often, these photographers begin with the site of their own home, using the camera to perform an excavation of the everyday, to see anew the banal details that usually fade into the background. In the series *Of Light, Dust and Passing* (2011), Julie Quon photographs her family home in New York's Chinatown, where her parents have lived since 1980. Still living with them at the time, Quon lingered over ordinary objects bathed in early morning light, seeking out the incidental traces that index her parents' particular presence, without needing to show their faces: her mother's slippers under the chair, her father's cigarettes hidden behind the radio, the makeshift dust covering over the washing machine. These still lifes reflect Quon's architecture training with their clean lines and geometric compositions, but they are also portraits, years in the making, that patiently tease out the inner lives of their elusive subjects through a visual vernacular of the quotidian.

Miraj Patel takes the portrayal of the family home in a different direction, using elements of performance and self-portraiture to create playful, moody meditations on immigrant life in American suburbia. He began the series *Do you see what I see, when I look at me?* (2020–present) while cloistered at home with his parents during the first year of the pandemic. In one image, *Sunday Morning* (2020), Patel snuggles in bed with his parents and dog, reenacting a childhood ritual; this unusual arrangement of bodies contrasts humorously with the generic, symmetrical furnishings of the room. Other photographs show Patel creatively misusing various corners of their home. These performative interventions heighten a sense of incongruity between the Southern California house, a symbol of assimilation and upward mobility, and its Indian American inhabitants. "In trying to fit into the cookie-cutter formula," Patel pondered, "what is this third thing we exist as?"

Likewise, Tommy Kha, whose family was part of the Chinese diaspora in Vietnam before immigrating to the United States, recalled noticing as a child that his house was "set up differently" from those of his friends: "every room had different walls and textures." In his series *Shrines* (2013–ongoing), Kha explores this distinctive heterogeneity by tracing the presence and placement of religious and ancestral shrines, first in his own home, then in the homes and businesses of others across Memphis and New York. Kha calls the mismatched assemblage of incense holder and offerings in *Stations (Kitchen God)* (2015) "my mom's curation"; set amidst other details bearing her touch over the years—a large burn mark on the counter, aluminum foil lining the stove tops and range hood—it forms a palimpsest of immigrant life. "It was a part of my childhood," Kha said of the shrine, "but no one ever explained the ritual to me." The project thus began with a

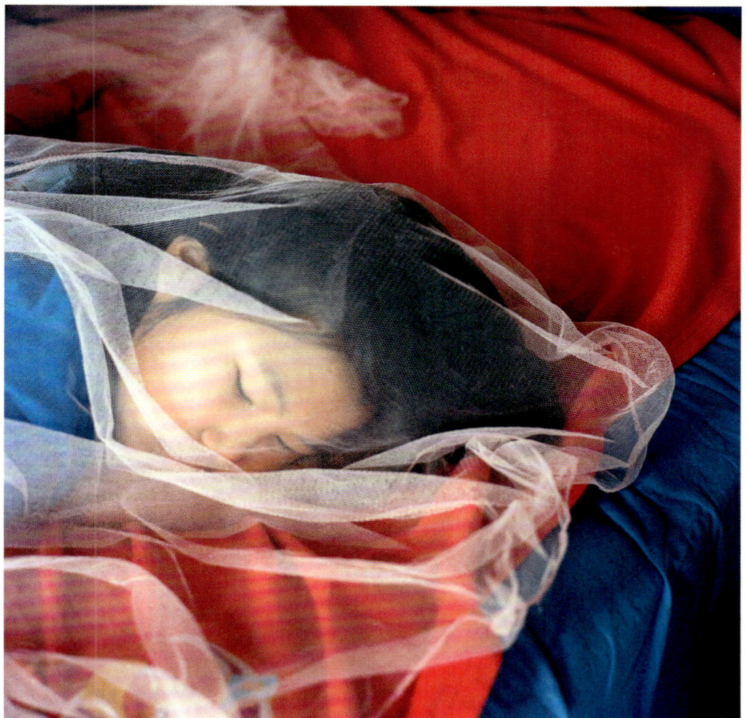

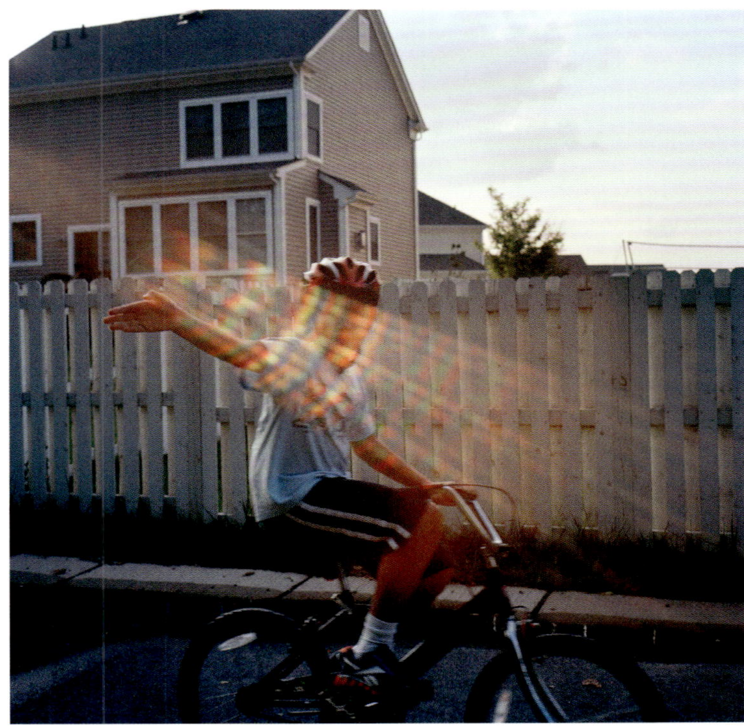

Top:
Julie Quon, *Amanda*, from the series *Nine to Thirteen*, 2011; bottom: Julie Quon, *Nolan*, from the series *Nine to Thirteen*, 2011
Courtesy the artist

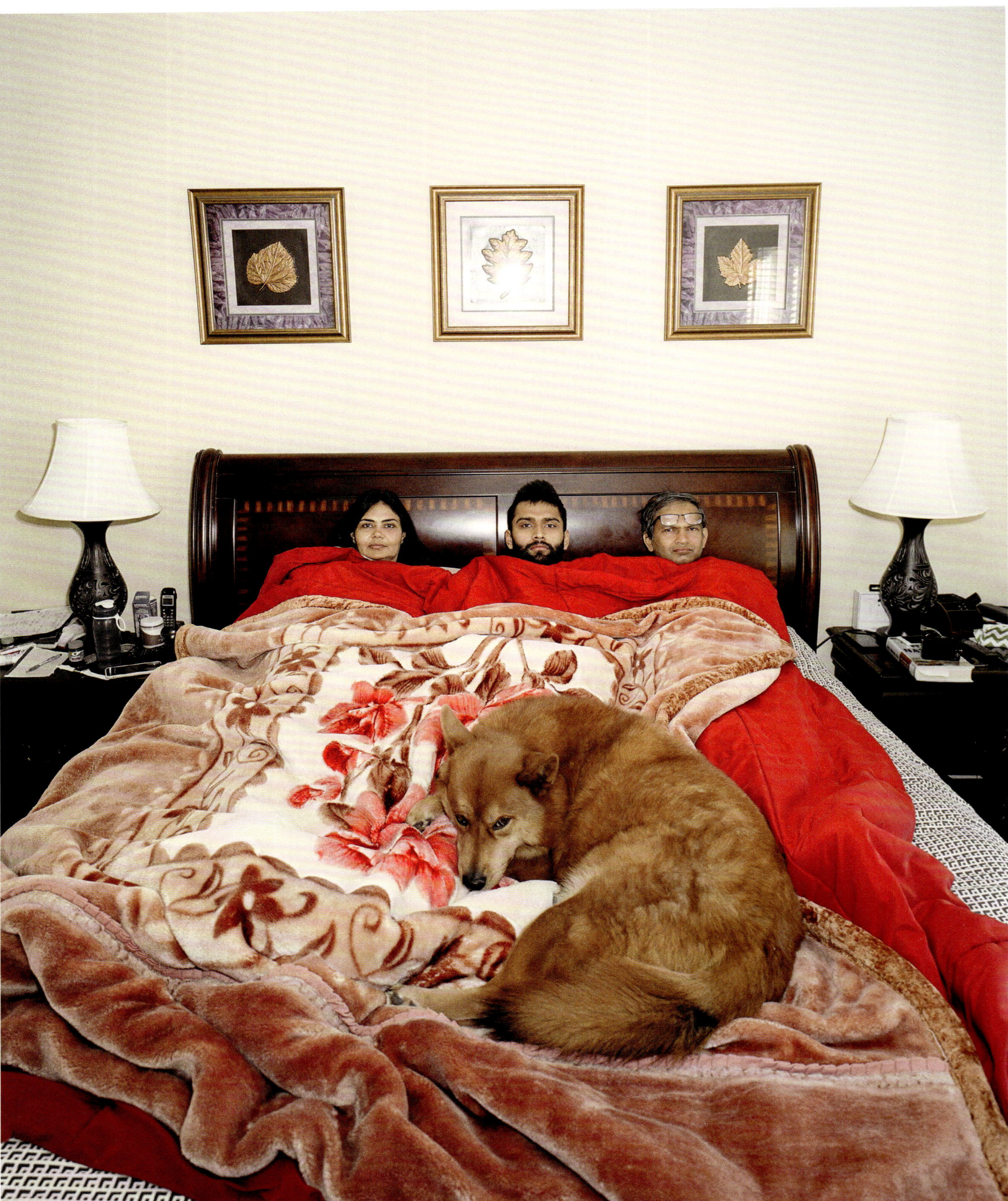

This page:
Miraj Patel, *Sunday
Morning*, 2020
Courtesy the artist

Opposite:
Tommy Kha, *Stations
(Kitchen God),
Whitehaven*, 2015
© and courtesy the artist and
Higher Pictures Generation,
New York

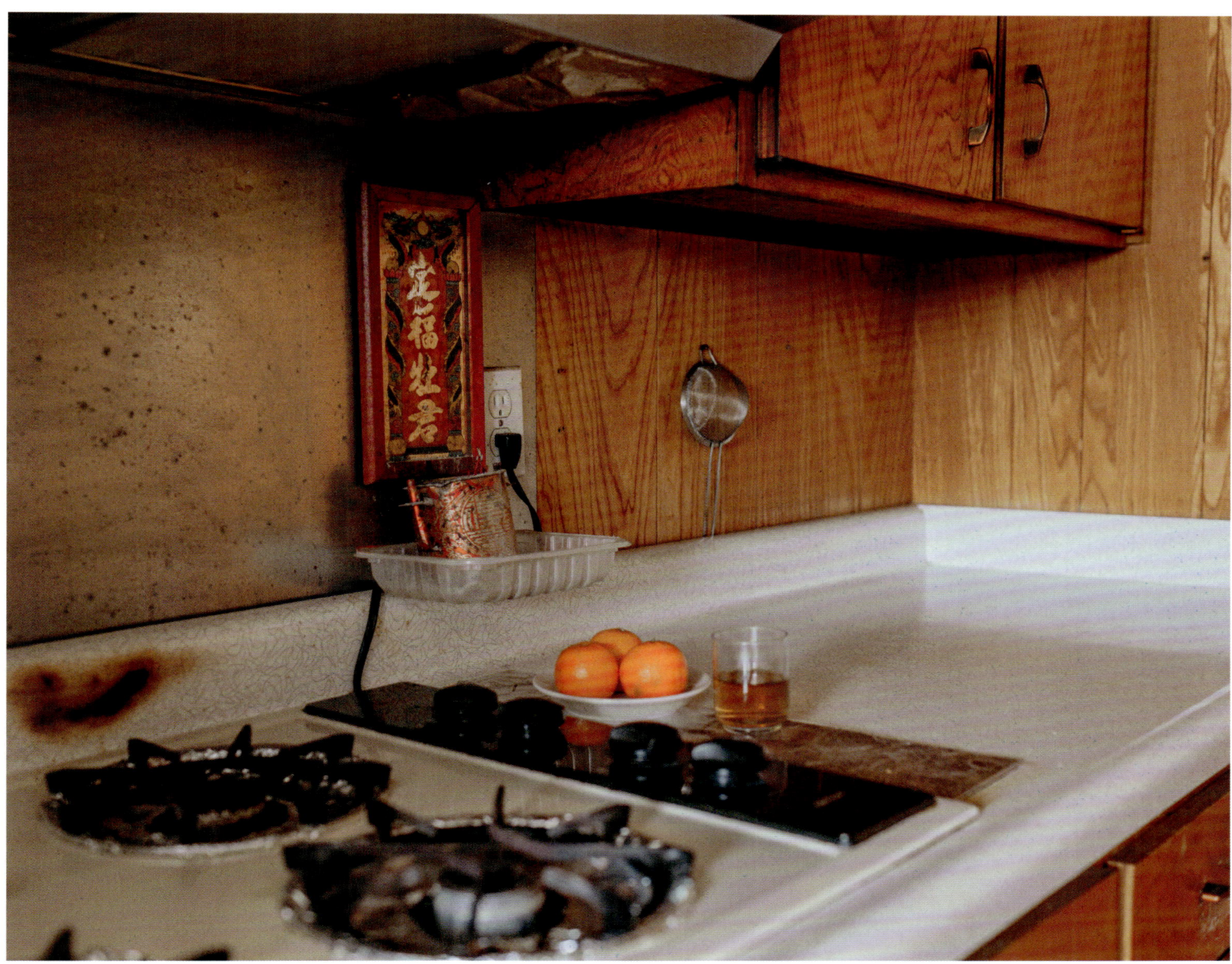

reconfiguration of Kha's own vision, a shuffling of the background into the foreground. For the past seven years, Kha has photographed more shrines—in restaurants, stores, and multigenerational homes—in an effort to locate and survey a shared, everyday Asian American iconography.

Jarod Lew similarly tries to find a shared language of the home in his series *Please Take Off Your Shoes* (2016–ongoing), which took him to the houses of relatives, friends, and strangers around Michigan and San Francisco. Lew, whose work is featured in a portfolio in this issue, began the series as much to seek community as to make pictures, an interest reflected in the deeply collaborative nature of his process. "A lot of these photographs stem from conversations I have with the person I'm photographing, building trust, coming up with ideas of portraying them in a way they're comfortable with," Lew told me. Like Quon, Lew looks to still life as the key to portraiture. In his unwavering attention to some of the most mundane sights of domestic life—furniture covered with sheets, a plate of cut fruit, shoes by the entrance— there is an argument about the home itself as performative, a rich sensory world that wordlessly conveys entire histories of intimacy, relation, and feeling.

What does Asian America look like from the inside? What does it mean to live in the blind spots of American history? For over a century, Asian American photographers have explored these questions by crafting ways of seeing that paradoxically protect from the trap of visibility, the trap of being defined by external policies and historical flashpoints. By treasuring the least remarkable recesses of everyday life, these photographs enact radical shifts in vision. To see ourselves in the shared spaces of staying in, unburdened by legibility or relatability—this, they suggest, is the only kind of seeing that will free us.

Xueli Wang is a writer and PhD candidate at Yale. Her research for this piece was supported by the Andy Warhol Foundation Arts Writers Grant.

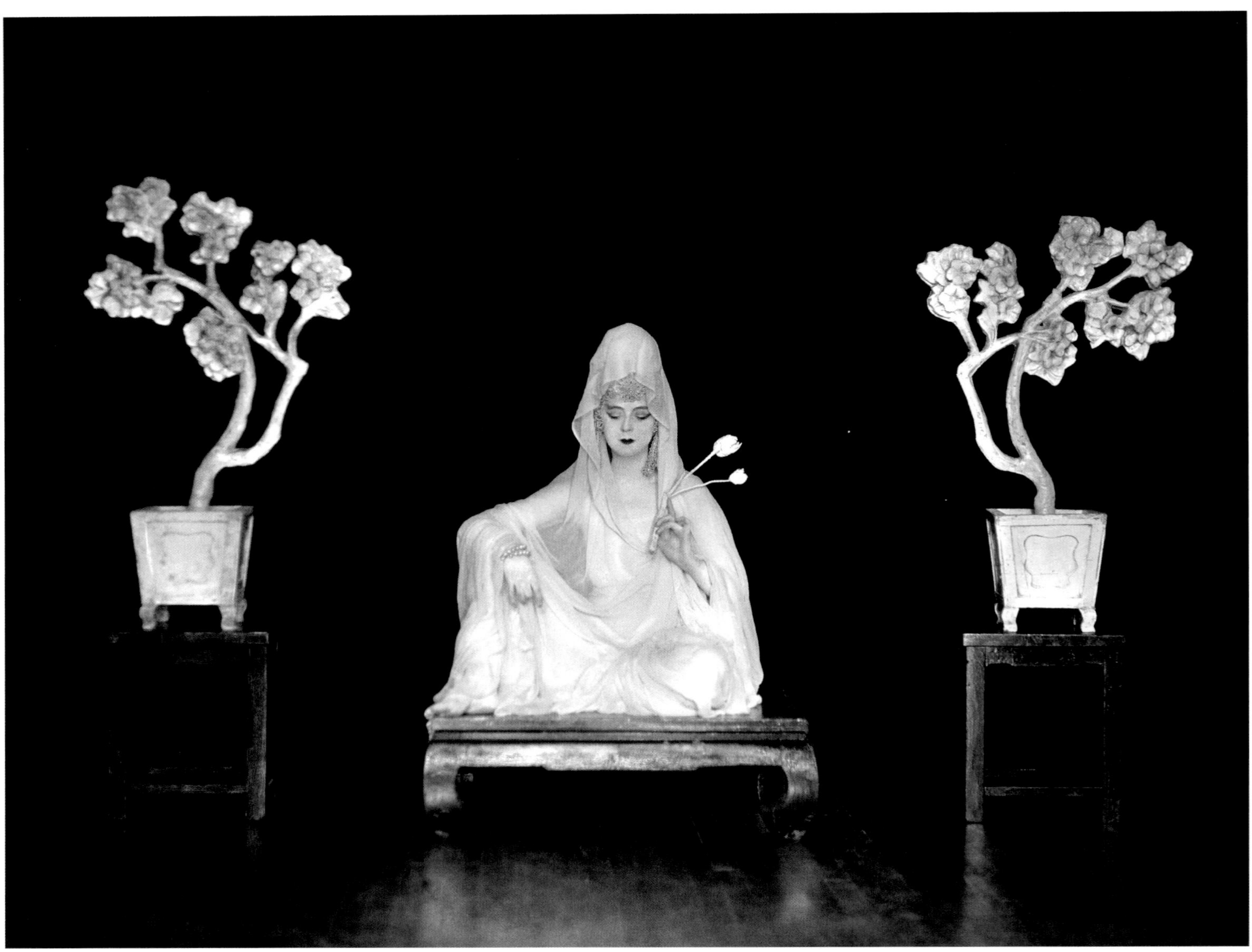

Soichi Sunami
Movement &
Form

Yechen Zhao

On January 5, 1942, a month after the attack on Pearl Harbor and the United States' entry into World War II, the Museum of Modern Art (MoMA) director Alfred Barr Jr. wrote a letter vouching for the "good character" of Soichi Sunami, a first-generation Japanese immigrant artist employed by the museum. This brief letter offered Sunami's decade of photographing exhibitions at MoMA as a guarantee of loyalty to his adopted country. Though Japanese Americans on the East Coast were never interned like their counterparts on the West Coast, Sunami faced an unprecedented new level of racialized scrutiny. Barr's letter invites us to not only recognize the importance of Sunami's photographic career but also consider—in the context of this issue on "Asian in America"—what it means to use the quality of his work as proof of political loyalties.

Born in 1885 in Okayama City, Japan, Sunami came to the United States in 1907, just before the two nations informally agreed to eliminate Japanese immigration. In 1919, while living in Seattle, he found work as an assistant in the commercial studio run by the photographers Wayne Albee and Ella E. McBride. Sunami used the skills he gained in their darkroom to create Pictorialist portraits and landscapes of his own. Taken around 1920 and rendered with a subtlety of tone achievable only through platinum printing, Sunami's moody view of Mount Rainier cradles the peak within a silvery envelope of water and sky.

He simultaneously cultivated talents in painting and sculpture under the tutelage of Fokko Tadama, an Indonesian-born Dutch

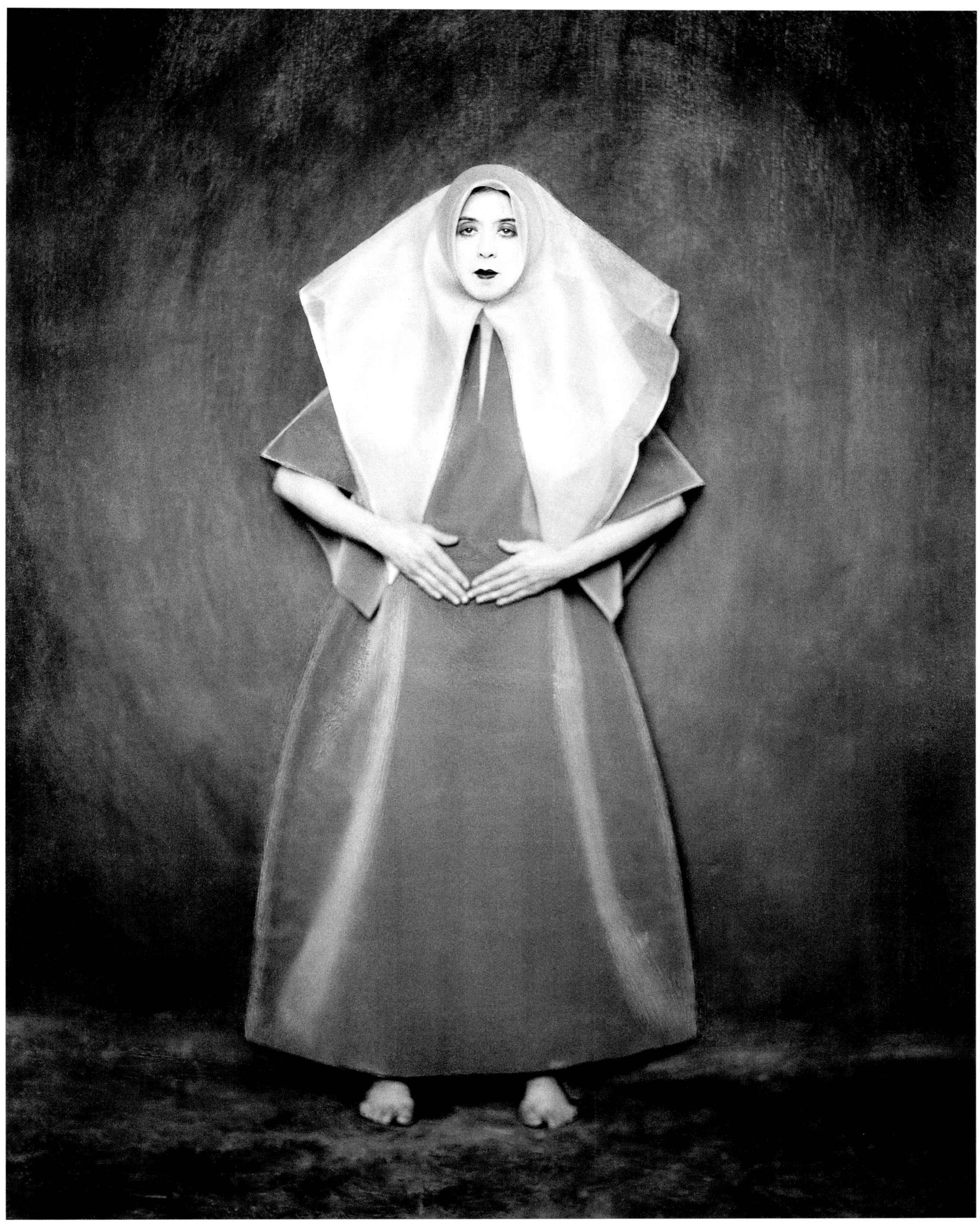

Previous page:
Ruth St. Denis in *White Jade*, 1926

This page:
Martha Graham in *Poems of 1917, The Dance of Death*, 1928
Courtesy Martha Graham Resources

Over their five-year partnership, Sunami captured Graham's virtuosic expression in pictures.

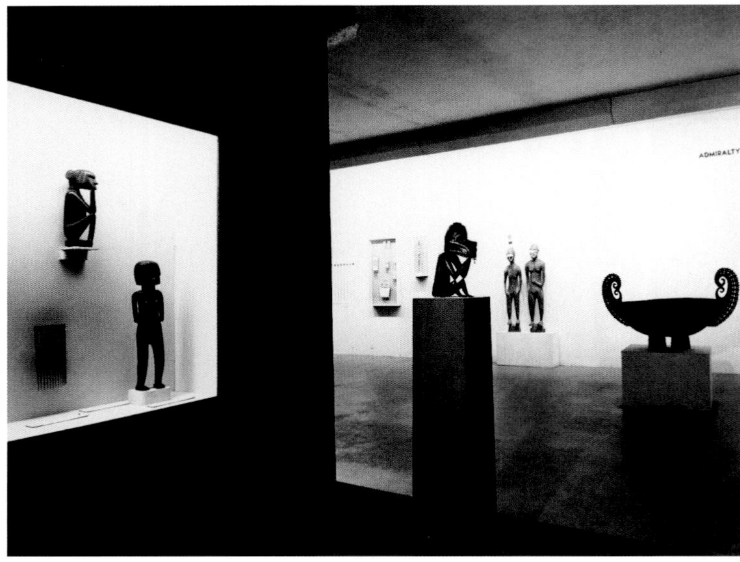

painter living in Seattle. Keen to further this training, Sunami left Seattle in 1922 to enroll at the Art Students League of New York, where he studied with John Sloan and George Grosz. Though he immersed himself among painters and sculptors— Alexander Calder, Edward Hopper, Yasuo Kuniyoshi—Sunami was increasingly recognized for his photography.

His friendship with the dancers Ruth St. Denis and Ted Shawn led to photographic collaborations within New York's performing arts community, including with Martha Graham, Doris Humphrey, and Charles Weidman. St. Denis writes in her autobiography of the flurried activity that accompanied Sunami's arrivals to her dance center in the Bronx: "a scurrying of the household in all directions" to help him create "exquisite poems of photography." In a 1929 photograph promoting her dance *Tagore Poem*, St. Denis arcs her body in a manner reminiscent of a bow being drawn, her torso and arm pulling at her costume to instill a sense of physical tension within the image. Seeking publicity photographs for her first independent dance recital in 1926, Graham chose Sunami as a collaborator; his studio was conveniently just five blocks away from her apartment. Over their five-year partnership, Sunami captured Graham's virtuosic

expression of movement and form in pictures, including her performance of *Lamentation* in 1930. Graham's limbs and head explode against the fabric sheath she wears, threatening to rip it completely apart.

These jobs were artistically rewarding but poorly compensated. With the onset of the Great Depression, Sunami could not live on a bohemian salary of exchanged artworks and intangible recognition. He was already freelancing as an exhibition photographer. Sunami's reputation as an excellent technician, combined with personal connections, landed him work at the newly opened Museum of Modern Art.

Traveling regularly between MoMA and his darkroom on Fifteenth Street, Sunami used an 8-by-10-inch view camera to document the museum's collection and exhibitions. While writing his letter, Barr could easily have called to mind Sunami's photographs of the 1941 *Modern Primitives: Artists of the People* exhibition, which had opened a few weeks before the attack on Pearl Harbor. The pictures deliver the hallmark visual experience of installation photography: a highly legible, inhumanly sharp reveal of the gallery that simulates a human vantage point. What makes such images successful is their illusion of authorless indexicality, as if the exhibition had recorded itself. For more than thirty years at MoMA, Sunami practiced this form of self-effacement through photography.

By his retirement in 1968, Sunami had produced more than twenty thousand large-format negatives for the institution but remained inconsistently credited. Until 1961, the museum paid him two-thirds the amount received by his white peers. The images remain an undeniably important record of modern art in America, and it is no exaggeration to say that most students of modernism have seen a photograph by Sunami. His ability to minimize an authorial presence from these images set a standard for installation photography to such an extent that some scholars would later interpret the genre as reproducing an idealized, *white* gaze toward art.

That achievement required him to forego a career as an independent artist, a strategic move made out of economic necessity but also a tacit acceptance of the inequitable terms that defined Sunami's place in the country. But the professional work of hiding his subjectivity produces a melancholy art of its own— a quality seen more clearly through historical hindsight. Take, for example, a photograph from *Arts of the South Seas* (1946). Held at MoMA just months after the atomic bombings of Hiroshima and Nagasaki, this display of Oceanic art explicitly contextualized its curatorial conceit in relation to World War II's Pacific theater. Using the dramatic division of light and dark between two galleries, Sunami throws the biomorphic and stylized forms of the sculptures into relief against the museum's austere architecture. The image is aesthetically potent because Sunami presents, with restrained impartiality, an exhibition utterly enmeshed within the imperialist ambitions of his adopted country. It speaks to the vexing position of immigrant Americans whose survival required speaking the norm even as they faced persecution for embodying difference.

Yechen Zhao received his PhD in art
history from Stanford University. He is
the Marcia Brady Tucker Fellow in the
Department of Photography at the Yale
University Art Gallery.

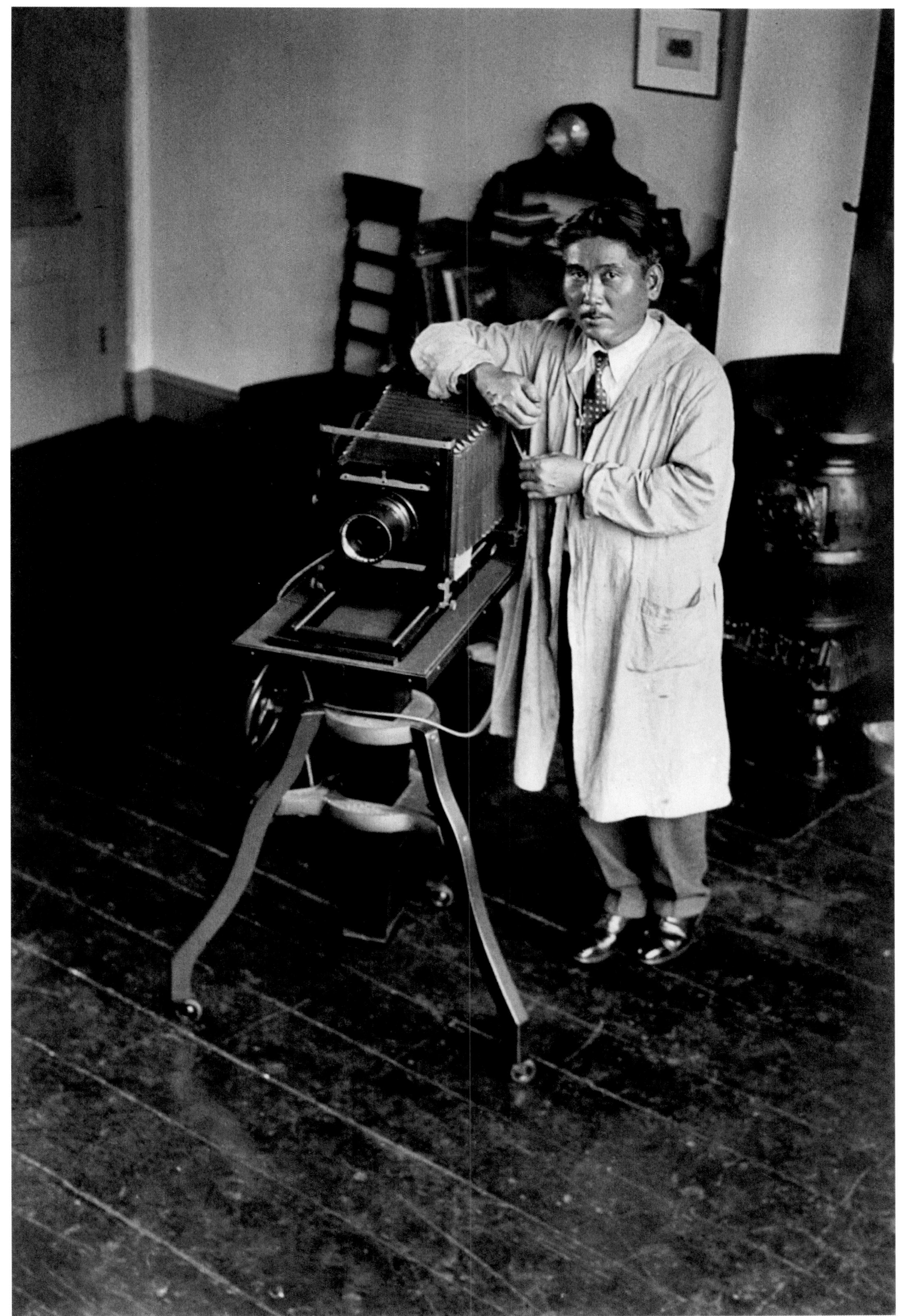

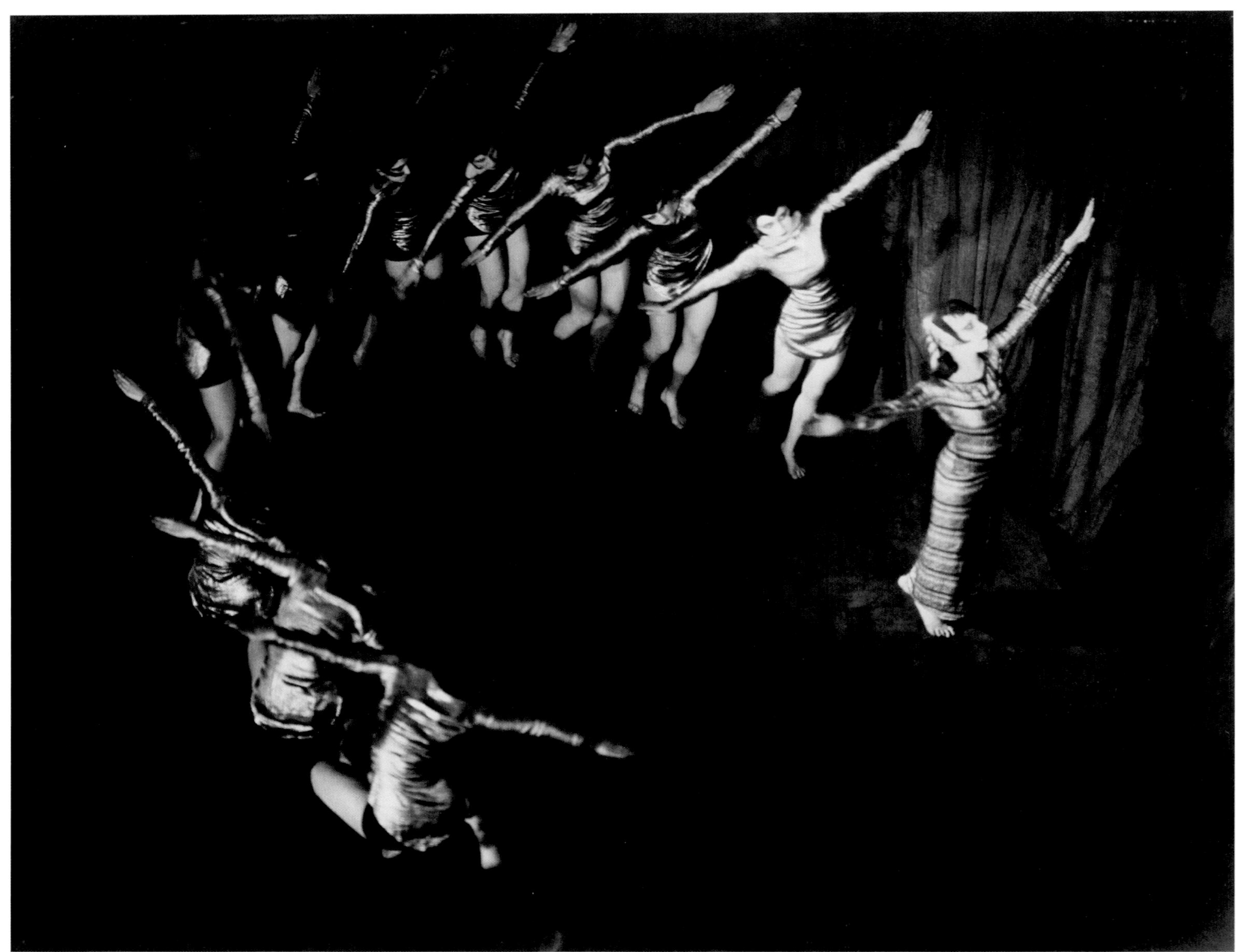

Doris Humphrey and
company in *Life of the Bee*,
1929

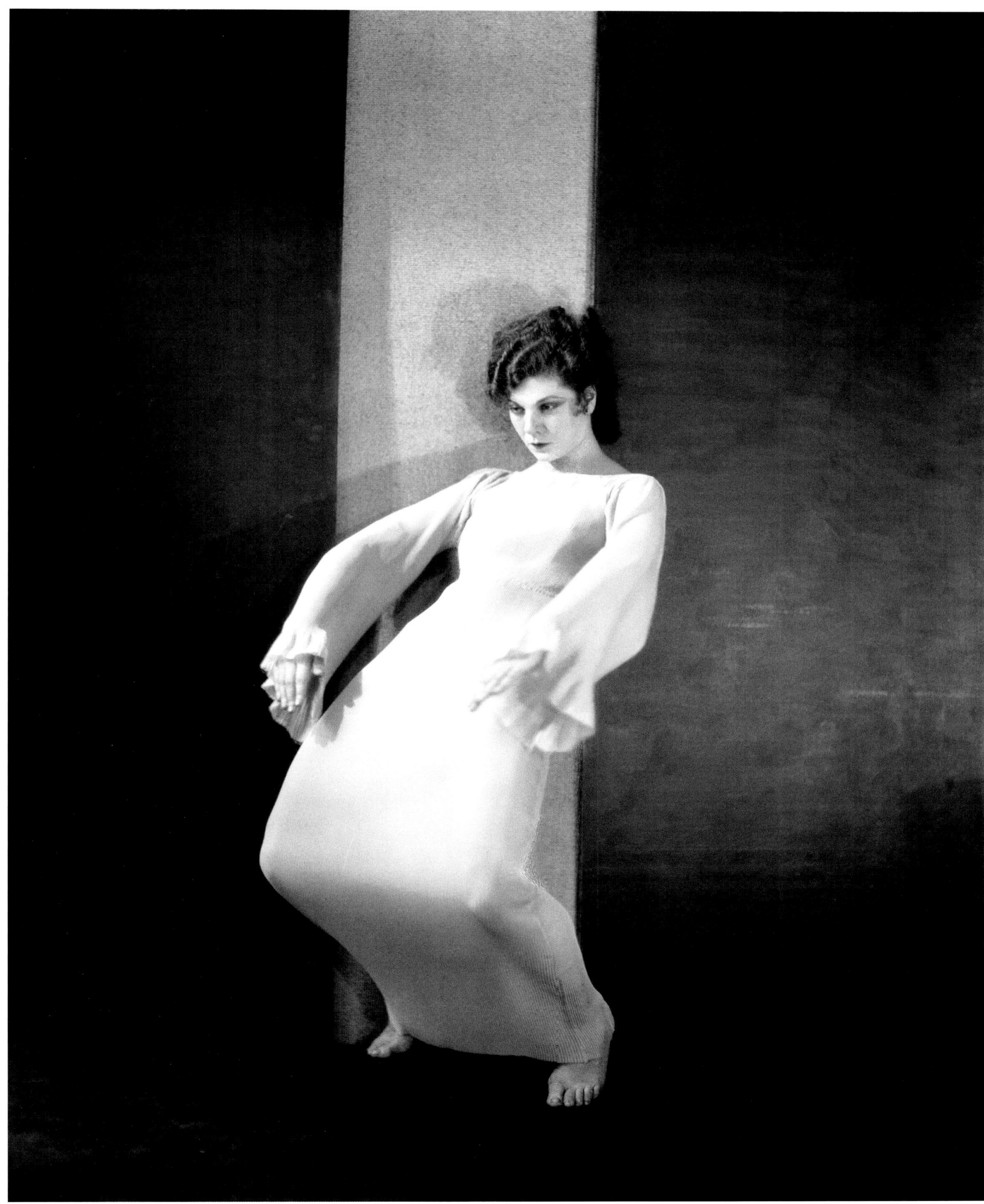

Helen Tamiris, ca. 1930
Unless otherwise noted,
all photographs courtesy
Collection of the Sunami
Family; David Martin; and
Cascadia Art Museum,
Edmonds, Washington

When she was four or five years old, Priya Suresh Kambli watched her mother cut out her own face from family photographs. Kambli's mother left the pictures of her daughters, Priya and her elder sister, Sona, intact. This act of simultaneous erasure and preservation fascinated Kambli. Decades later, she brings the same dialectic into play when creating her own artworks drawn from family photo-albums.

Kambli was born in 1975, in the Indian city of Mumbai, then called Bombay, and came to the United States at the age of eighteen. A few years earlier, Kambli's mother had died from cancer, and just six months later, her father had suffered a fatal heart attack. In the period that followed, Kambli was adrift. One of her aunts, a pediatrician in Louisiana, sponsored Kambli's move. Art hadn't, so far, been a part of her repertoire, and photography was even less attractive to her. Kambli's father, however, a trained pastry chef, had been an avid amateur photographer. As a child, her father's fussiness over his pictures, and the time he took arranging his family's poses, felt like punishment. But, as an undergrad, Kambli enjoyed her photography class. She didn't have her father's Minolta, so she borrowed a camera from her aunt's husband.

By graduate school she had discovered the excitement of creating art. She was learning from the work of artists such as Carrie Mae Weems and Lorna Simpson, who were interested in issues of identity, but she also experienced a sense of dissatisfaction with Western image making. In 2003, Kambli traveled to New York to see an exhibition from the Alkazi Collection of Photography. The pictures were mostly taken in India, and Kambli remembers being "blown away" by the hand-painted portraits showing some parts of the figure in black and white while other parts, particularly clothing and jewelry, were rendered in glittering color. These vernacular images in the pristine white gallery space, Kambli says, were very much like those in the two albums of family photographs she had brought in her suitcase from India. She began to work with those familial pictures, embellishing them in different ways, making connections between her present and her past.

As Kambli was telling me all this over Zoom from her home in Kirksville, Missouri, I was thinking about her images in which faces are obscured—in one depicting her maternal aunt, *Mami* (2016), the face is left only partially visible under a decorative arrangement of flour. Flour was always at hand in the home of a pastry chef, and the patterns are borrowed from the traditional Indian practice of *rangoli* drawings, which are used during festivals or seen printed on textiles. It is difficult not to think of Kambli's practice as therapeutic: the artist returns to a disquieting memory of her mother disfiguring photographs and then produces a transformed object that bears traces of its past but is altogether new and beautiful.

In his book *Camera Indica: The Social Life of Indian Photographs* (1997), a classic study of the role of portraiture in India, Christopher Pinney describes a photography studio as a "chamber of dreams." Pinney observes that in the small town in India where he was conducting his anthropological study, the creativity of the studio photographer as well as his subjects lay in their envisioning fluid selves that defied any narrow, realistic self-representation. In Kambli's images, we are no longer in small-town India, but the impulse is the same. There is imaginative storytelling about possible selves, among them a cosmopolitan iteration stretching across continents. What we see over and over again, in collagelike constructions, are numerous selves tied to different temporalities and identities.

Many years ago, Kambli was watching *Sesame Street* with her child. On the show, the characters were demonstrating how to make a rainbow. That idea stuck in her head. Photography plays with light, and Kambli wanted to explore light's mercurial nature. For her fortieth birthday, Kambli asked her husband for a prism. For the longest time, she couldn't figure out how to make it work. The prism sat in her studio for two years until, one day, she picked it up and, as if by magic, the colors appeared.

Priya Suresh Kambli
Cut-ups

Amitava Kumar

Sona and Me (Breaux's Studio), 2017

Amitava Kumar is a professor of English at Vassar College. His most recent book is *A Time Outside This Time* (2021).

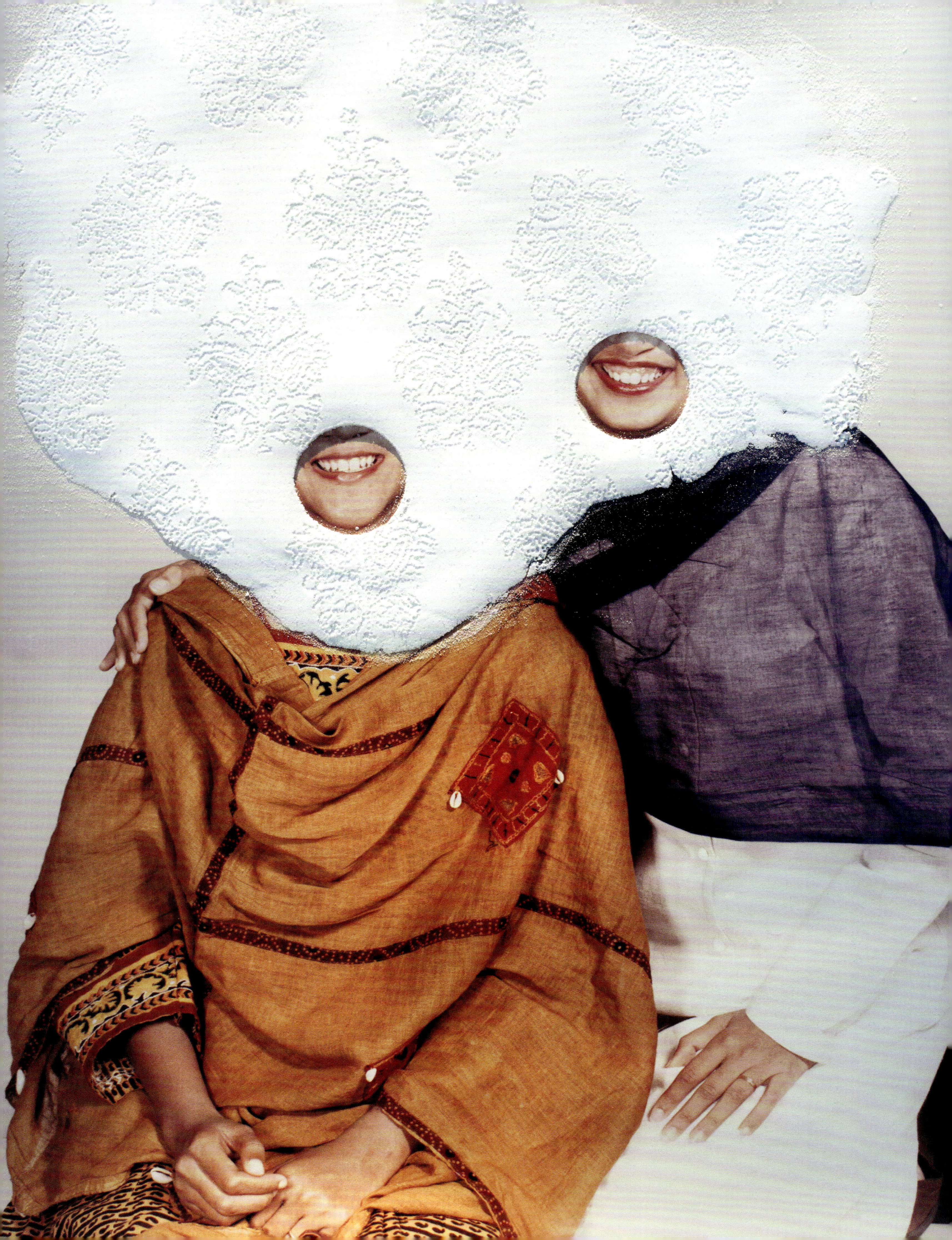

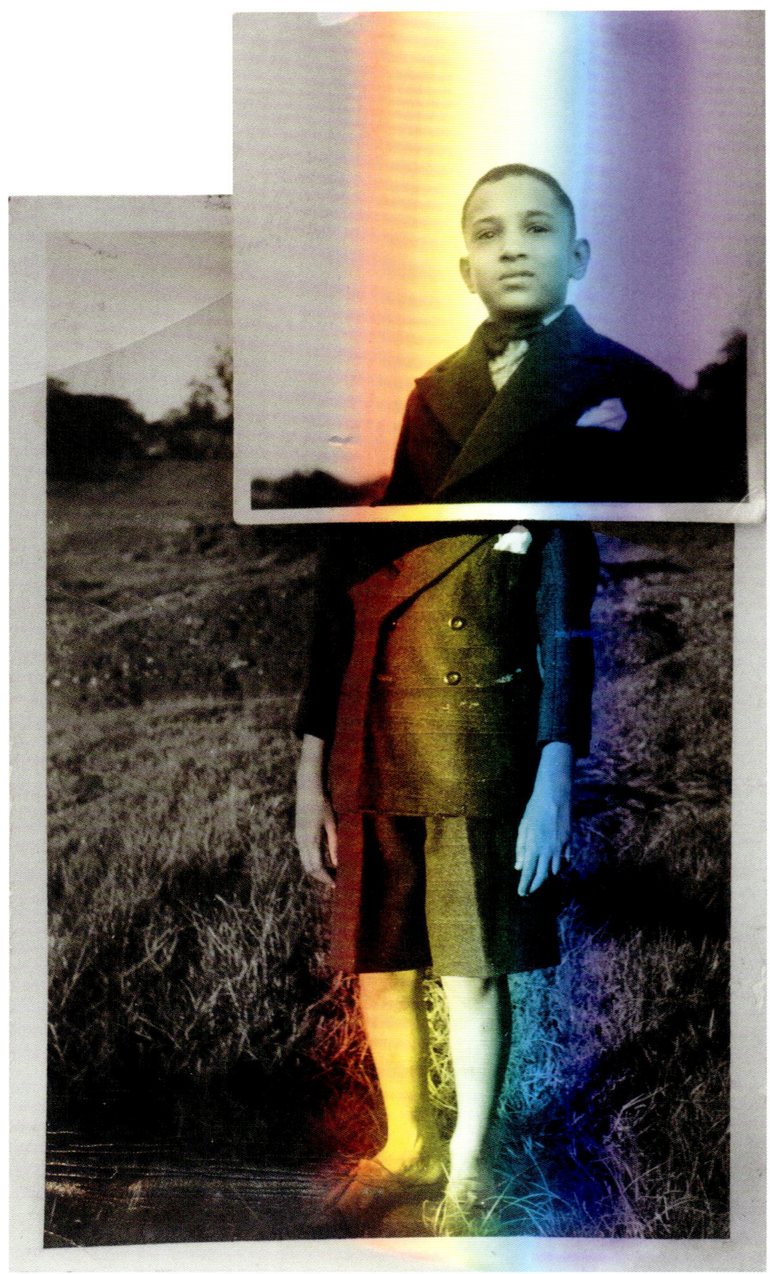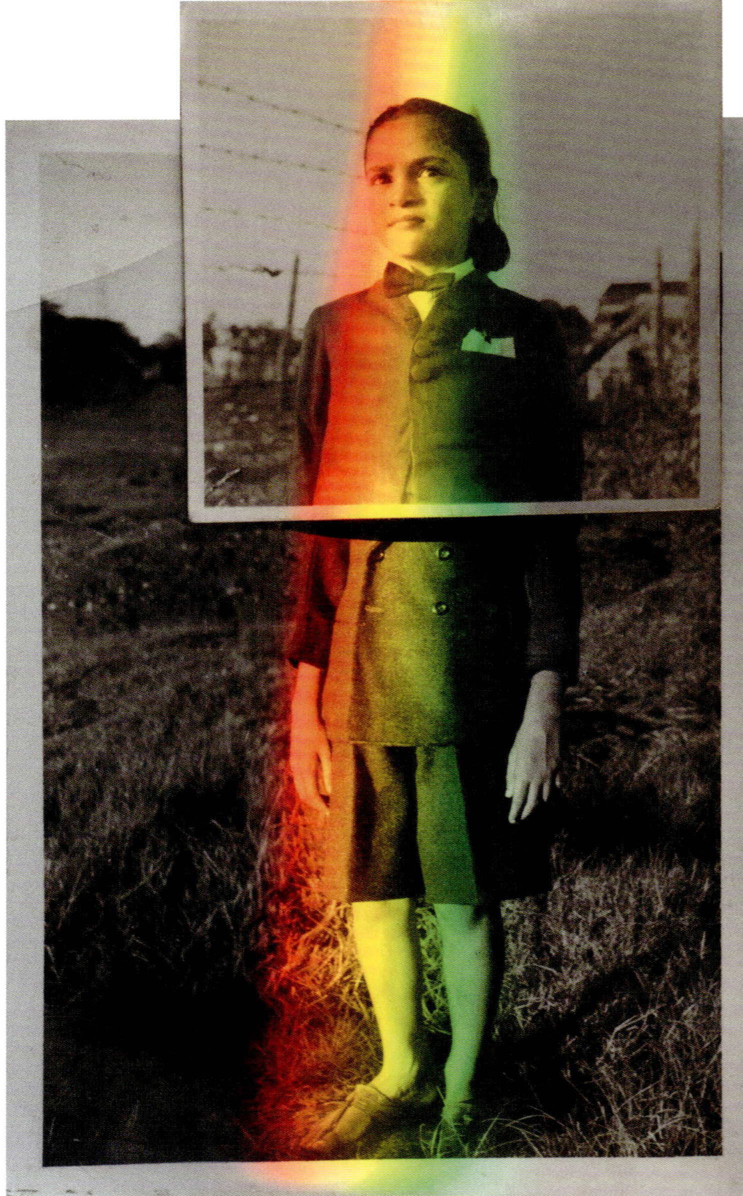

Mama and Muma, 2019

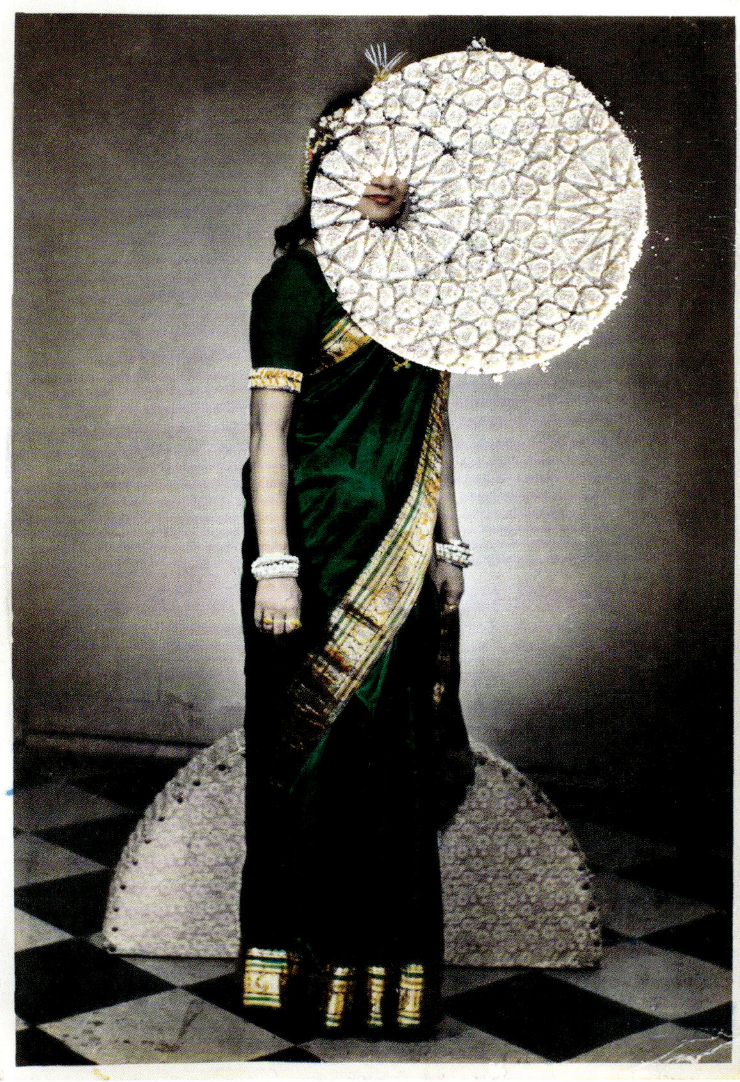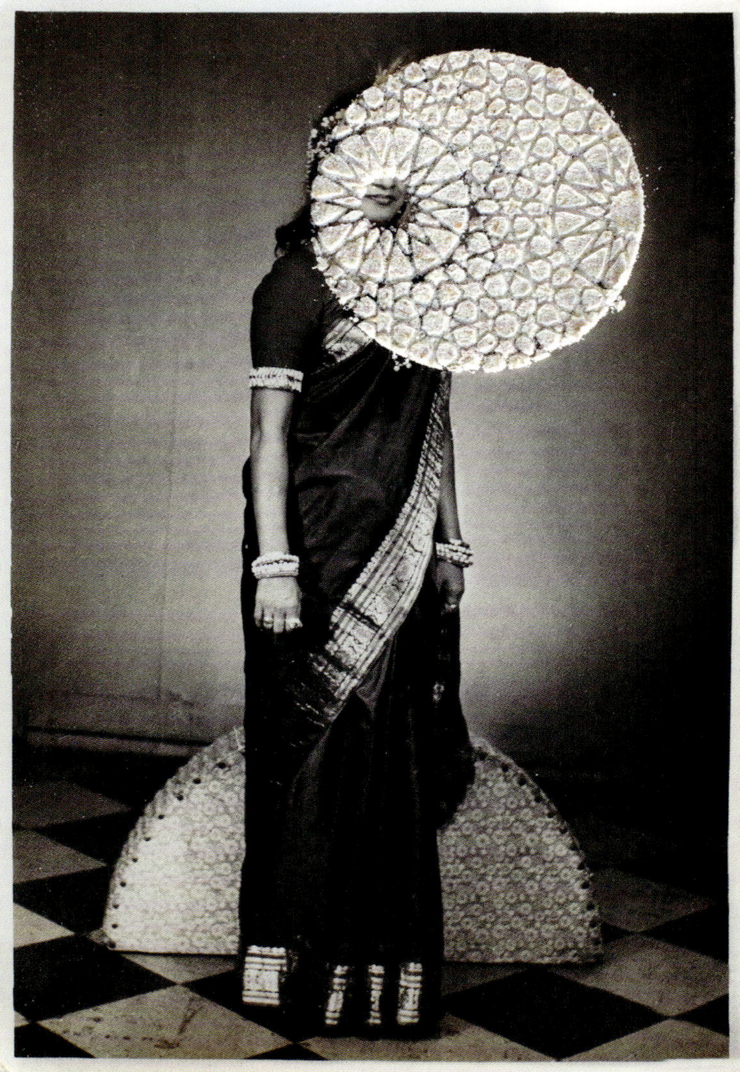

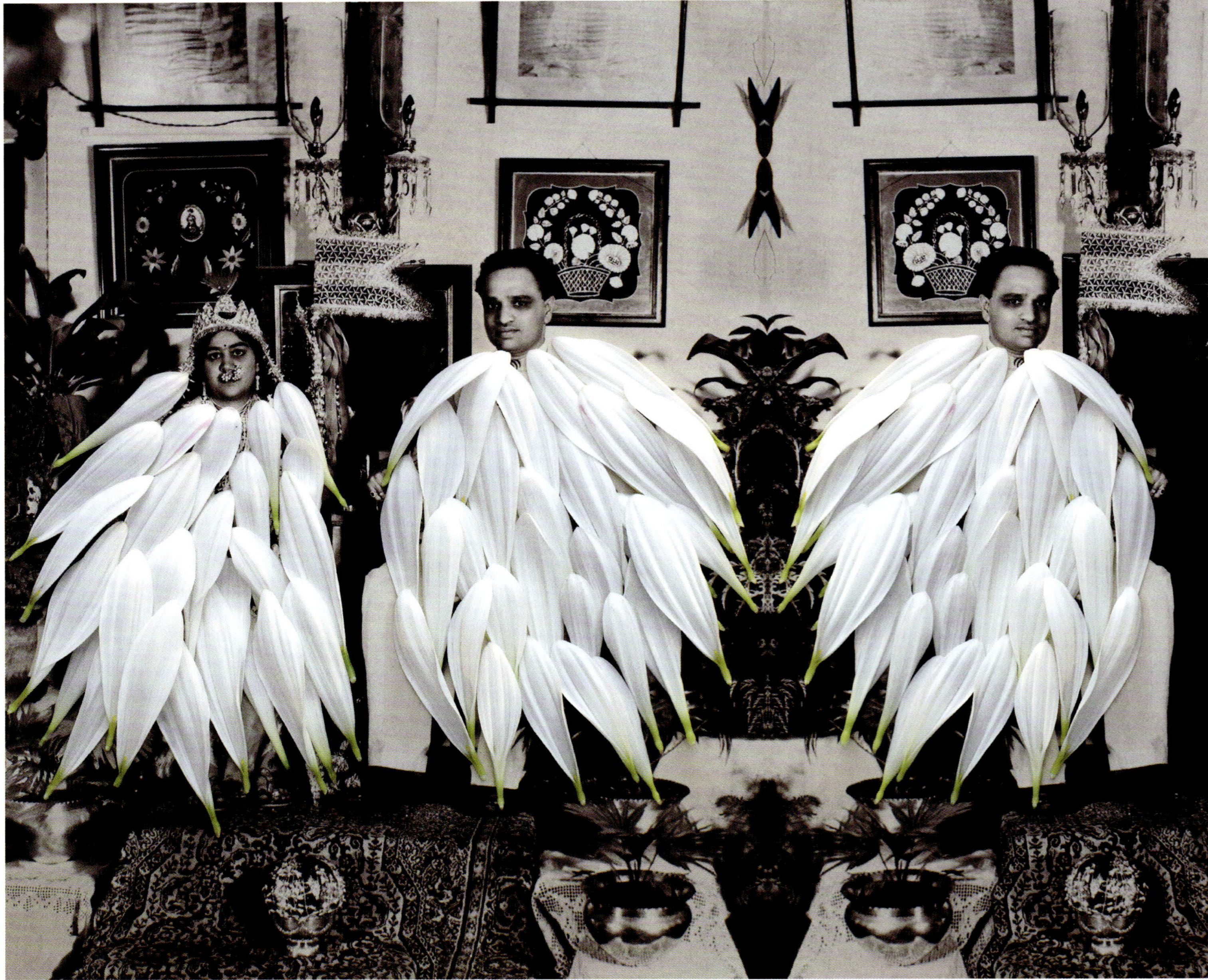

This page:
Dada Aajooba and Dadi Aaji, 2012

Opposite:
Baba (Dodging Tools), 2017
All works courtesy the artist

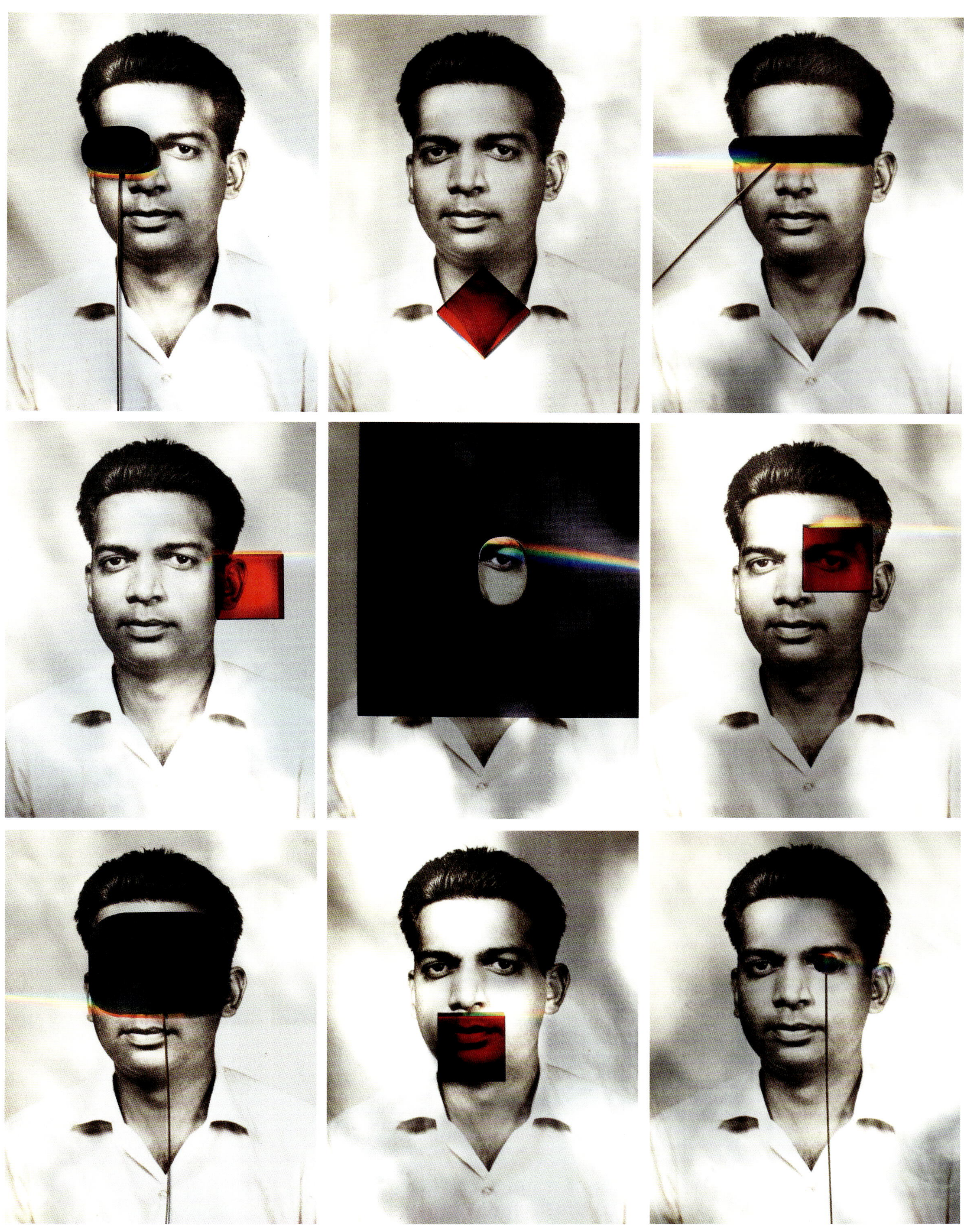

Context is rarely tidy. Even as it clarifies, it confounds. Consider this: in 1982, Vincent Chin was beaten to death by two Detroit autoworkers on the night of his bachelor party. In the aftermath, he became an enduring icon of the Asian American civil rights movement. Thirty years after Chin's murder, the photographer Jarod Lew discovered that his mother had been the one engaged to him. If this is context, I wondered, viewing Lew's family portraits in his series *In Between You and Your Shadow* (2021– ongoing), what to do with it?

In one photograph, Lew's mother hides her face behind a bouquet of bright spring flowers. In another, two vacant chairs sit against the wall of his aunt's Chinese restaurant in Metro Detroit. I admit I tried to make such images carry the loss of a man the photographer never knew, could never know, his absence making it possible (though who knows) for Lew to be here in the first place. Forking paths and multiverses, they're in the air, imbuing our traumas and silences with the infinite weight of context—not just the past, present, and future but the *what if*. Yet if conveying such weight is a maximalist project, Lew's portraits interest me because they're deliberately uncluttered.

Still figures are neatly framed between window shutters, an open car door, shadows, light. In the restaurant, plastic tulips take the spotlight next to a Michigan Chinese mainstay, almond boneless chicken. At home, Lew's now retired father sits in his socks and his old work uniform. One can draw a straight line from the lamp in the background, to the United States Postal Service logo, to the floor vase in the foreground—the symbol of an American institution floating between two objects that could have been acquired by googling "oriental decor."

Not so, Lew tells me. He grew up in this house, with that lamp and vase. After coming home from the post office, his father would sit at that ottoman to decompress and chat. Lew has his family reenact everyday rituals, from the trimming of flowers to his mother slipping food to his brother before he drives off.

There's a private intimacy here, from which the photographs also provoke a more public meaning. The lamp, the vase, the logo, the father, the socks—are the relationships among these elements complementary? Contradictory? Depends who's looking.

Set mid-meal, mid-chat, some of the images also indicate an interruption. The subjects look back, as if aware of our looking. But these, too, are replicated scenes, the usual motion of spontaneity channeled into the stillness of control. To be aware of such control is to question the very connections that you can't help but make.

"The connection I have for Vincent Chin was through the documentaries that I watched, based on so much pain. I can't fully embed myself into that," Lew explains. I question, too, the line that we feel compelled to draw from Chin to more recent incidents of violence toward Asians, from the Atlanta spa shootings, to the assaults on Asian elders, to the Monterey Park and Half Moon Bay shootings, committed by Asian male elders. As though a line would make all this tragedy more meaningful. As though there were such a thing as *more meaningful*.

Lew's work resists this pressure: control is also a means to build a protective structure around the living. When posing for the camera, Lew's mother felt, at first, as though she were playing a character; now she's happy playing herself. Afterward, Lew shows her the pictures on his camera, a method of instant collaboration that was one of the reasons he switched to digital from his usual film. If these photographs obscure a larger context, they do so as an act of care. I think of Grace Paley's short story "A Conversation with My Father," in which a writer tells her dying father different versions of a sad tale, to mixed results. "How long will it be?" he finally asks her. "Tragedy! You too. When will you look it in the face?"

The story ends on that question. But perhaps Lew's portraits pick up the thread. Look or don't look, they say. I'll listen all the same.

Jarod Lew
In Between You and Your Shadow

Simon Han

Untitled (Mom and Dad),
2022

Simon Han is the author of the novel *Nights When Nothing Happened* (2020).

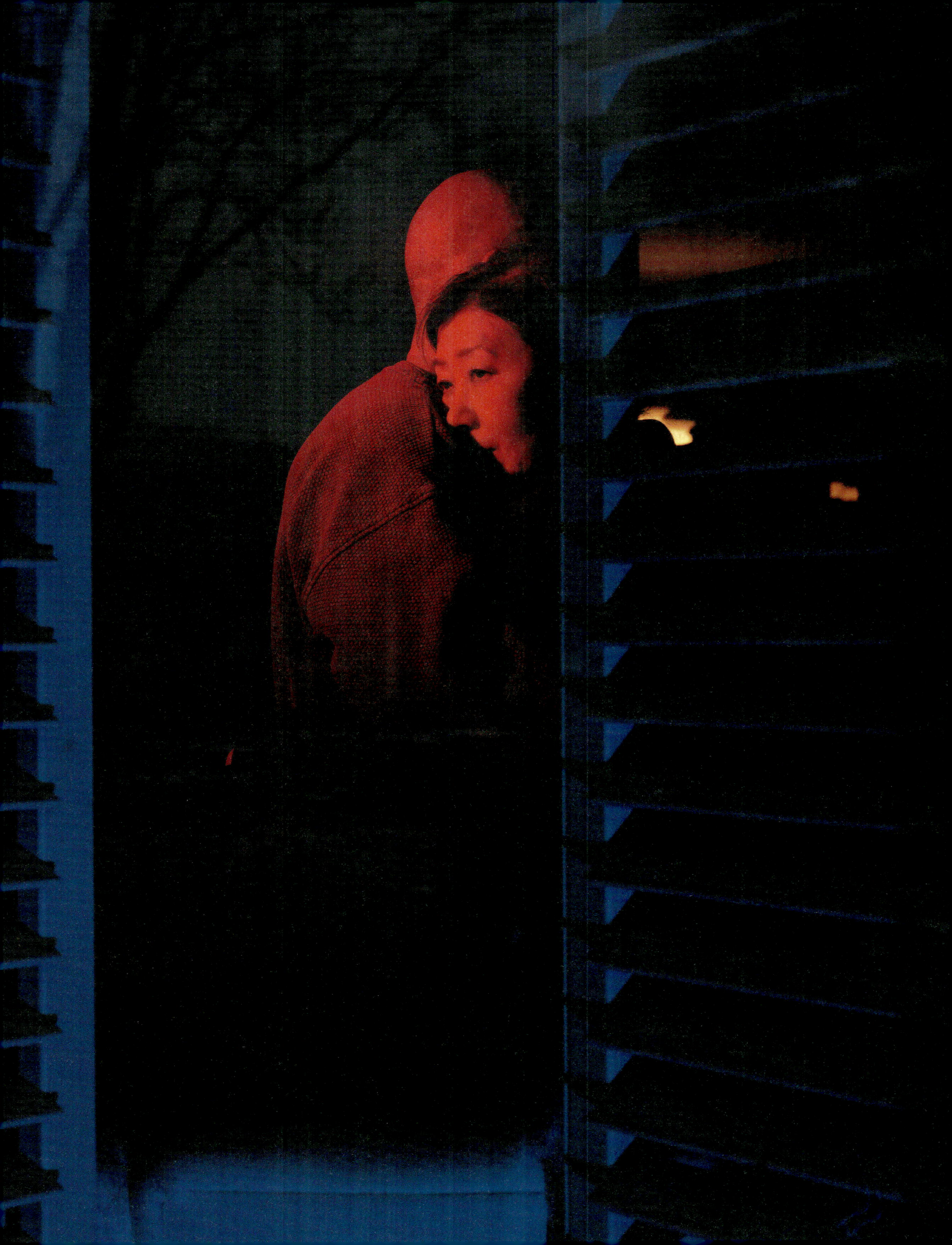

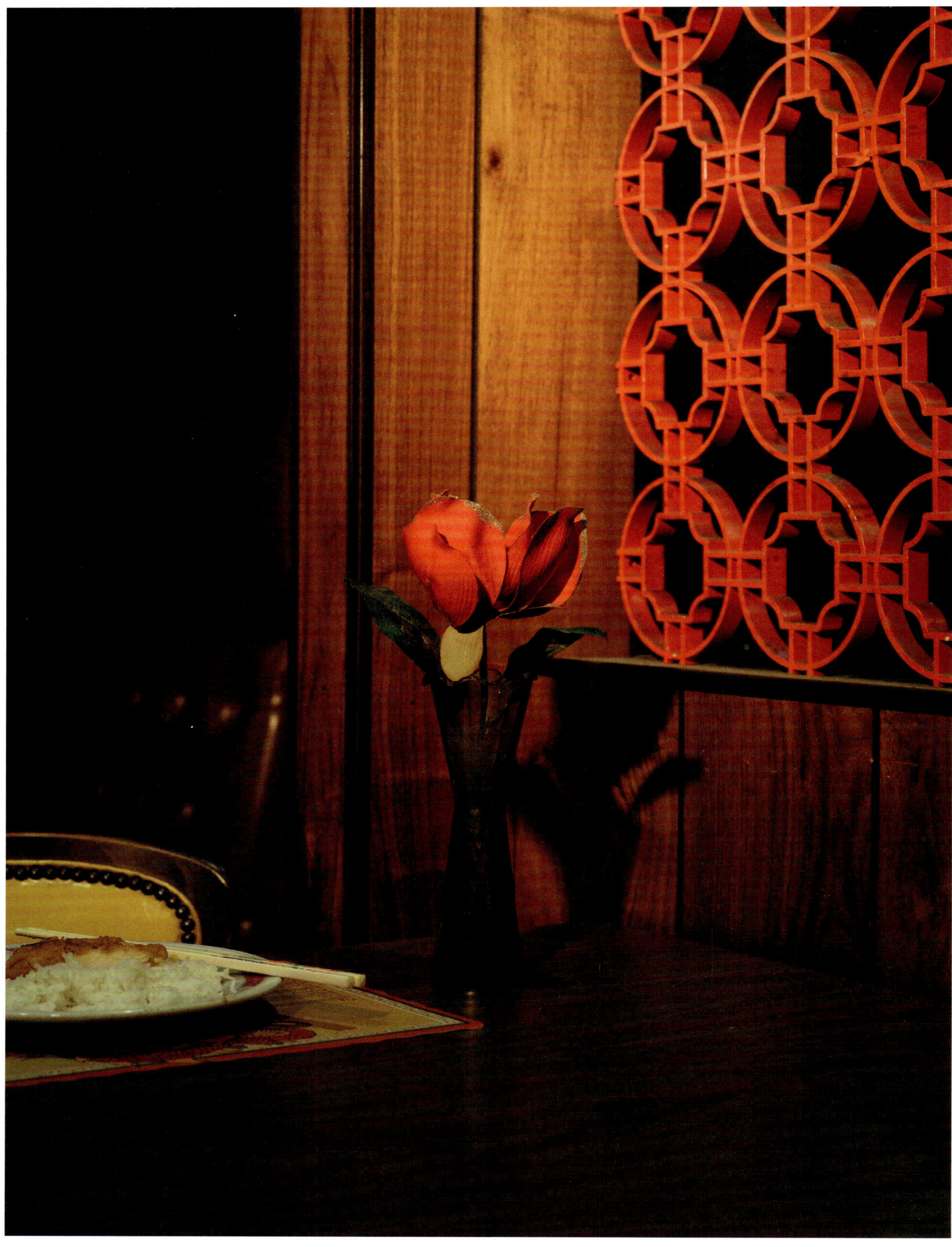

This page:
Untitled (Red Flower),
2023; opposite: *Untitled
(Family Restaurant)*, 2023

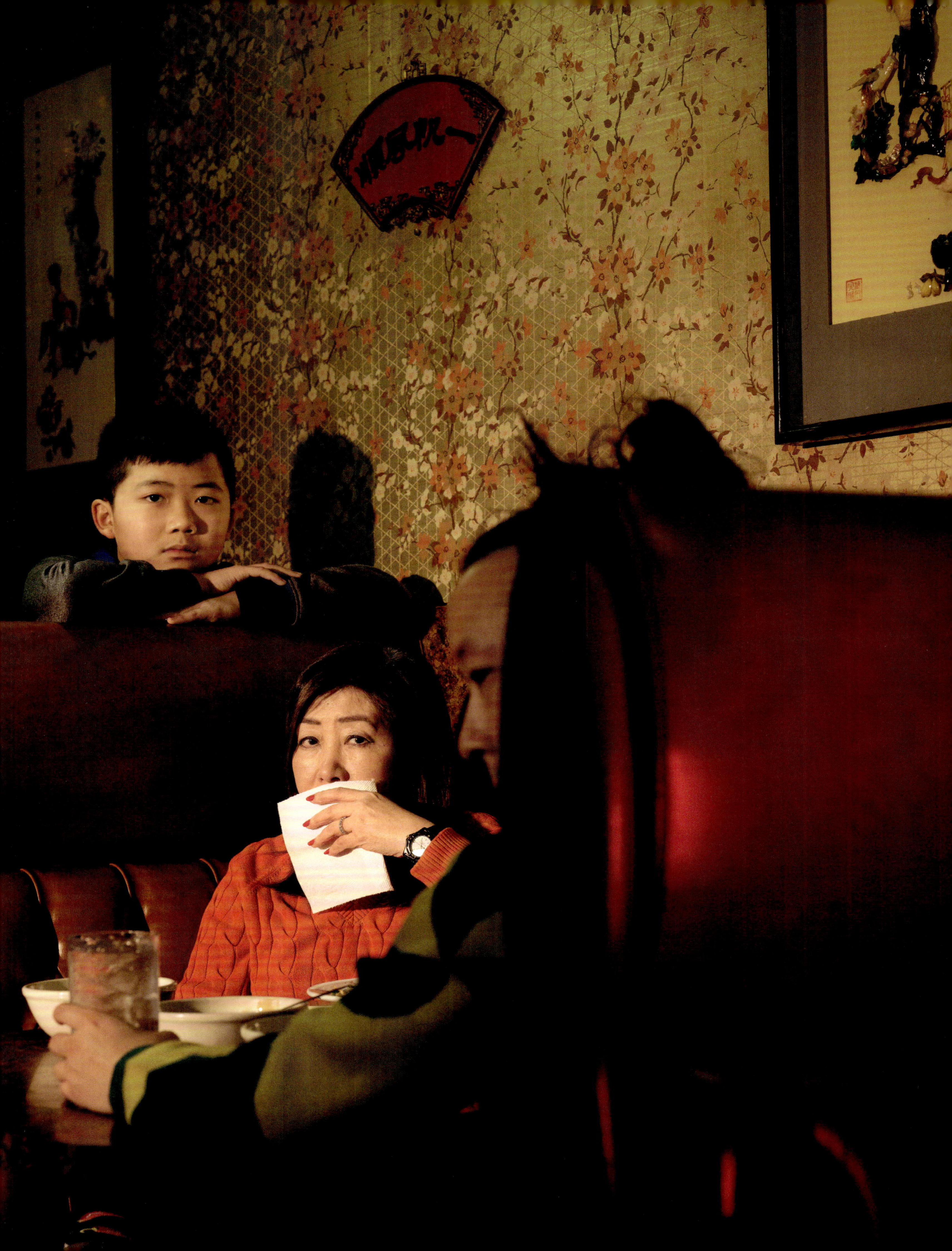

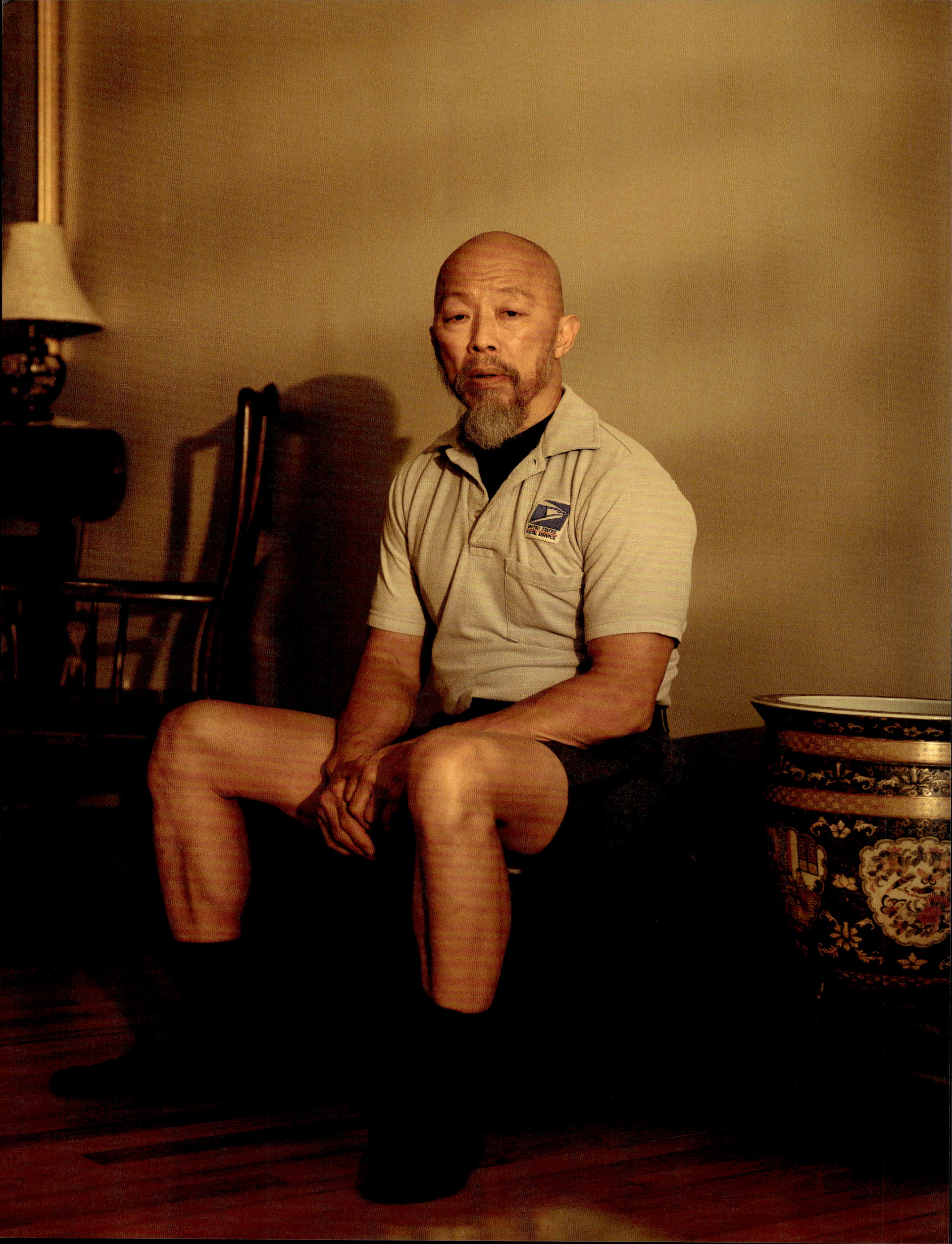

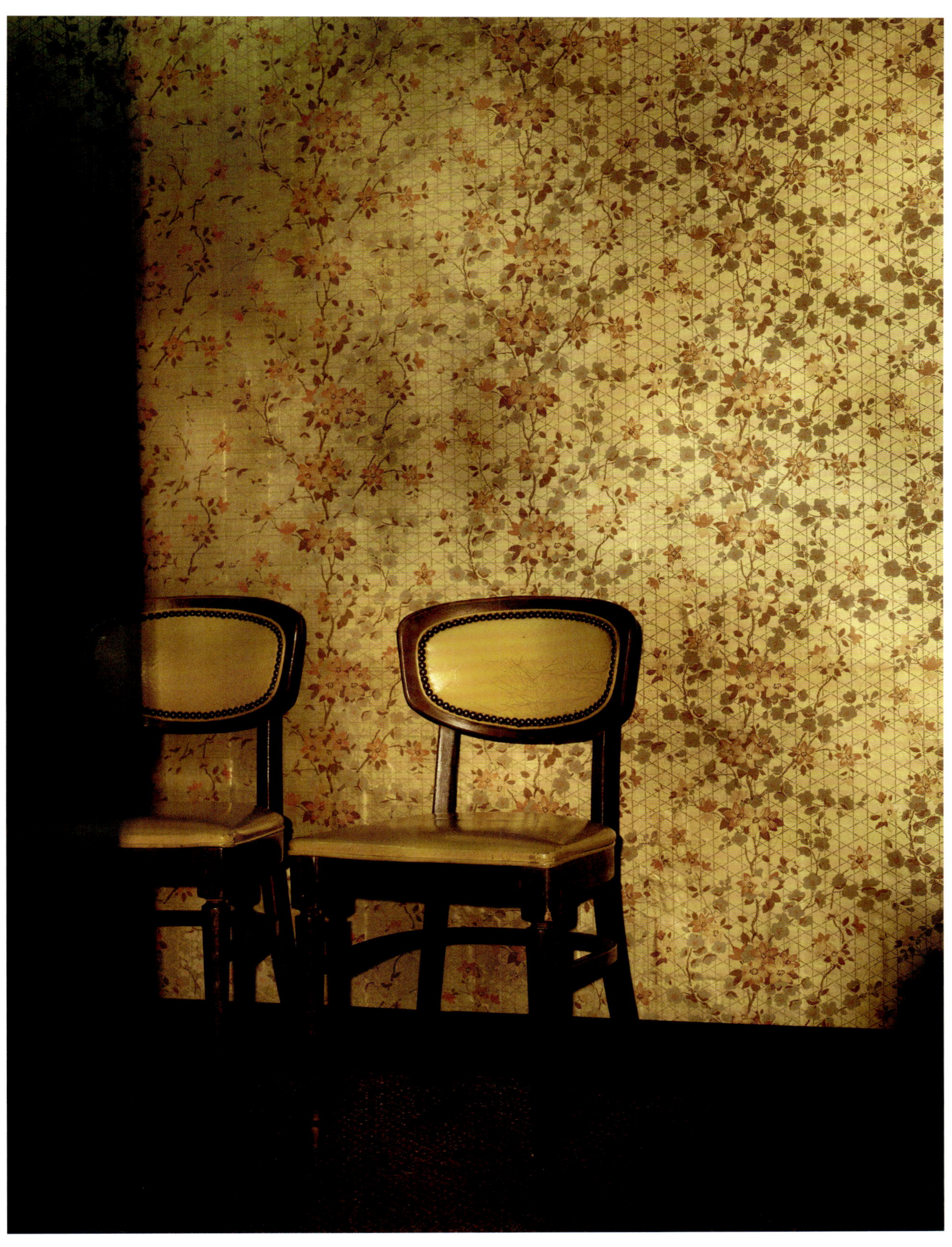

This page:
Untitled (Yellow Chairs),
2023; opposite: *Untitled
(Dad the Mail Carrier),*
2023

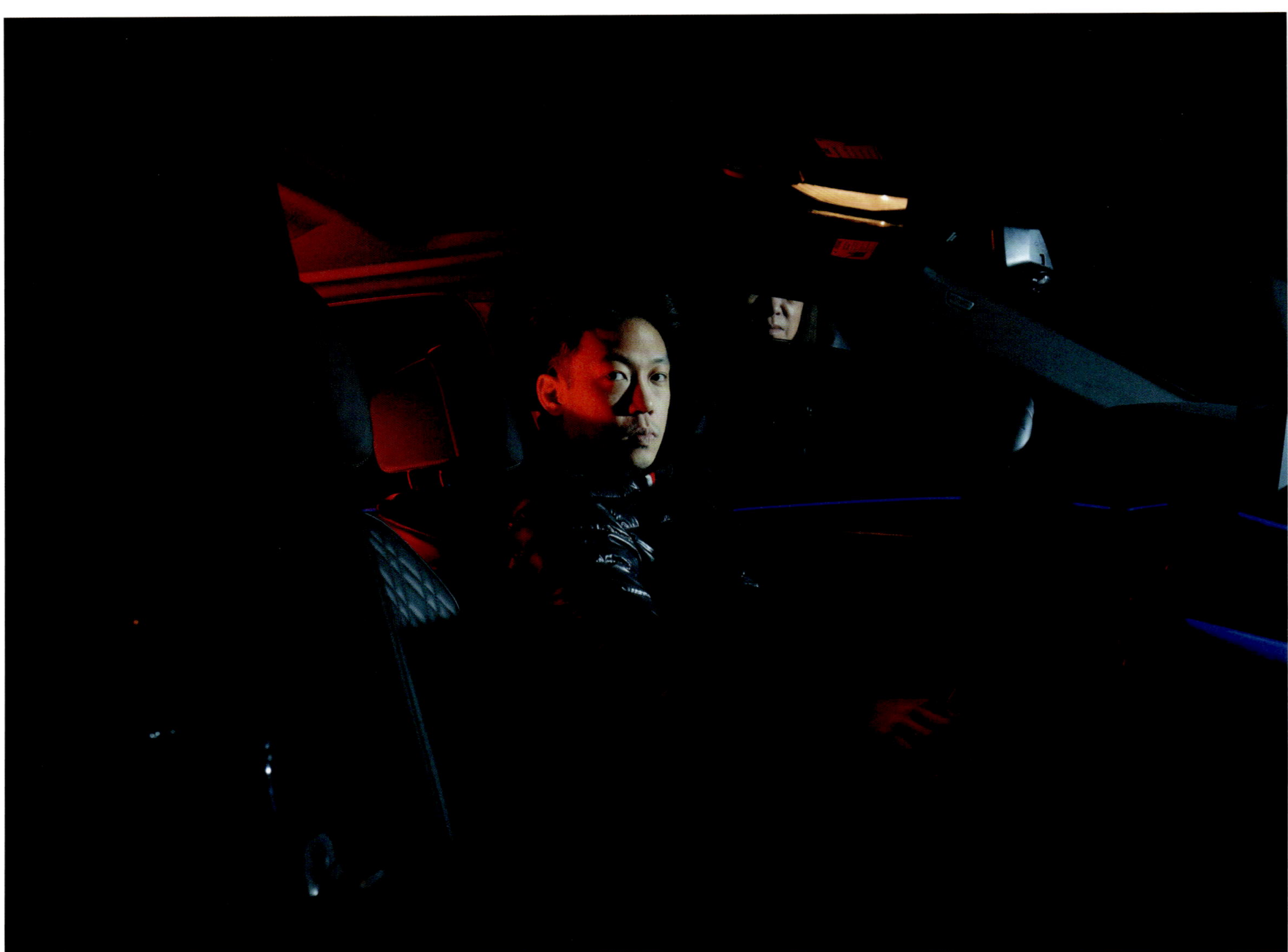

This page:
Untitled (Mom and Jake),
2023; opposite: *Untitled
(Cutting Flowers),* 2023

All photographs from
the series *In Between
You and Your Shadow,*
2021–ongoing
Courtesy the artist

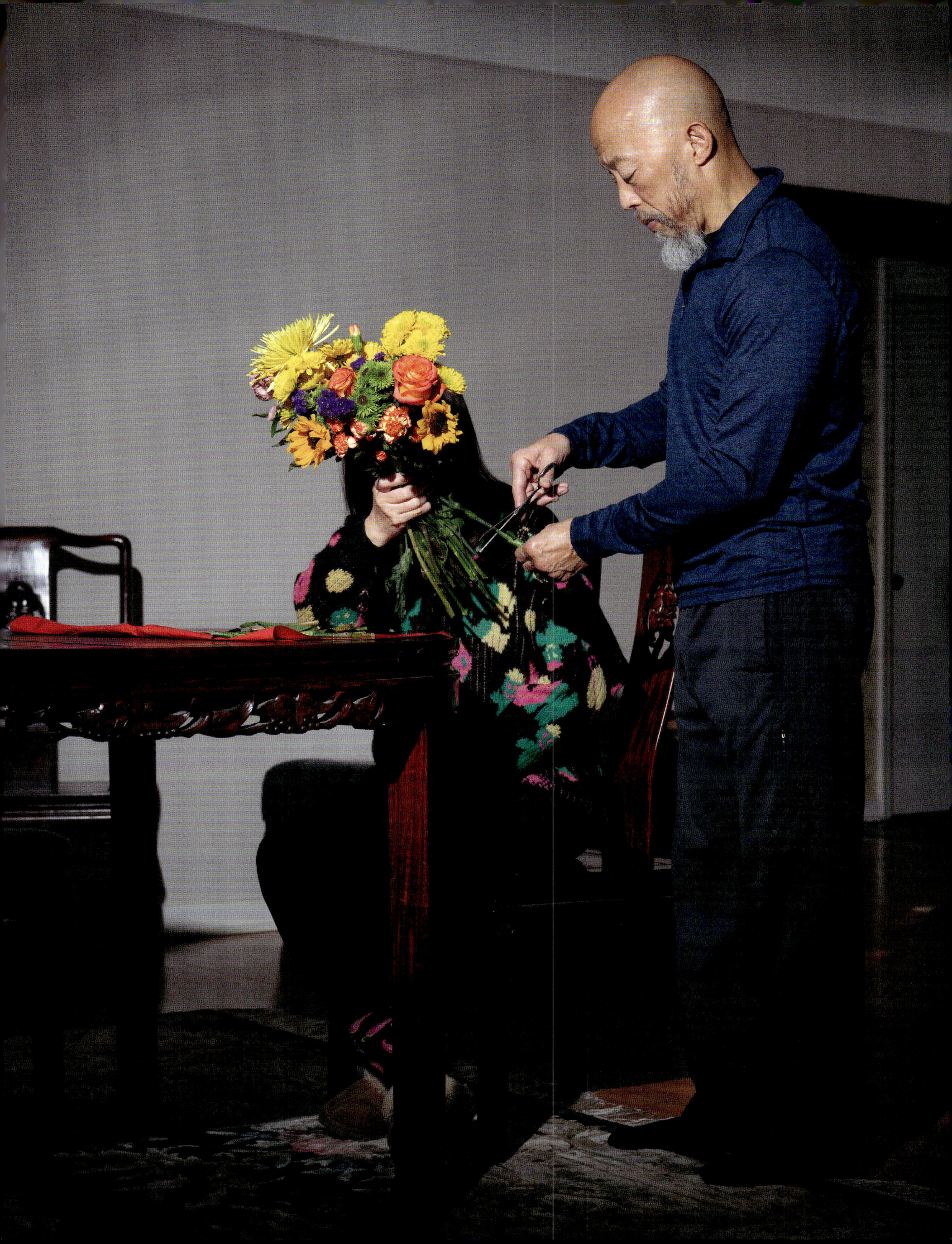

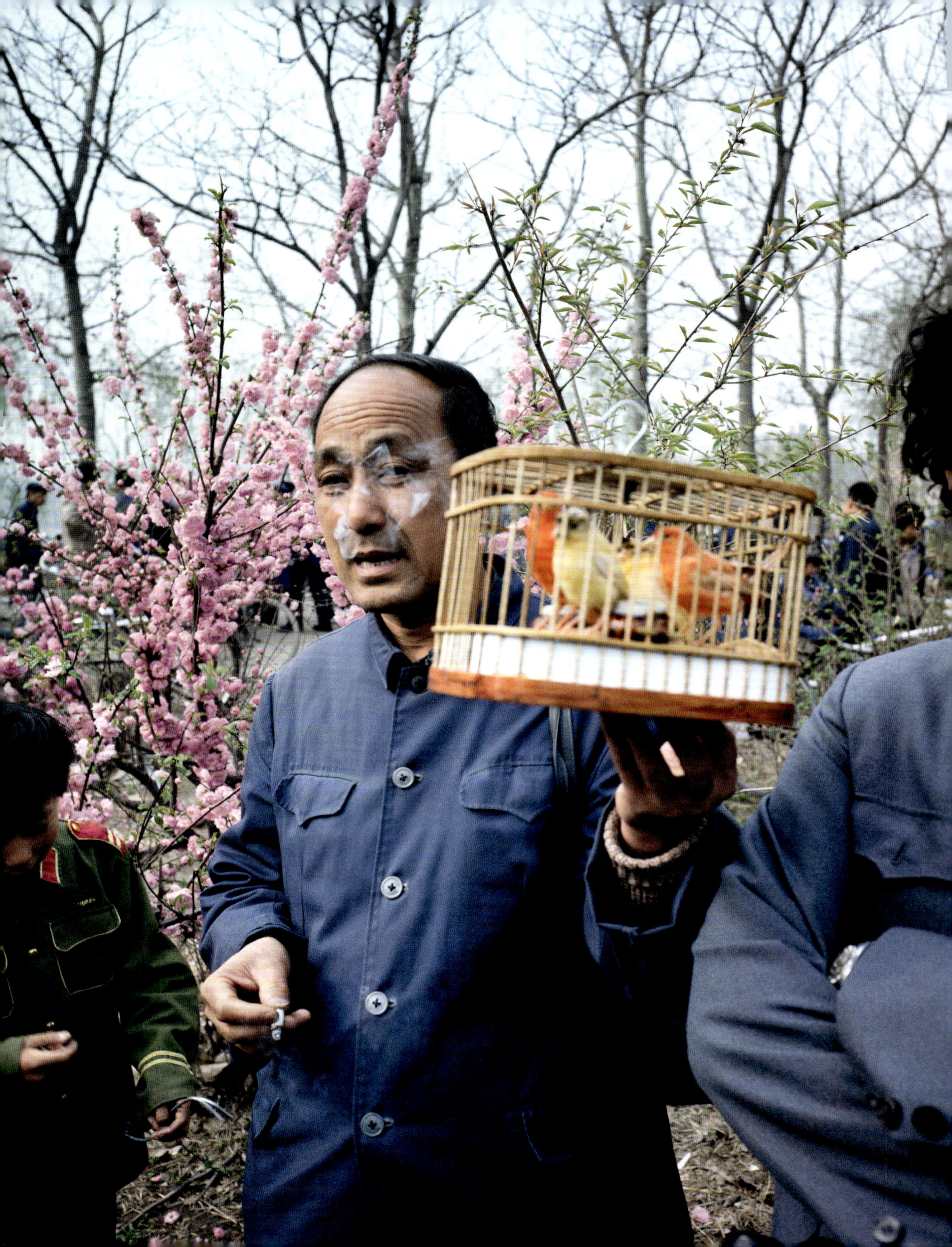

How to Survive the American Dream

Reagan Louie in Conversation with Aleesa Pitchamarn Alexander

In the 1970s Reagan Louie moved to San Francisco to take a teaching job. The city still had a countercultural flair, and Louie, who at the time considered himself something of a rebel, began documenting the streets and vibrant businesses of its Chinatown. He later traveled to China, connecting to his family's history and capturing the country's rapid pace of change. By now, he has spent more than fifty years exploring issues of migration, cultural transformation, and intergenerational dialogue through photography.

As the son of immigrant parents, Louie's decision to take an art path was a bold one. He studied with such major figures as Robert Heinecken and Walker Evans, and considers Chauncey Hare, the photographer-activist who famously abandoned the art world to focus on the plight of workers, a mentor, even though technically Hare was Louie's own student. Louie also often felt estranged from the art world. After graduate school at Yale, he almost gave up on art, taking odd jobs digging sewers before pushing himself to return to photography so that he could pursue his original "intent to understand and discover the world."

In 2022, Louie's work was included in one of three inaugural exhibitions related to the Asian American Art Initiative (AAAI) at the Cantor Arts Center at Stanford University, an ongoing initiative dedicated to the study of Asian American art. Here, Louie speaks with Aleesa Pitchamarn Alexander, codirector of AAAI, about his artistic journey and the stakes today for Asian American visibility.

Aleesa Pitchamarn Alexander: **Let's talk about this particular moment we're in, which is both difficult and celebratory for Asian Americans.**

Reagan Louie: Yes. Our talk is taking place at the beginning of the Lunar New Year and a few days after two mass shootings by Asian American men. For me, it represents the kind of ultimate American assimilation—these two men shot and killed as Americans, not as Asians. The tragedy illustrates a lot of things that I felt. They were unseen and isolated. That reveals to me this irony of the promise of the American dream, which can never be fully realized by people of color. They can never become white. For Asians, that foreclosure is double, because we're still perceived as being quite exotic and inscrutable, and, therefore, forever alien.

This is, I think, what my work is about—being both Asian and American. It's kind of like a Venn diagram, where the Asian circle and the American circle overlap. That union between the two circles of identity is what matters. Perseverance is the hallmark of my life, a quality I share with all Asian American artists, if not all artists. I'm not really sure where it comes from. But surely it has to do with survival, this profound need we have, or I have as an artist, and the success, if I've had any successes—I've had

some—has been accompanied by many moments of feeling unseen and marginalized. In fact, I first believed that I had to turn my back on my Chinese culture to achieve the American dream, to be successful.

APA: **You're reflecting on your more than fifty-year-long career from a certain vantage point. In the early phases of your career, how much do you feel these factors of identity, both from your position as an Asian American and from how you and your work were seen, impacted the way that you moved through school or the art world? I'm thinking, of course, of your early experiences with Robert Heinecken and, later, Walker Evans, both of whom you studied with. To what extent did these questions come up then for you?**

RL: Almost never. Because at that time, it was all about formalism, and any other conversation was irrelevant. In the 1970s, there was no interest, like there is now, in any of the other questions, particularly around identity. There was always this struggle going on between my Asian side, which was almost the opposite sometimes of American behavior and values, which had privilege over your Eastern ideas or

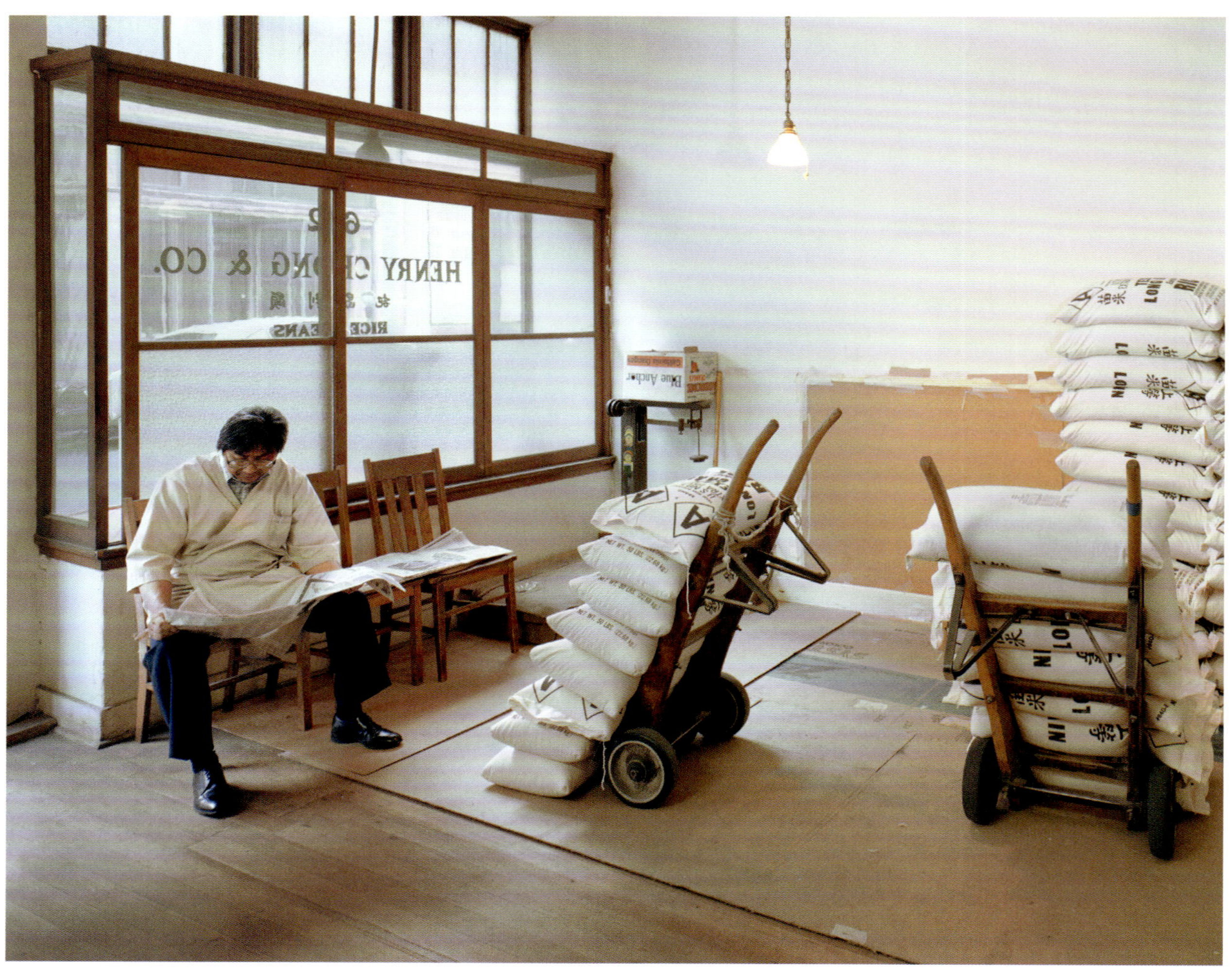

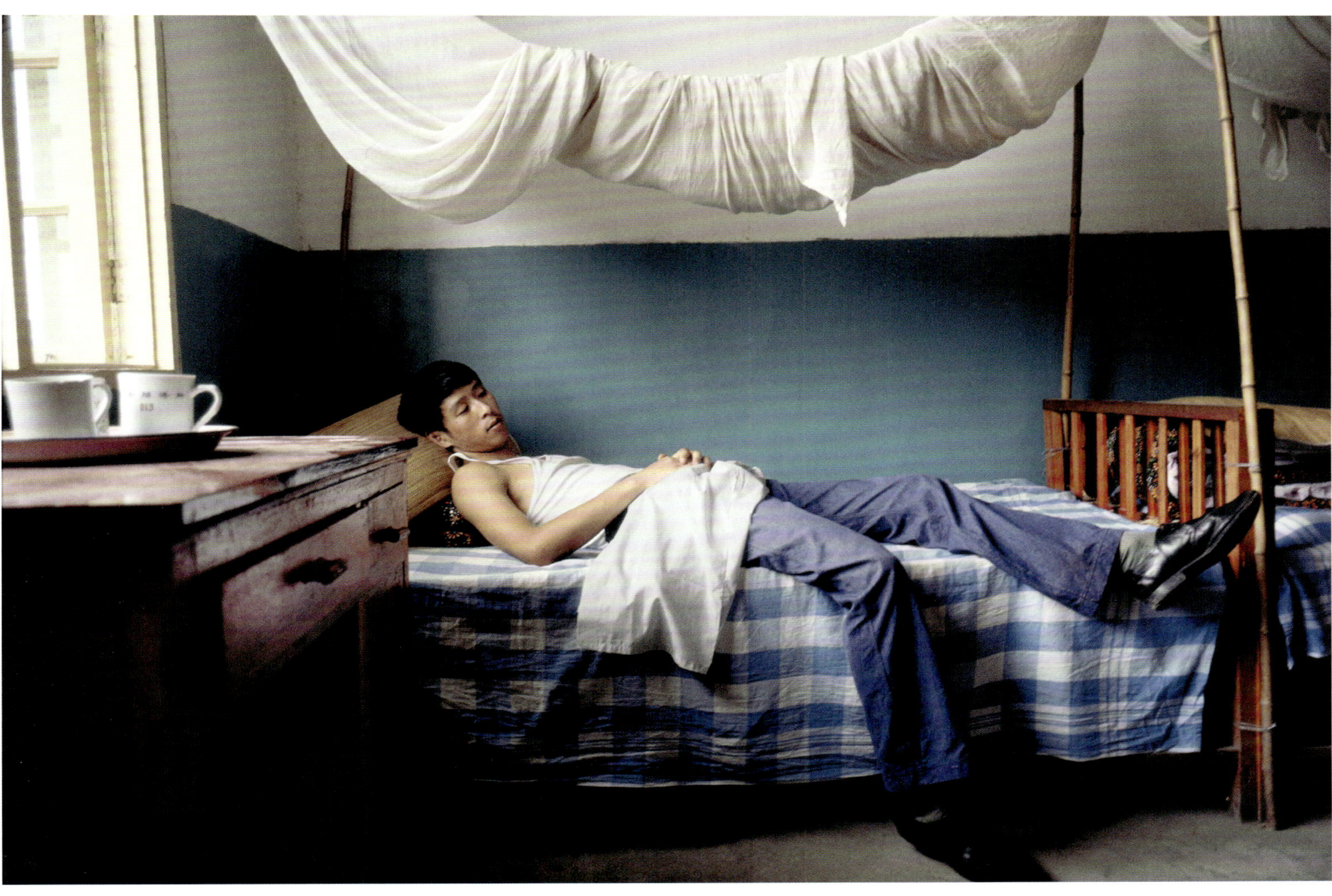

Jiao, Hefei, China, 1980

This fusion in using the camera to find my Chinese, non-Western self comes with many obstacles, including adopting its logic and its values.

values or culture. You had to be extroverted, boisterous in America, not stoic. Hubris always triumphs over humility, and individualism over the collective. So these were all dynamics that were internal in the work I did.

Until college, I was a pretty indifferent student. I wasn't your typical model Asian American student. I nearly flunked all my math and science classes. But somehow, in my first year, I took an art class as a gut course. But I was enchanted. It opened me up to new ways of looking and being and understanding the world, a new way of communicating, and I developed a curiosity that has remained to this day. This was a moment when the world was changing. I'm a child of the 1960s, and there was a bit of a rebel in me. I was seeking truth and light and beauty and all that. I was a romantic. I still am in a lot of ways.

APA: **That also makes me think about going back even further into your life— your mother and your father, and their roots, and how you came to be.**

RL: There was no precedent for becoming an artist. Growing up, I recall going to a museum only once. My family didn't have time or interest in cultural matters, really. They were too busy making a living, like most people in that generation. So when I decided to become an artist, and not become a lawyer or a doctor, or at least a pharmacist, and studied art instead, I really knew deep down I had to abandon my family for the moment. Abandon those obligations, familial obligations of being the oldest son, and all those expectations that come along with it. I had to turn away from my Chinese self. I mean, literally, physically. I just didn't see them for a while.

I chose this tool, photography, which is the quintessential Western invention, a paradox that both estranged me from my Chinese self and my family but also gave me a way back to discover and to integrate those two selves. This fusion in using the camera to find my Chinese, non-Western self comes with many obstacles, including adopting its logic and its values, the machine logic, which you kind of resist.

There's a critical divide that needs to be recognized, or reckoned: immigration to America before 1965, and after. I'm a boomer. My generation's experiences are more connected to that first wave of Chinese immigration that began in the nineteenth century. But I'm somewhere in the middle if we consider that the Chinese American experience is a continuum from the 1800s until now. My father was born in China. Even though I'm fourth generation

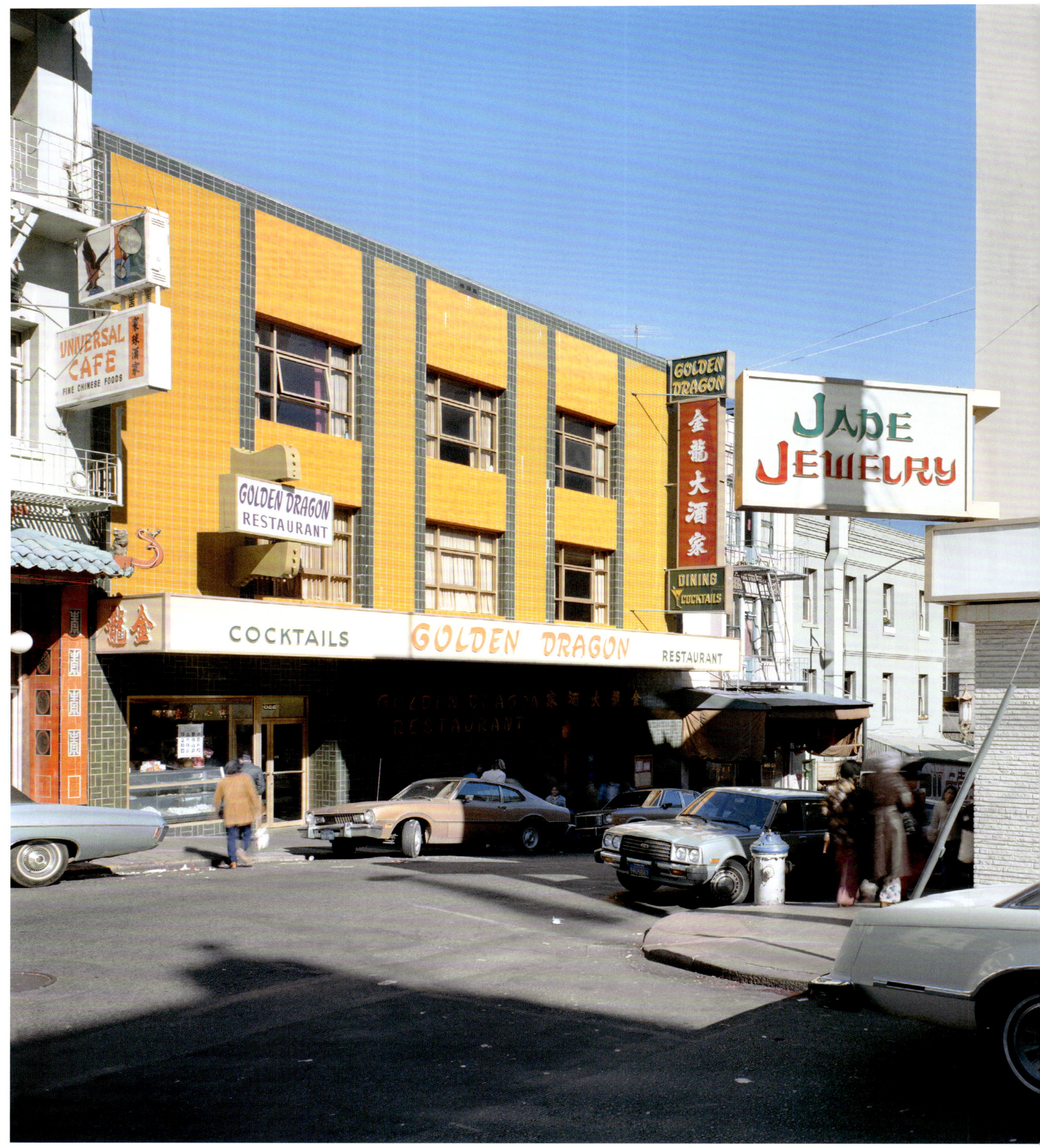

San Francisco Chinatown,
Golden Dragon
Restaurant, 1979

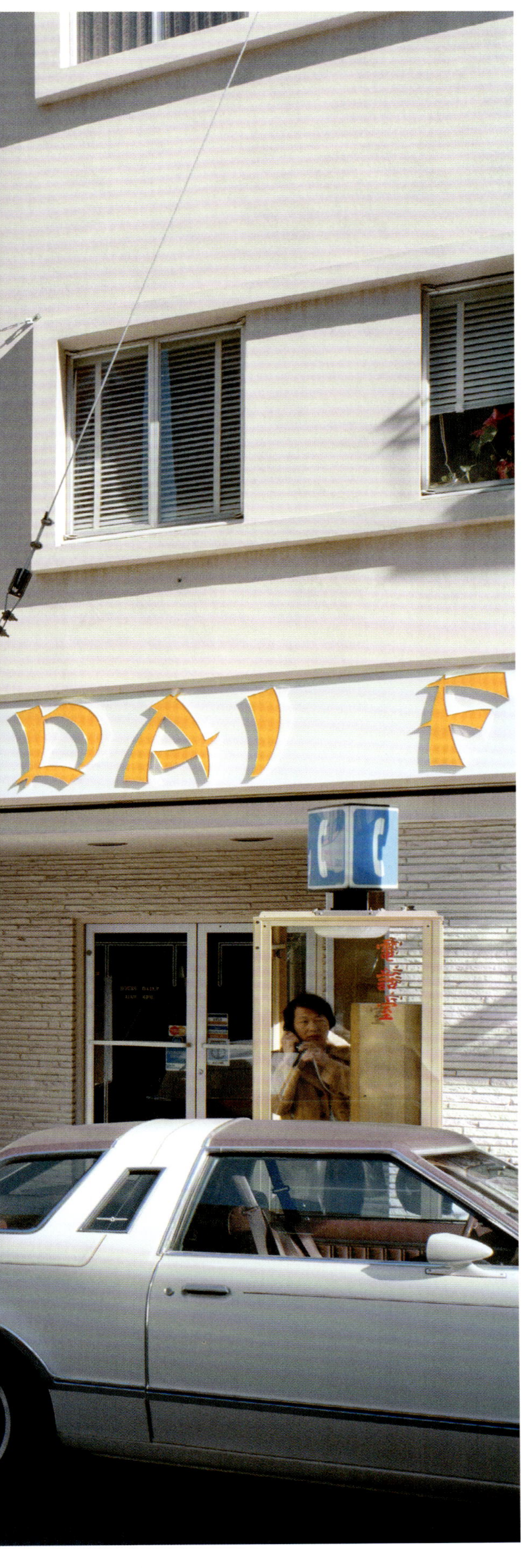

on my mother's side, which is very unusual, I identify as a second-generation citizen because my mother's family really grew up in isolation, away from the surrounding communities. My first language is Cantonese. We lived in a pretty enclosed world. Both waves of Chinese immigrants came for the same reasons—for a better life for their families, for themselves. But we faced very different kinds of receptions. The pre-1965 immigrants faced open hostilities, physical violence, whereas the post-1965 generation was welcomed, albeit with more subtle forms of racism and suspicion.

APA: We see that continuing through today, especially during the pandemic. So, in order to pursue photography, you essentially had to turn away from your family. But then, it comes back around that your work is, in many respects, largely about your family—and family in general. I wonder if you might share a little about that process, from arriving at your subject matter in San Francisco's Chinatown in the earlier part of your career to how you ended up in China.

RL: There was no way I could explain, even to myself, why I wanted to be an artist—and especially to my family. They took comfort that I went to good schools, and then later on, I became a professor—so that's how they saw me. Art? They just couldn't figure it out.

It was only when I came with my father to China in 1981, into his village that he had left when he was nine years old, that my photography made sense to them. That's when the circle closed, and I really understood for the first time what my work meant to me, what I was trying to do. Eventually, I reconnected with my family.

I moved to San Francisco to accept a teaching job at the San Francisco Art Institute in the 1970s. San Francisco was a beautiful place then. It was still basking in the afterglow of the '60s. I began photographing in San Francisco's Chinatown really out of convenience. I lived there, and it looked exotic. I lived around the outskirts, the border of Chinatown and North Beach, in this alleyway called Fresno Alley. Its claim to fame was that my building was the location of a Woody Allen film. It was still really boho life there. You saw the North Beach poets still wandering around, trying to channel Ginsberg.

While I began photographing there out of convenience, it was also a place of my ancestors and memories. Many of my family members, including my grandfather and father, lived and worked in Chinatown

initially. I deployed a nineteenth-century stand camera, 4-by-5. I wanted to contrast the incredible detail that camera renders with the motion blurs of people's movements. I saw them as my ancestors, as ghosts.

Chinatown led to China. In 1980, I answered an ad in a Chinese newspaper to study in China. That's when I began my forty-year odyssey. Unbeknownst to me, what I was doing was attempting to find another way, a truer life. Again, finding your cultural roots, or even thinking about that as a source for your art, wasn't heard of then in high-art circles. That was taboo, really. I thought that's what I was doing, but I didn't tell myself that was the goal. In fact, I said the opposite: I was taking my educated eyes to picture this new exotic world. I couldn't really acknowledge the real reason for going to China, my need for some kind of authenticity.

APA: Why do you think it is that it took both you and your father going to China for him to understand your practice more fully?

RL: It was less what we spoke about than our actions. Toisanese especially, and my family in particular, are very laconic. My dad, me, my son, we're all men of few words. So what spoke to me was watching him become a nine-year-old again. He had tears in his eyes most of the time. I saw his gentleness, which I had never seen, because to survive as an Asian male at that time, when I was growing up (and still, maybe), you had to be a tough guy.

With the two eras of Chinese immigrants, the work that's produced by the artists of those eras really manifests their time, the conditions they faced. The art made in internment camps, photographically—like the pictures made by Toyo Miyatake—is a declaration that they were here. Right? They weren't going away. I feel really strongly about that. Whereas the work being made now, which is wonderful and celebratory, it's about living life out loud.

APA: Why do you think it was difficult for you to acknowledge that the need for authenticity was a primary driving force for you to go back to China?

RL: Again, I drank the Kool-Aid. It was all about formalism and nothing else.

APA: Many of the early Chinese immigrants to the United States came from a specific province, Guangdong. This is to say, there are many distinct provinces in China with their own

dialects, mores, and histories. Yet here, sometimes, there's a tendency to view China, this massive country, as a kind of monolith.

RL: Before I began working in China, I vaguely knew that China was vast and diverse, filled with different dialects and cultural practices. But I didn't realize to what extent until I got there. I really detest anything pan-Asian right now. I don't even like the word *Asian American*.

APA: Speaking of the term *Asian American*, we got to know each other through the Asian American Art Initiative, a project I codirect. Your work was included last year in the exhibition *At Home/On Stage: Asian American Representation in Photography and Film*, curated by my colleague Maggie Dethloff at the Cantor. I recall that you wrote beautifully in a private note to Maggie and me about what it means to be included in an exhibition like that, even when you don't love the term *Asian American*.

RL: I was struck by how much art in the exhibition came from suffering pain and grief, which I could identify with. We know the pain and suffering caused by internment, or the history of violence directed at Asian Americans, which continues to this day. But equally important for me was the daily pushing against grief and loss that we face, that's faced by every Asian American every day—racism and discrimination, not being fully seen, just those daily microaggressions against people of color. But in the exhibition, we see Asian American artists pushing back against all that discrimination and hate; from their pain and hardship they made tremendous meaning. Art that gave them solace. Which is why all the work for me is filled with healing joy. It was never bitter. The art in the show reminded us that beauty and grace can arise from pain and loss. It's that irrepressible human spirit.

APA: Recently there's been a lot of critique of the racially specific exhibition model. From your perspective, working all these decades both within and on the perimeter of the art world, what's your thought on this kind of model of inclusion in the museum space?

RL: Super complicated question. I refuse to do this, to perform our Asian-ness. Right? I think it's great that museums and institutions are recognizing that we're coming from a different place than just formalism. But I am skeptical sometimes

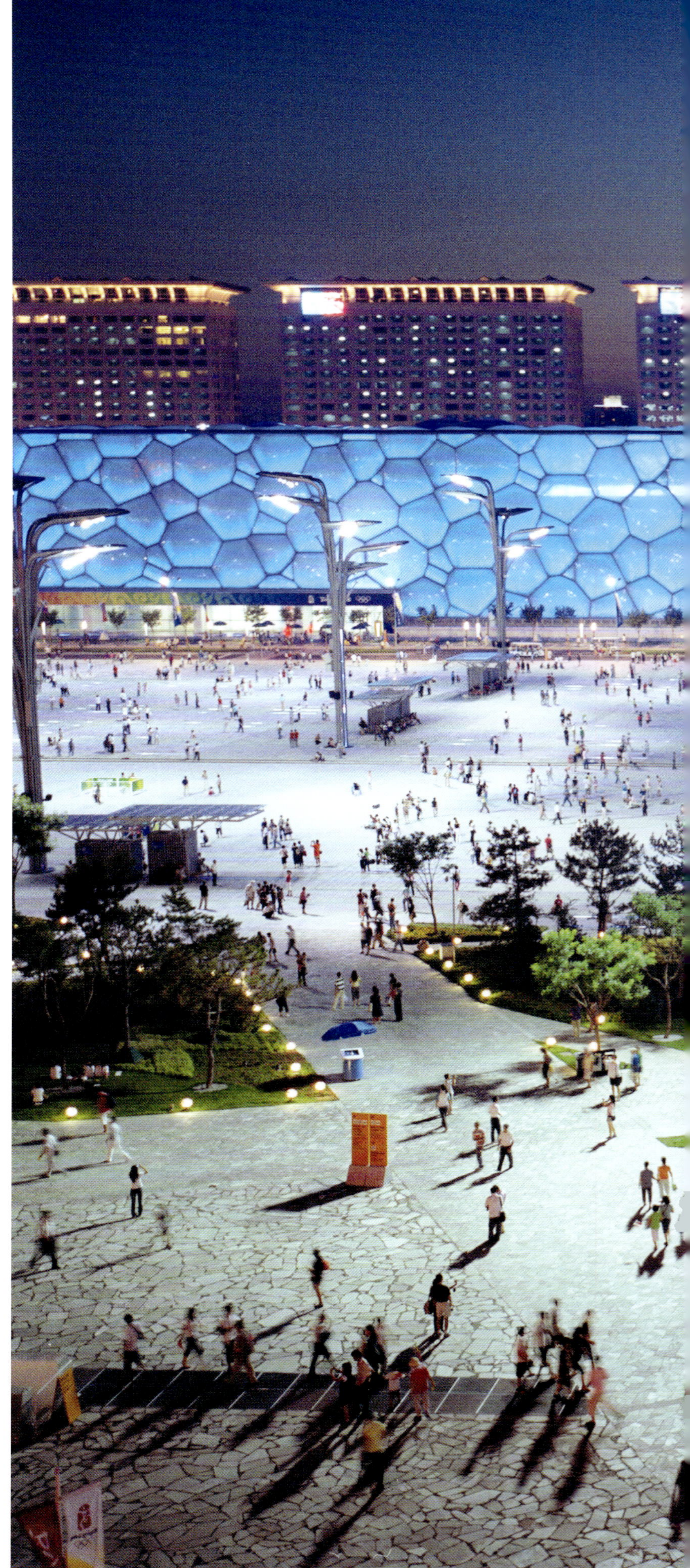

Olympic Park, Beijing, 2008

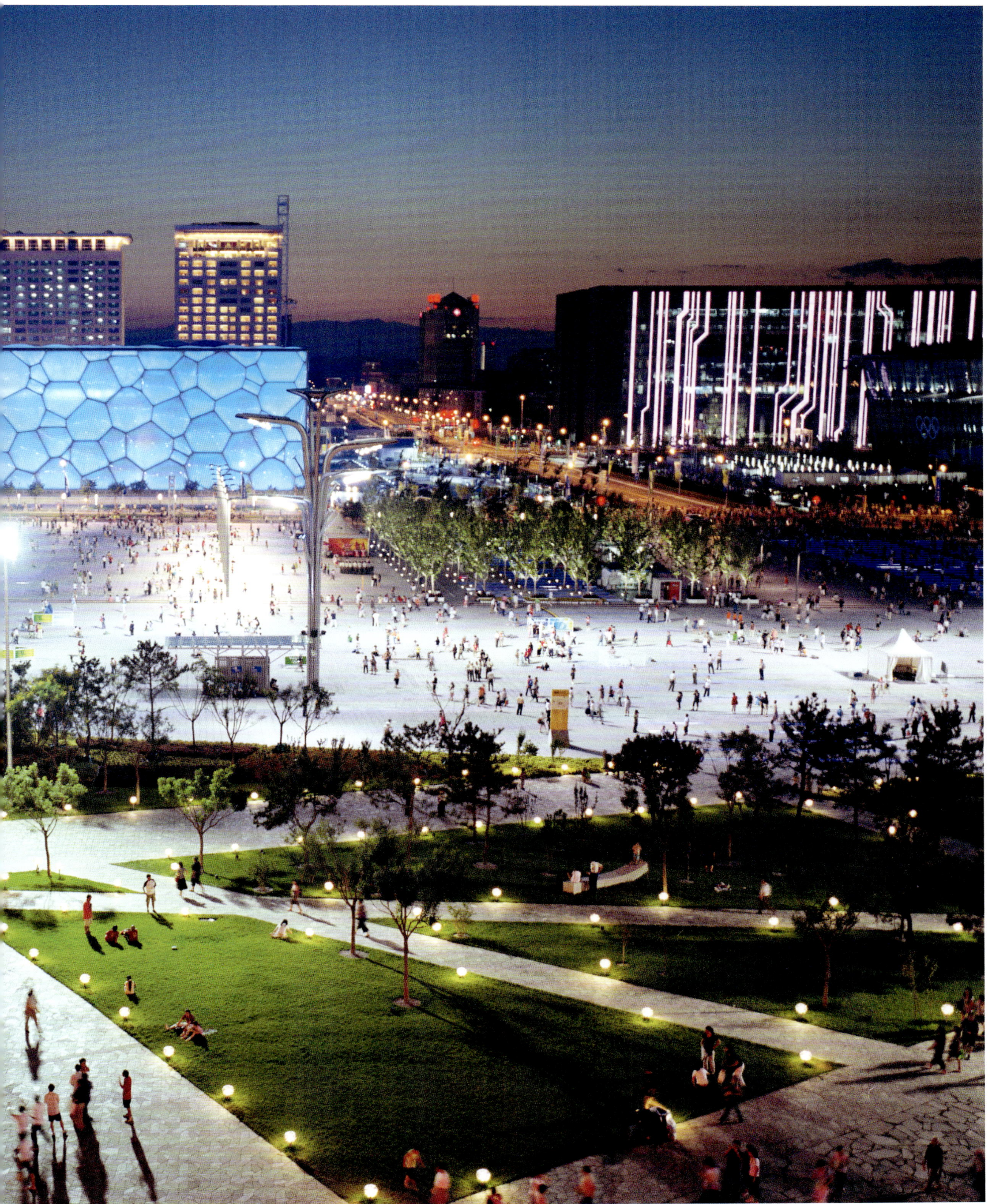

**I'm embracing values
that I once rejected.
Inclusion, not exclusion.
Authenticity,
not artificiality.**

about putting in one or two pictures of an Asian American artist, or whatever. How much difference does that really make? Is it really transformative? I've seen too many instances where it's not. In fact, it's reductive. It diminishes the work of that artist, seen in that context. If you truly want to make a statement, you've got to make the big move. Turn the entire museum inside out. Not just one or two pictures but an entire show. That's what's going to pull in new audiences.

Maybe this is a good moment to give you an example of an experience I had with all this in the '70s. I was a photographer during the very beginning of photography as a fine art. At the top was MoMA, in New York. The museum had a generous portfolio-review policy. The drill was you'd drop off your portfolio and return to pick up the work a few days later. The first time I dropped off the work, it was a tray of color slides I'd made while I was in California that year after I'd returned. They were of places around Sacramento, where I grew up, and they were very formal, beautiful pictures—and I was surprised when I was invited to come in and speak with the curators. They thought the pictures had a sweet quality and asked me to keep them updated. But the reception for my work made in China was much chillier. I couldn't articulate what it meant.

As I've talked about, I didn't know why I had gone back to China. And there were awkward silences with the curator when the conversation veered away from formal aesthetic issues. At one point, I remember I was trying to talk about my feelings, to try to communicate what was at stake for me. The curator was dismissive. He said he didn't care about my feelings, only his. It just shut down that conversation. I was really pondering whether I had what it took to be an artist. I was really dejected after that encounter. I tried to step away from art and tried to quit. I applied to business school. I was convinced I didn't measure up. And I was also tired of always being in debt.

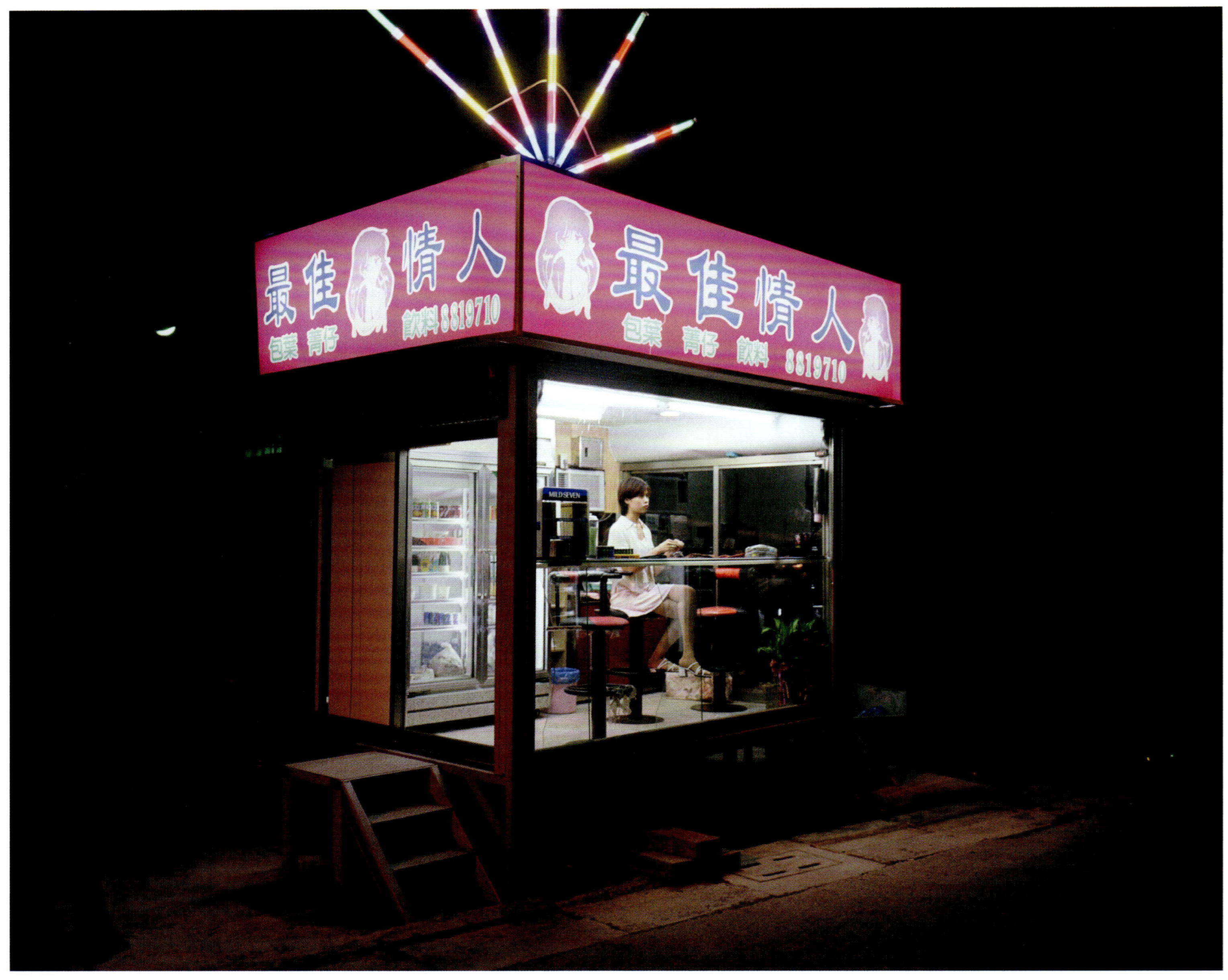

Fortunately, no business school accepted me. But I didn't know what else to do. Art was the only thing I knew. So, I rolled the dice again. I went into more debt and moved to Beijing, a decision that wreaked havoc on my marriage. I photographed with crazy, wild abandon. Every day, I would wake up as early as I could and stay out as late as I could, taking as many pictures as I could. I shot over three thousand rolls of film that year, 1987. I tried to find aspects of my Chinese self in them, especially the men. I was unknowingly trying to find my Chinese soul that could coexist with my American self. That year something had shifted. I really felt I had broken new ground.

I returned to MoMA with my portfolio, having no expectations. This time, it was even worse—the receptionist just returned the portfolio with no comment. But then, one of the curators at MoMA left a message that said, "We returned your portfolio by mistake. Could you please come back tomorrow with the portfolio?" Which led to, the following year, in 1988, the show at MoMA—*New Photography 4: Patrick Faigenbaum, Reagan Louie, and Michael Schmidt.*

APA: So, in the end, the result was positive. But it still gives me tremendous unease, as I'm sure it gives you— this unstable and unproductive ground of constantly thinking about or relying on forms of validation from predominantly white institutions. And yet, we want to forge careers in the arts. What do we do? What should we do to not be beholden to these types of external forms of validation when that is the most obvious path to mainstream success?

RL: We have to take nonobvious paths. We're in a much better place than when I was coming up. Back then, there was so much power concentrated in one institution, almost in one person. It kind of was mimicking, maybe, the time of Abstract Expressionism, when you had Clement Greenberg or Harold Rosenberg creating a school of painting.

APA: When we first came into contact, I know you were at a difficult moment in your life, and you were feeling like that was the end of your artistic career, essentially. And yet, here you are in a moment when there has been increased interest in your work. What does it mean for you to step into that reception rather than recede from it?

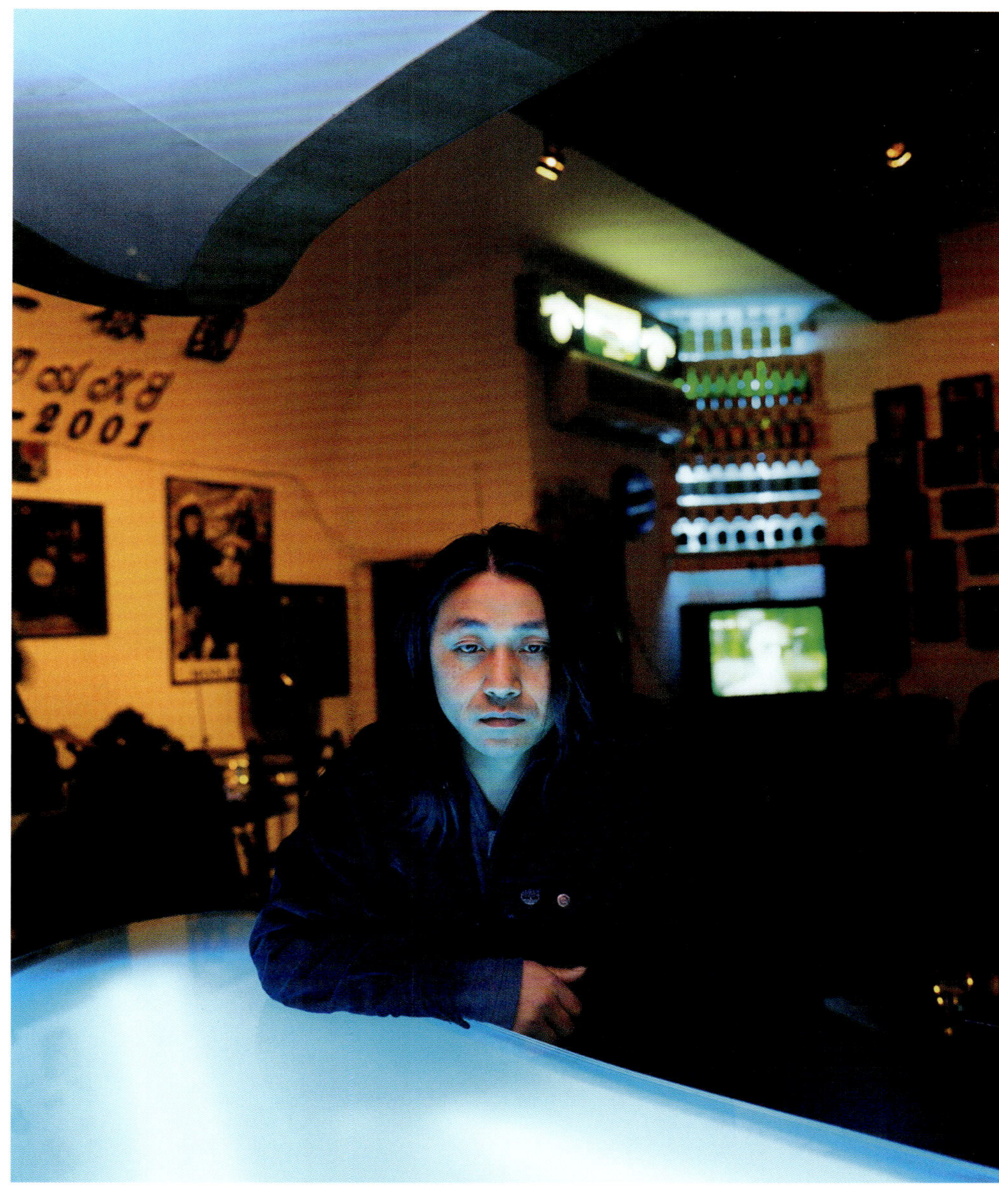

Chengdu, 2002
All photographs courtesy the artist

RL: It's been a struggle. I've found new allies, new communities. It really pulled me back from the brink. When we first met, I was just realizing the price I had paid, the price we have to pay to succeed in this country, to be a Chinese American. I was in a very dark void. I really thought I was finished and would disappear. But now, I'm embracing values that I once rejected. Inclusion, not exclusion. Authenticity, not artificiality. Heart values, not head values. And joy, not suffering. I'm not fully there yet. But I can see that these are options. And I'm trying to get back to work.

Aleesa Pitchamarn Alexander is the Halperin Associate Curator of Modern and Contemporary Art and codirector of the Asian American Art Initiative at Stanford University's Cantor Arts Center.

NEW PHOTO BOOKS

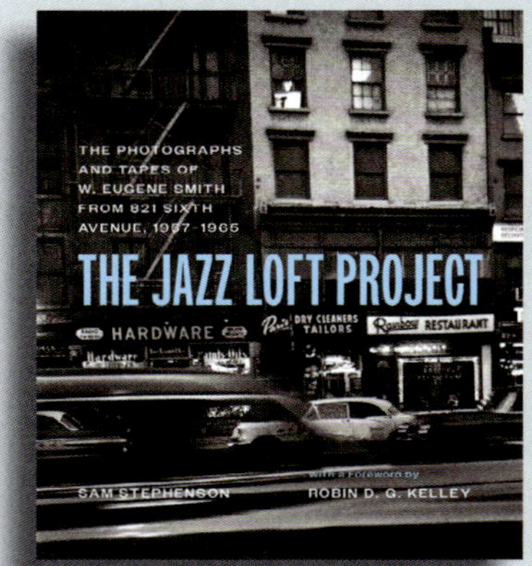

From **CHICAGO**

The Jazz Loft Project
Photographs and Tapes of W. Eugene Smith from 821 Sixth Avenue, 1957–1965
W. Eugene Smith and Sam Stephenson
With a Foreword by Robin D. G. Kelley
Cloth $40.00

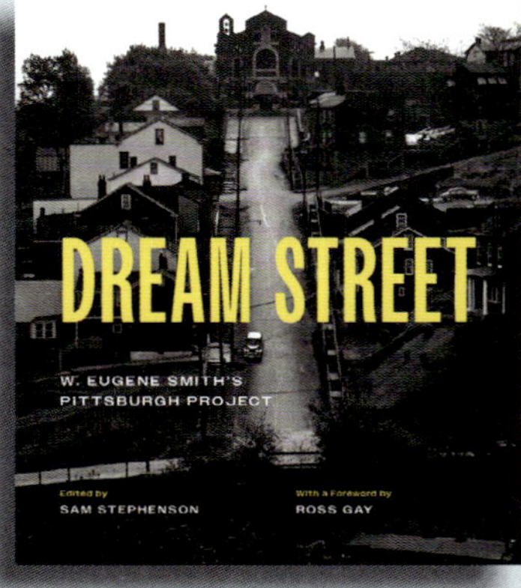

From **CHICAGO**

Dream Street
W. Eugene Smith's Pittsburgh Project
W. Eugene Smith
Edited by Sam Stephenson
With a Foreword by Ross Gay and an Essay by Alan Trachtenberg
Cloth $30.00

From **Scheidegger & Spiess**
Art | Photography | Architecture

HR Giger by Camille Vivier
Edited by Beda Achermann
With Photography and Contributions by Camille Vivier
Cloth $110.00

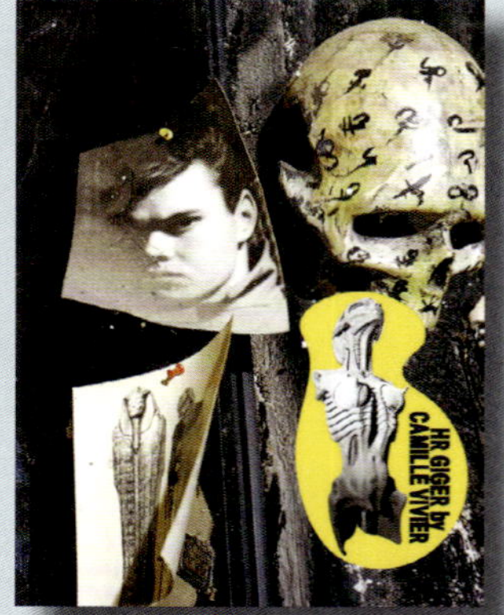

From **BODLEIAN LIBRARY PUBLISHING**

Dark Room
Garry Fabian Miller
With an Introduction by Edmund de Waal
Cloth $65.00

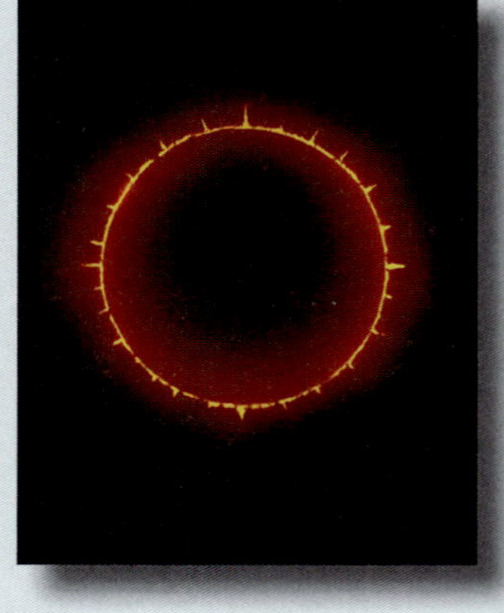

The University of Chicago Press www.press.uchicago.edu

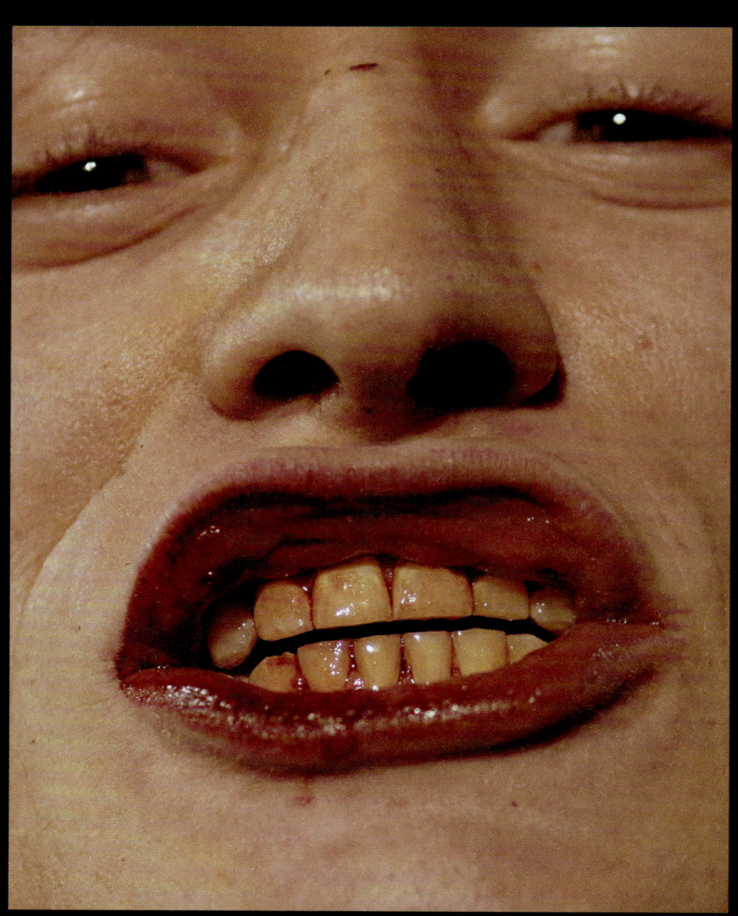

mica.edu/aperture

M|I|C|A
PHOTOGRAPHY

Jack Sorokin '15 (Photography BFA) from *Rodeo Boys*

His recent film titled 'Landfall' was accepted and screened at 16 film festivals around the world in 2022 and won Best Experimental Short Film at three of those festivals, including the Paris Short Film Festival.

The PhotoBook Review

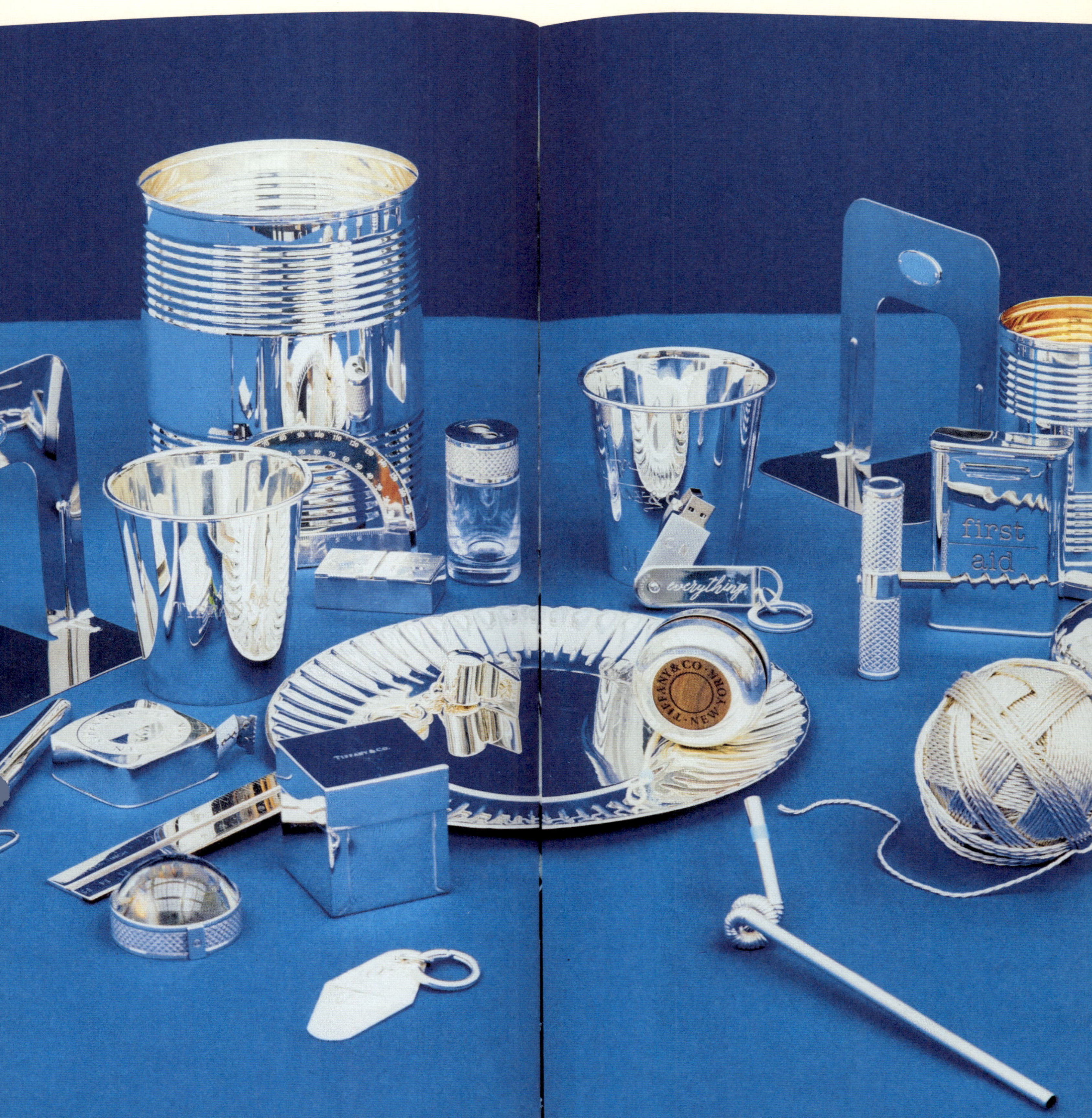

Looking, Watching, Trying, Doing

Cécile Poimboeuf-Koizumi in Conversation with Taous Dahmani

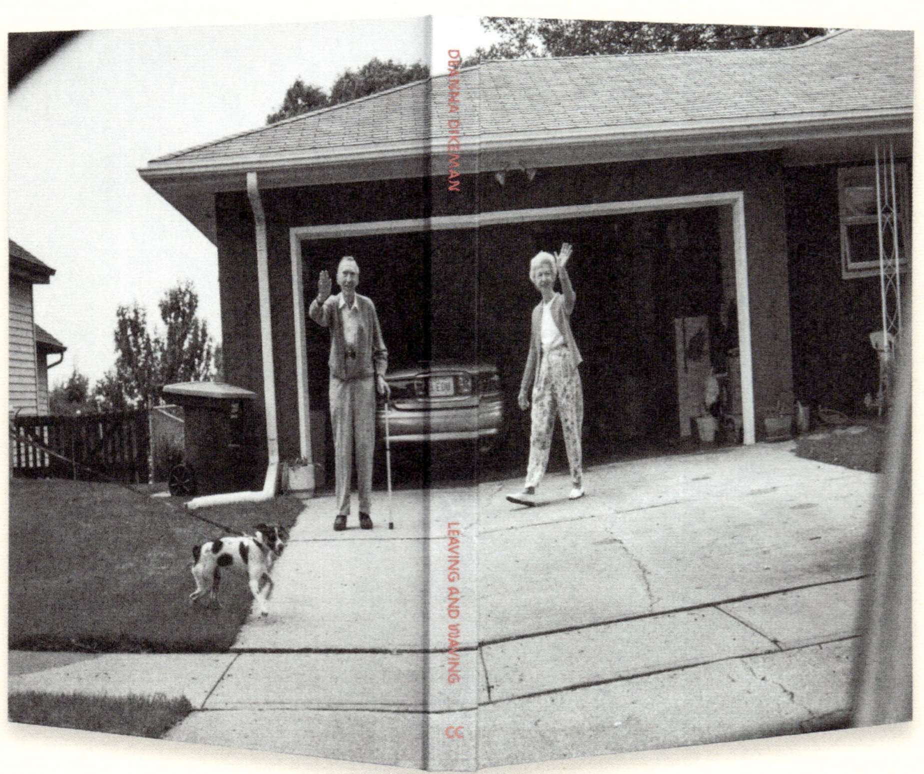

Cécile Poimboeuf-Koizumi has been making books since 2014. Founded in Paris in collaboration with the photographer Vasantha Yogananthan, her independent publishing house, Chose Commune—a reference to things that are both familiar and simple—has for nearly a decade created unique publications and objects. The press focuses on photography and works on paper in a manner that is meticulous, creative, and deftly attuned to the physical form of the book. Over the years, Poimboeuf-Koizumi has made striking publications with an acute graphic awareness and a collaborative outlook, including those with emerging artists such as Moe Suzuki and Deanna Dikeman as well as Japanese legends such as Issei Suda and contemporary photographers like Daniel Gordon. In a moment crowded with talented independent publishers, Chose Commune distinguishes itself with a singular touch.

Taous Dahmani: In 2020, you moved Chose Commune's offices from Paris to Marseille, where we also became close friends. Being such a charismatic place, how has the city influenced you and your work?

Cécile Poimboeuf-Koizumi: I guess Marseille has had more of an impact on my daily life than on my actual projects. The city instantly felt like home when I moved here—which is something I don't say often, because I've never really felt at home anywhere. Marseille is not an uncomplicated city, but I love how people-driven it is; I would never be able to have coffee with the delivery guy back in Paris! The sunny, warm weather fills me with energy and inspires me to work. I couldn't be under Paris's gray skies anymore.

TD: Moving around and navigating new cultures is not new for you. You traveled a lot in your youth, and still do. How has that shaped your interests and your vision for Chose Commune?

CPK: Chose Commune is basically me. Whatever direction I take in my life has an impact on the publishing house. So, yes, my upbringing has definitely shaped Chose Commune. I've never done anything I don't feel strongly connected with. I think it really comes with knowing what I like and knowing what I'm drawn to. Growing up in China, Japan, Thailand, Australia, and Taiwan, I was in contact with so many different—mainly Asian—cultures. It was an incredibly rich cultural experience, and probably explains why I'm drawn to working internationally. But it came naturally, nothing was that conscious. I came to live permanently in Paris when I was eighteen; I remember not knowing much about France's culture and not knowing that many French people. Also,

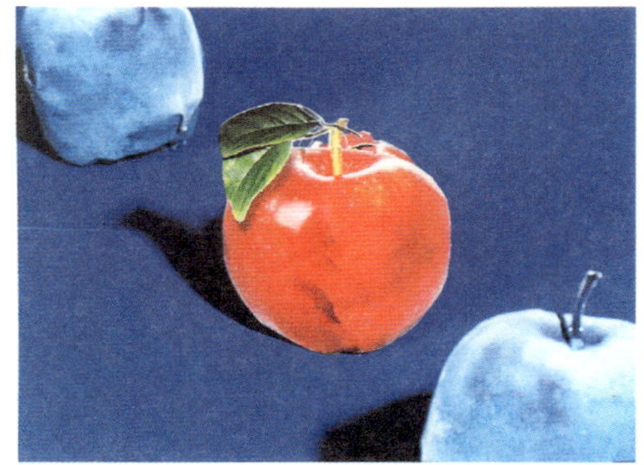

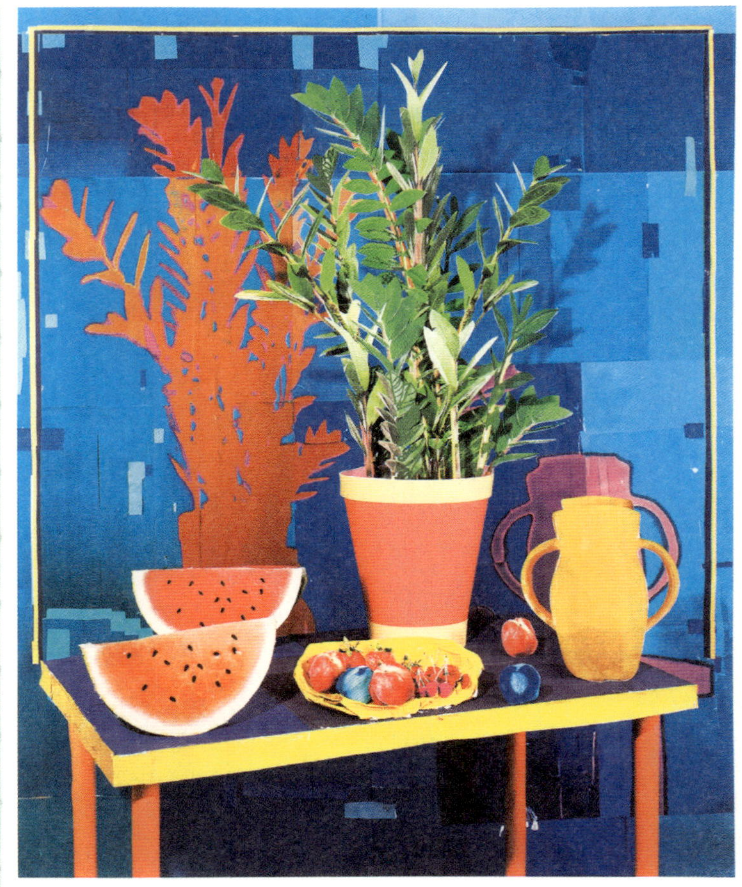

I studied Chinese and Japanese languages and cultures—not photography—so that was another unusual pathway into creating my own publishing house.

TD: **It's interesting that you say that. I have a special appreciation for people who come to the field of photography from elsewhere, or are on the edge of that space, almost as outsiders. Do you think that lens has helped your work?**

CPK: It definitely helped me and Chose Commune. I believe in charting my own path and starting from nothing. I knew almost nothing about photography and bookmaking, and learned by looking and watching and then trying and doing. It was always very instinctive, and it has proven to be quite a humbling process, because I don't think you can ever reach an exhaustive knowledge of bookmaking. I was very interested in production and learned on the job, going on press and talking to printers. Production was what I was most drawn to, and I loved getting to know every aspect of it. I'm still very hands-on with our projects, and I think the readers can feel that difference. There's no formula. I would never do the same thing twice.

This page, top: Spread from Daniel Gordon, *New Canvas*, 2022; bottom: Cover of Vasantha Yogananthan, *Amma*, 2021

Opposite: Cover of Deanna Dikeman, *Leaving and Waving*, 2021

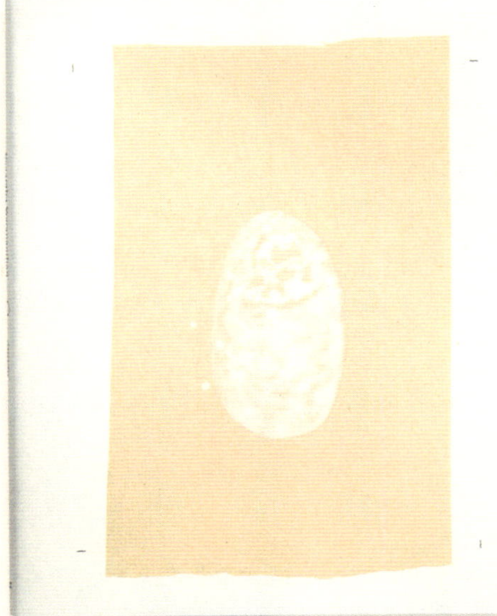

TD: **Your mother is from Japan and you were educated in an omnipresent Japanese culture. So I wanted to ask you about Chose Commune's links to Japan.**

CPK: Because I've been publishing a lot of Japanese photography for the past two to three years people think it's my "thing," which is something I don't really like. I don't want to be put in a box. But, because whatever I do is, in the end, quite personal, I find within my work a way to stay very connected to Japan and to Japanese people. I don't really see that as making books about Japanese photography, but rather as having the ability to understand these photographers' working culture and process, which has enabled me to make books with Seiichi Furuya, Rinko Kawauchi, or Issei Suda. I think it's really more about finding something I'm drawn to. Sometimes I just see a body of work and picture it as a book. I use my knowledge to show something that is slightly different. What I end up picking for these books are often bodies of work or aesthetic routes that are unknown or unexpected.

TD: **You are extremely sensitive to aesthetics and receptive to beauty in objects, and you also have a passion for**

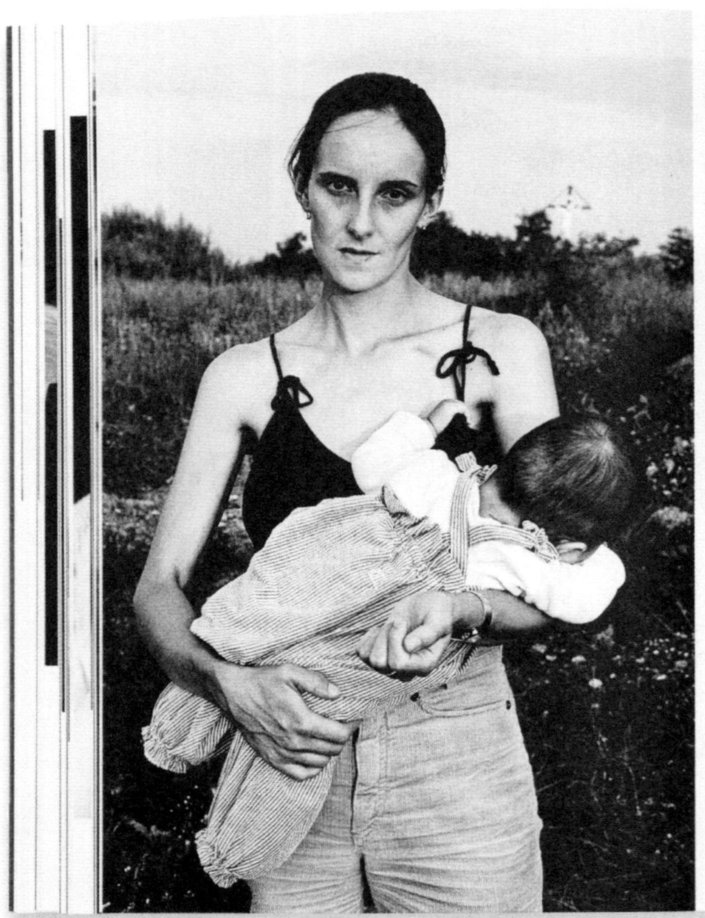

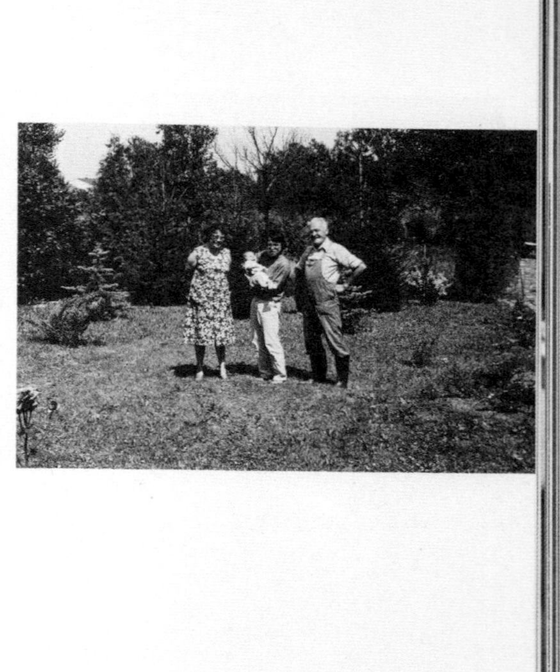

Inspiration can come from anything: a ray of light on the wall, a stain on the street, or the shape of a tree.

ceramics, crafts, and vintage books. How does this inform your own process?

CPK: Inspiration can come from anything: a ray of light on the wall, a stain on the street, or the shape of a tree. Shapes and colors are important, especially the ones you find in the most mundane of things. I'm very interested in what was made before. I love old books— mostly 1950s French literature that I find at flea markets. The designs are always on point. They are filled with a wide range of bookmaking techniques, and great attention was given to papers and spines.

TD: **Finally, I wanted to ask you about connections, friendships, relationships, and even love, as I know they are key guides in your life and work. For instance, you started Chose Commune with your partner, the photographer Vasantha Yogananthan.**

CPK: Vasantha is no longer fully involved with Chose Commune—so that he can focus on his own practice—but he still has a very important place. I trust his judgment and vision the most. I would not be able to do whatever I do now if it wasn't for our relationship. Beyond Vasantha, there's always a strong connection to the people I work with, even if I wouldn't always call all my collaborations friendships. Making a book is a long and intimate process; I spend hours talking to photographers. At the point when we're producing a publication together, we need to have a close connection to make things work. Then there are always "post-publication blues" once a book is released and goes on to live a life of its own. It's a real thing! I also work with a few senior photographers, who might be my mother's age, for example, and the relationship can be similar to a family dynamic. Whatever the relation, there's always the pleasure of working together and a necessary mutual trust. So, for me, the human connection is really important when making an object that is going to be in the world, hopefully for generations.

Taous Dahmani is a London-based French, British, and Algerian art historian, writer, and curator specializing in photography.

Magazine Culture

An expansive new book charts Japan's unparalleled history of photography in print.
Lena Fritsch

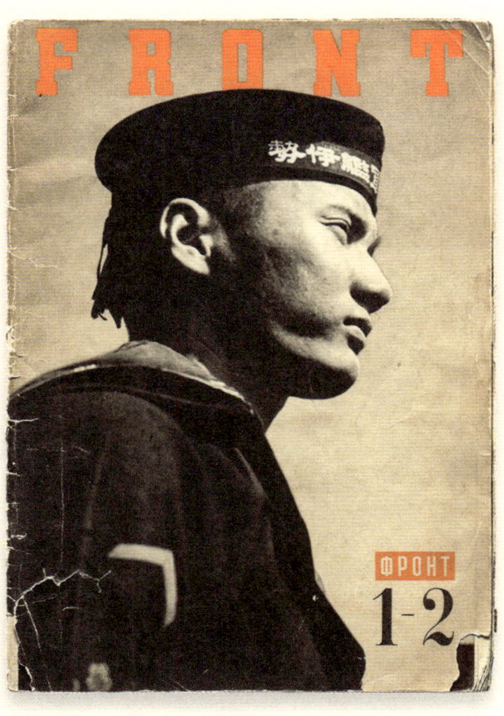

Cover of *Front*, Volumes 1 and 2, 1942, and spread from *Front*, Volumes 10 and 11, 1944, with photographs by Ihei Kimura

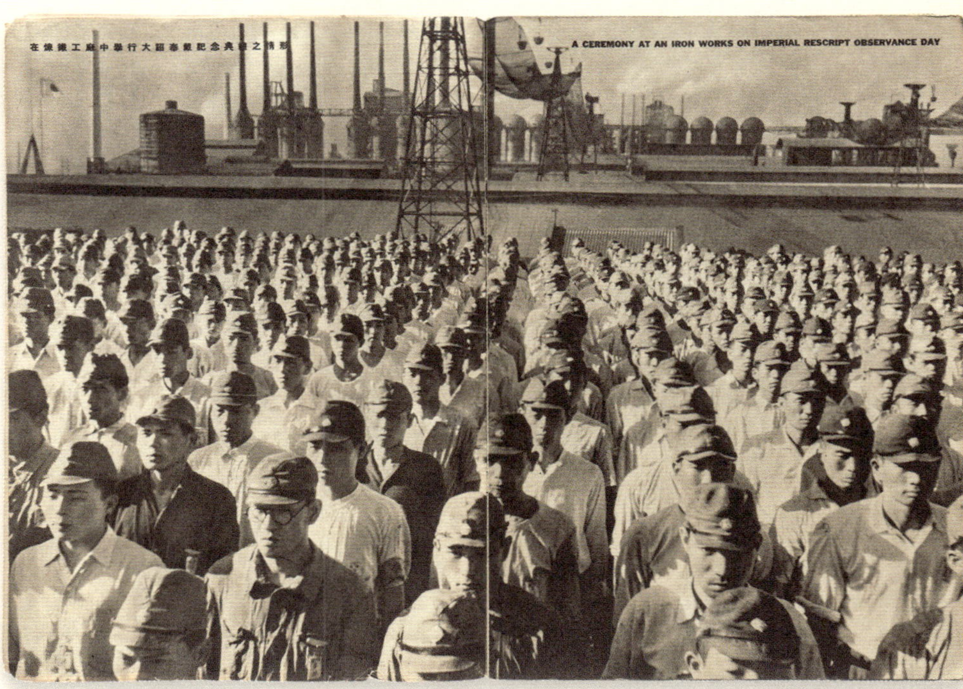

Not long ago, Daido Moriyama told me that his favorite way of encountering photographs is in a book or magazine. Nobuyoshi Araki has emphasized that "the photobook—not too big—is still the best way to show photographs." And Tomoko Sawada has proclaimed that her photobooks are "works of art in their own right." Indeed, many Japanese photographers understand books, as well as magazine features, as the ideal means of presenting their artistic output, often putting them on par with framed photographs on a wall. The importance of the printed page to Japanese photography cannot be overemphasized.

Over the last twenty years, images by a growing number of Japanese photographers have been shown in exhibitions worldwide. Simultaneously, the international photography community has begun to accept the photobook as a valid form of artistic expression, discovering, in the process, the innovativeness and significance of Japanese publishing. Yet there are still few comprehensive English-language books that consider the history of and specific sociocultural context for Japanese photography. Publications such as the 2003 exhibition catalog *The History of Japanese Photography*, by Anne Wilkes Tucker, Dana Friis-Hansen, Ryzichi Kaneko, and Joe Takeba, and my own book *Ravens & Red Lipstick: Japanese Photography since 1945* (2018) include select photobooks and periodicals but do not focus on them. The short-lived but influential 1960s journal *Provoke* was examined in a 2016–17 touring exhibition and related catalog. Even so, the history of Japanese photography magazines has remained largely underexplored.

Japanese Photography Magazines 1880s–1980s **(Goliga, 2022; 500 pages, $90)**, by Ryūichi Kaneko, Masako Toda, and Ivan Vartanian, sets out to change this by investigating one hundred years of photographic history in Japan, told through carefully chosen issues of camera and photography magazines. The book unfolds with an introduction describing the authors' approach and objectives. As an exhaustive overview is impossible, they aim to convey "one story of Japanese photography through the printed pages of periodicals . . . intentionally avoiding a western-oriented approach to ideas of photography, authorship, reading, and the relationship of images." It offers readers a chance to "see Japanese magazines within a Japanese context." Some selection criteria are explained. The stories and features highlight significant moments within the history of Japan and its photography scene,

The magazine format was a major, genre-defining space.

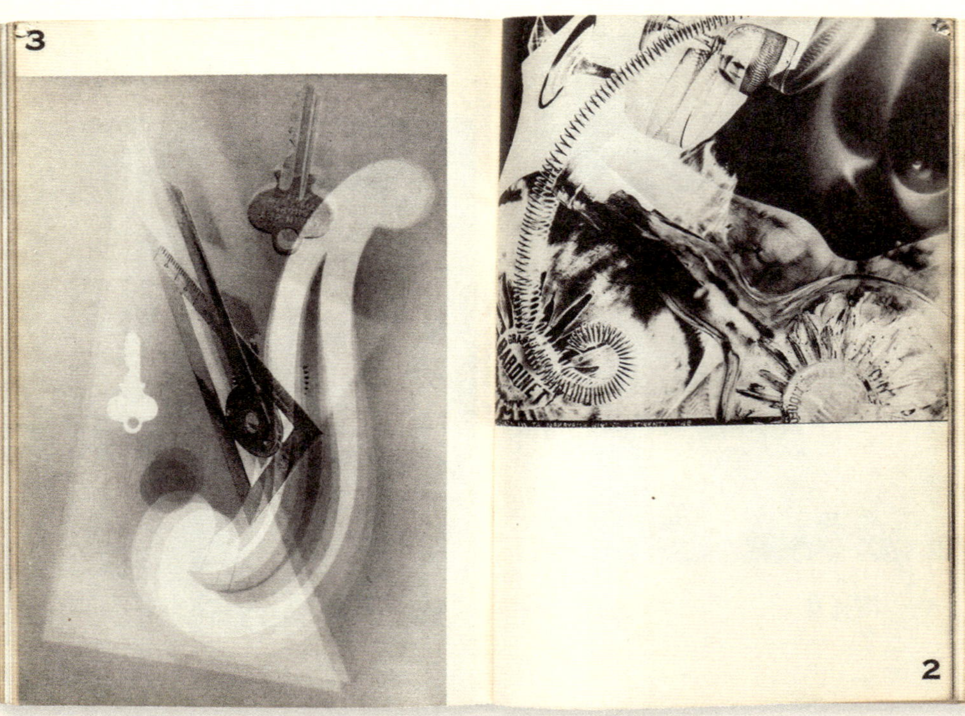

Top:
Spread from *Asahi Camera*, November 1936, with photographs by Nakayama Iwata; bottom: Cover of *Rokkor*, No. 8, January–June 1955

released at the end of the golden age of Japan's camera industry in the 1980s, the book immerses the reader in the work of internationally famous photographers, along with figures such as Shōji Ueda and Hiromi Tsuchida, who remain overlooked outside of Japan. The selection makes visible the diversity of Japanese imagery and approaches while also showing how magazines were a male domain that mostly excluded female photographers.

The authors have also compiled photographers' writings that accompanied their images in the magazines, ranging from the realist master Ihei Kimura's descriptions of his documentary approach toward photographing farming villages in Akita to an imagined, humorous dialogue, with erotic undertones, between a photographer and his subject by Araki. Often translated into English for the first time, these texts reveal how words were often significant components of the visual layouts.

Reproductions from difficult-to-access early magazines that appear in the book are particularly valuable. *Hanzai Kagaku*, from 1932, features captivating montages that were created collaboratively. An editor provided photographers with a theme: for example, "evoke the atmosphere of the train terminal" using specific motifs, such as a "bustling train platform." The resulting photographs were published as artistic collages with the editor's original prompts, creating a fascinating interplay of image and text, of assignment and photographic interpretation. The 1940s war propaganda magazine *Front* contains striking photographs by Kimura and designs by Hiromu Hara. It is also refreshing to see iconic photographs from the 1960s to 1980s in their original context, including Araki's first major work,

shedding light on the connection between magazines and photobooks as well as the roles of photographers and editors. Nude photographs—apart from those of women who were active participants in the creation of their photographs—were excluded, whereas camera advertisements that provide an indication of how technology developed over the years were deliberately left in. Linguistic and design challenges, such as having Japanese spreads, which are read top to bottom and right to left, reproduced in an English book, are addressed in an honest way, conveying the authors' awareness of their role in presenting Japanese photographic culture to "Western" readers.

This comprehensive volume is divided into three parts, eight chapters, and twenty-four thematic subsections in roughly chronological order. Starting with the first camera-related publications of the nineteenth century through to those

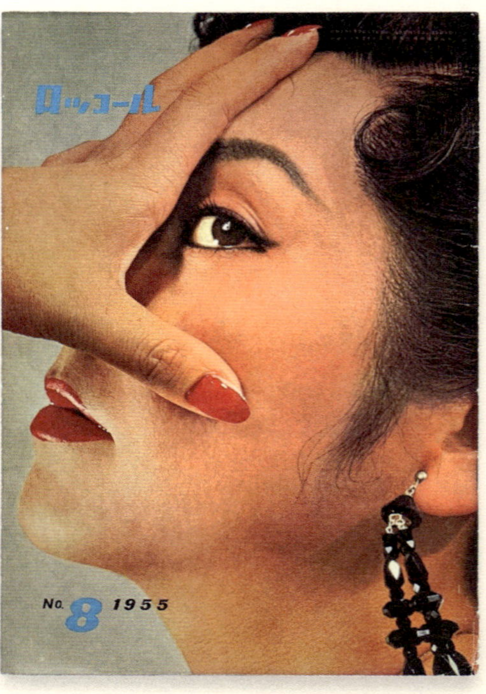

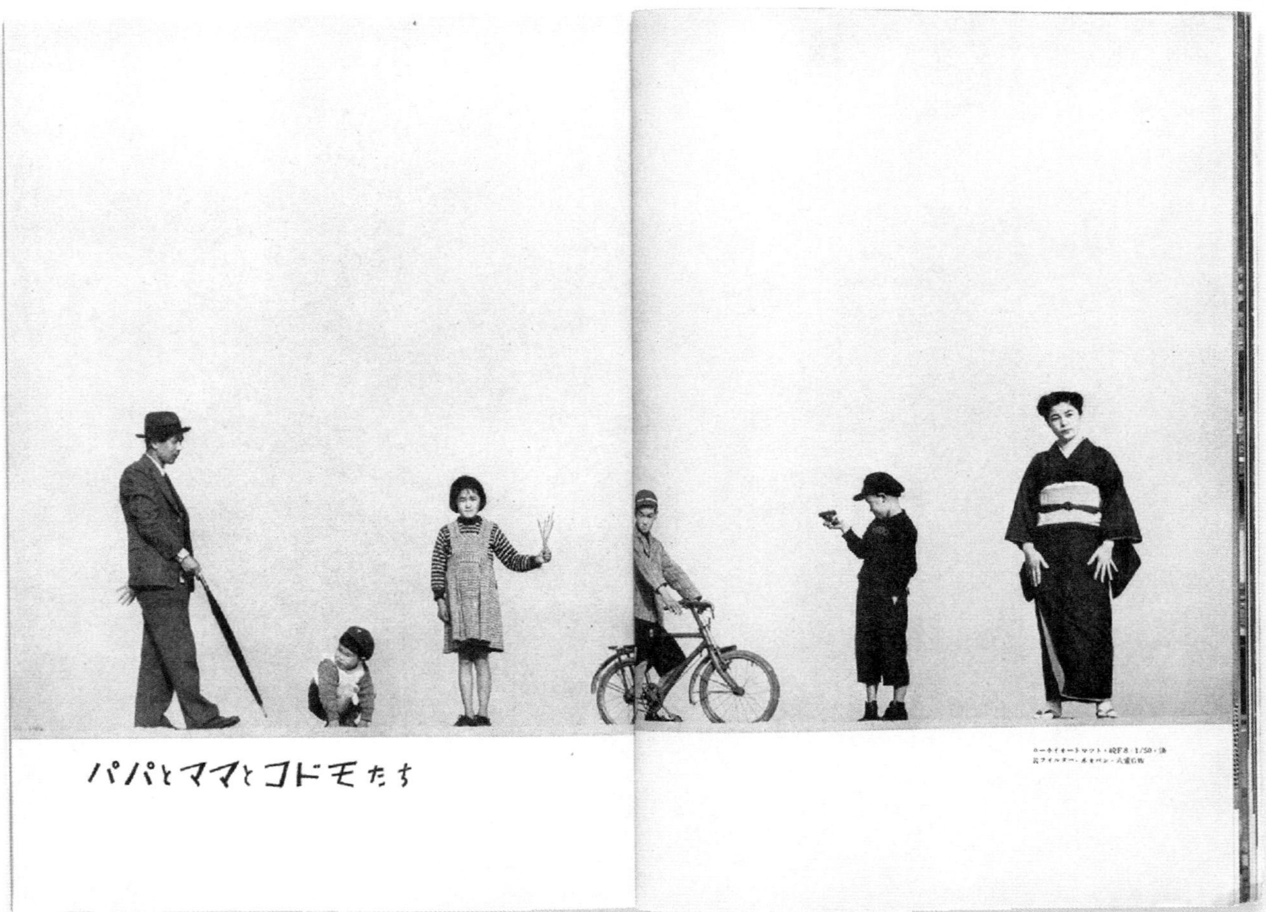

Sacchin, from 1964, Takuma Nakahira's *Fūkei* (1970), Masahisa Fukase's *Ravens* (1976–82), and Kikuji Kawada's series *Los Caprichos* (1972).

The idea for *Japanese Photography Magazines* was born when Kaneko and Vartanian collaborated on an earlier project about 1960s-to-1970s Japanese photobooks. Vartanian realized that "a discussion of photobooks required a considerable understanding of photography magazines, because that culture was the context and system through which the photobooks from Japan were greatly informed." *Japanese Photography Magazines*, a seven-year undertaking, is a well-researched, balanced, and sensitively designed book that provides a compelling story and convincingly presents the magazine format as a major, genre-defining space.

Japanese Photography Magazines is also the last major contribution by the legendary Kaneko, whose death in 2021 shocked the Japanese photography community. In addition to being thirty-second in the lineage of monks in charge of the Tokyo Buddhist temple Shogyo-in, he was a pioneering historian, teacher, and curator of Japanese photography, and an avid collector of magazines and books. Without Kaneko's expertise and collection, this impressive publication would not have taken shape. It will, hopefully, contribute to more in-depth research on overlooked Japanese photographers and Japan's unparalleled photography culture, beyond the "fetishizing" of vintage prints and photobooks as collectors' items.

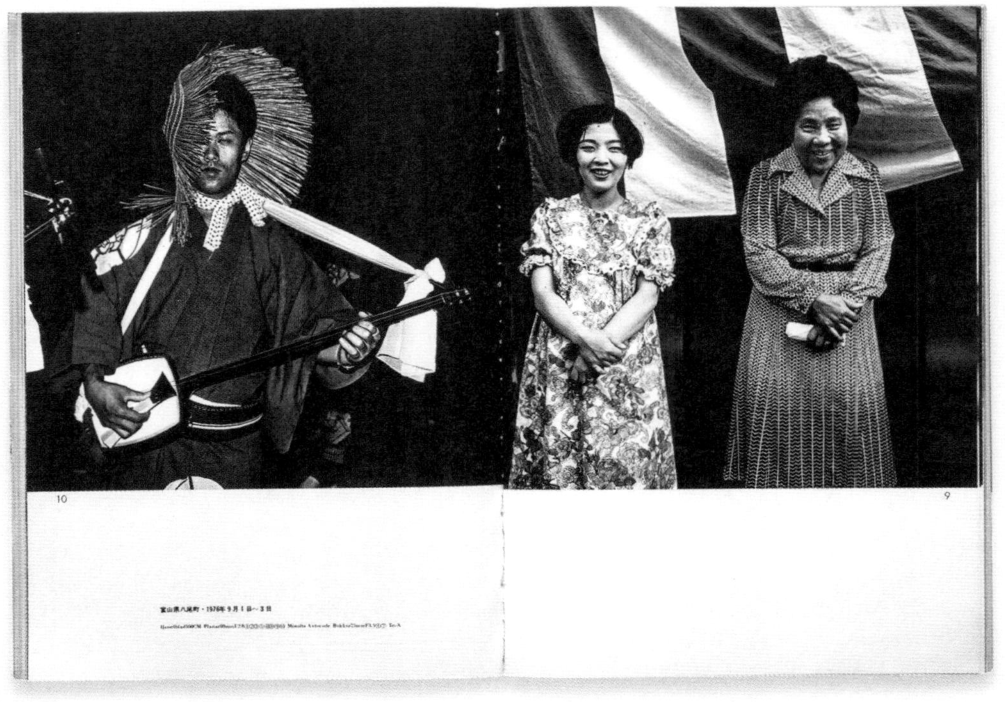

Lena Fritsch is the author of *Ravens & Red Lipstick: Japanese Photography since 1945* (2018). She is currently a guest curator at the Mori Art Museum, Tokyo.

Reviews

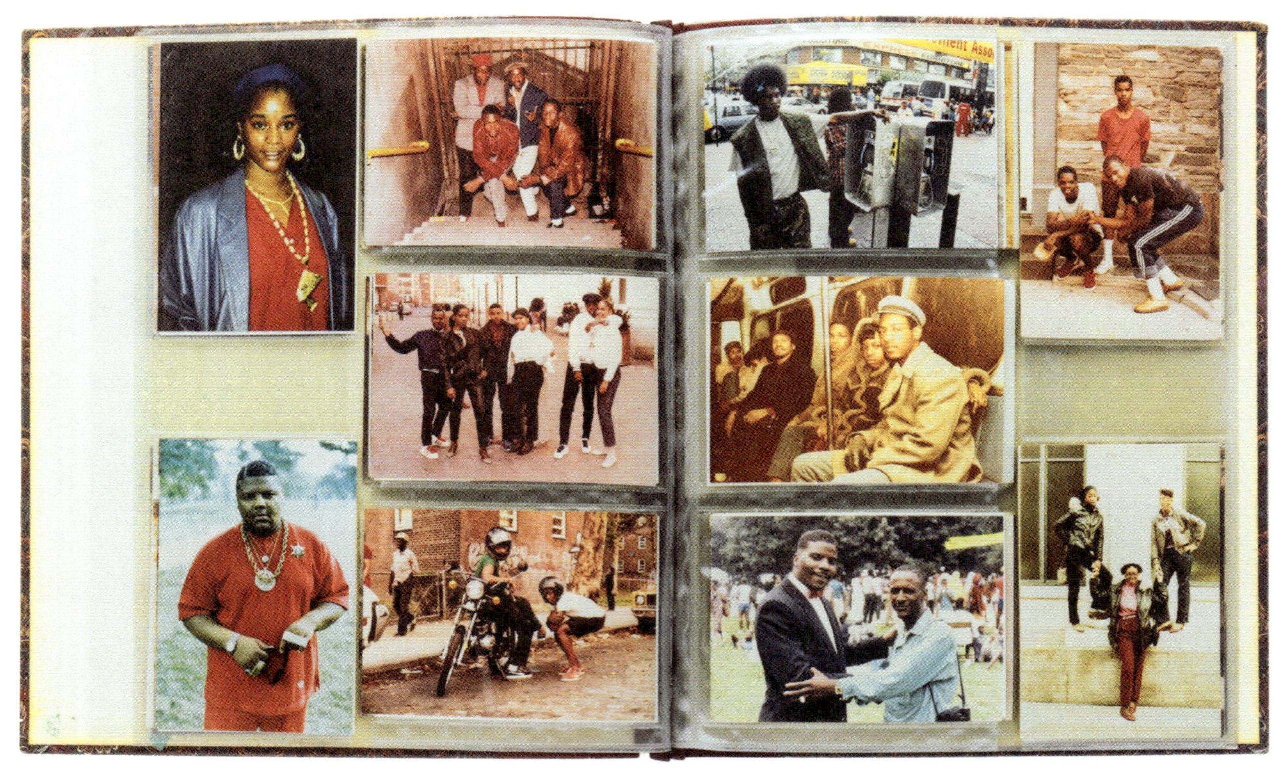

Spread from *Jamel Shabazz: Albums* (Steidl and the Gordon Parks Foundation, 2022)

Jamel Shabazz

If you want to understand the look of life on the streets of New York City in the 1980s, turn to Jamel Shabazz and his singular record of Black joy and sartorial flair. After a stint in the US Army, stationed in Germany, Shabazz returned to his home of New York. He worked on Wards Island and as a corrections officer on Rikers Island, the city's notorious jail, at the height of the crack epidemic and the "war on drugs," which devastated communities of color. On the weekends, he traversed the city, making portraits of individuals and collective portraits of friends and families in collaboratively choreographed poses. In an era of take-and-run street photography, Shabazz worked slowly. He spoke with people. "When I look at you, I see greatness," he'd say when approaching a potential subject. "If you don't mind, I'd like to take a photograph of you and your crew." The sidewalks and subway platforms of Brooklyn, Queens, and the Bronx were his studio.

The long-anticipated book *Jamel Shabazz: Albums* **(Steidl and the Gordon Parks Foundation, 2022; 320 pages, $50)** is not simply a record of how he archived his prints. Rather, it is a journey into his process. When he photographed, he carried an album of photographs, to earn the trust of those he wanted to picture by showing them the style, generosity, and care he brought to making a portrait. This smartly designed book reproduces these albums—conduits of human connection—at scale, in facsimile form, in their original arrangements. Spread by spread, we see couples embracing on graffiti-covered subway cars, friends posing in Kangol hats and fresh Cazal eyewear, loving fathers and mothers, children pausing from play to strike a pose. The cumulative effect is something between a yearbook, a lookbook, and a family album—it is a reminder that no one transmits the vitality of Black life and community in New York quite like Jamel Shabazz. **—Michael Famighetti**

Bharat Sikka

Bharat Sikka's long-term project about his father in ***The Sapper* (Fw:Books, 2022; 192 pages, €40)** is composed of fragments: a still life of his father's tools glinting in the sun; a portrait of his desk left unattended. Other images depict the impression of the elastic of his socks on his calves and shins, the constellation of age spots on his back. These oblique but telling observations leaven a series of studies of his father's face, of his figure in the landscape or caught up close in the burst of an off-camera flash. In *The Sapper*, Sikka's approach to portraiture resonates with *The Great Unreal* (Patrick Frey, 2015), the Swiss photographers Taiyo Onorato and Nico Krebs's American road-trip book.

Sikka was born in New Delhi and studied photography at Parsons School of Design in New York. He has frequently focused on the subject of masculinity, and his intervention with the artifacts of his father's career as a member of the Indian Army Corps of Engineers pays tribute to a man's life outside of traditional familial roles—in the book's evocative presentation of sharply observed elements there is a puzzle to be worked out. His construction and deconstruction of photographs as a means of teasing answers out of these otherwise mute details is effectively underwritten by the book's deft pairing and sequencing of images—patterns emerge and subside, only to return again. We remember, or think we do, but each moment of recall has been slightly altered from the last.

One segment in particular—an eight-page suite of full-bleed, black-and-white images reproduced to emulate cheap, Xerox-style copies—creates an enigmatic rupture in the otherwise gentle flow of images, confirming that something has been knocked asunder. An easy summation of Sikka's subject of consideration lies tantalizingly just beyond reach. Instead, *The Sapper* offers an affecting negotiation of meaning and understanding of a father by his son, and a bittersweet confirmation of the fragility of memory. —**Lesley A. Martin**

Newspaper

In 1968, Peter Hujar, Steve Lawrence, and Andrew Ullrick began printing and distributing *Newspaper*, a short-form, image-only, black-and-white newsprint publication. Over its brief three-year lifespan, *Newspaper* compiled a star-studded list of contributors—Diane Arbus, Richard Avedon, and Andy Warhol, among many others—and provided a platform for artists to exhibit different kinds of work from what was shown at galleries at the time. Unfortunately, scholarship about and recognition of *Newspaper* has been limited; the ephemeral nature of newsprint (which resists archiving)

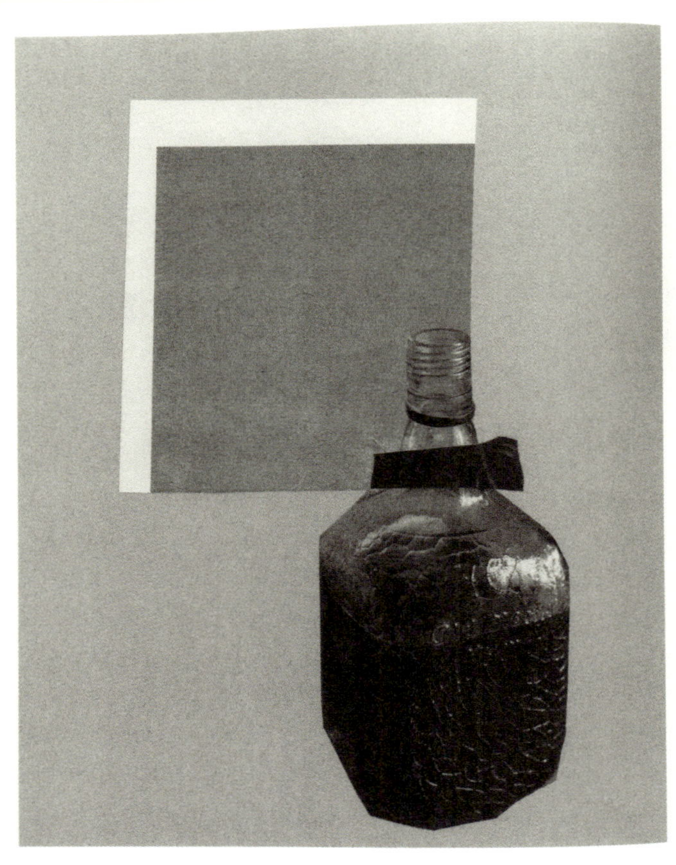
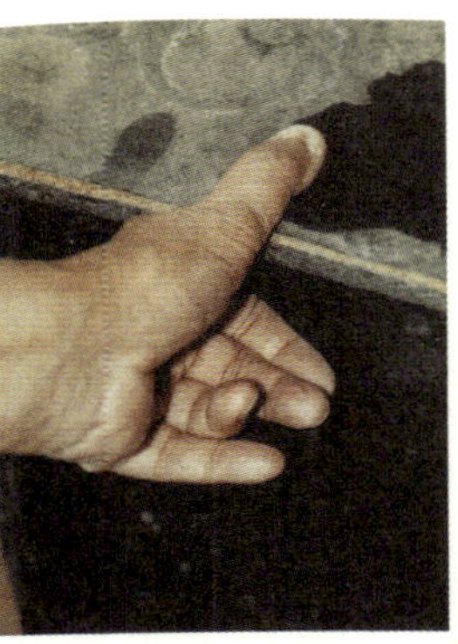
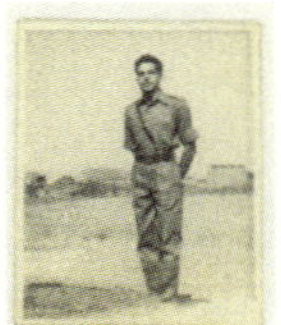
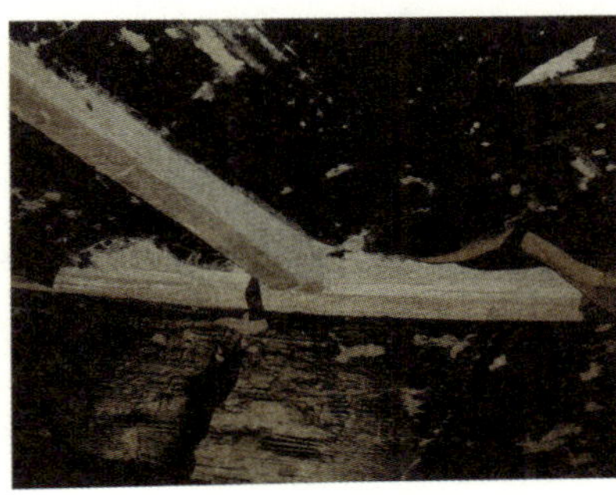

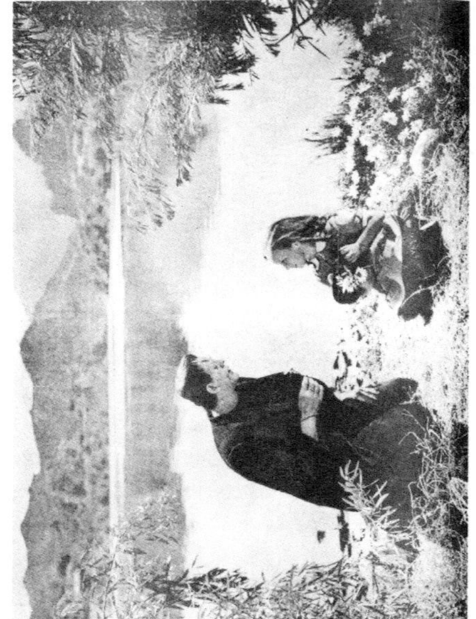

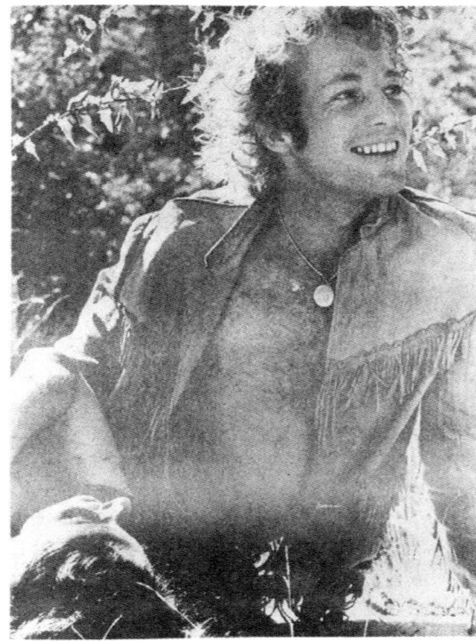

Spread from Steve
Lawrence, Peter Hujar,
Andrew Ullrick,
Newspaper (Primary
Information, 2023)

and the original publication's limited
distribution and print run meant that after
its end in 1971 it quickly faded into obscurity.

More than fifty years later, the Brooklyn-
based publisher Primary Information has
compiled the complete fourteen-issue
set of *Newspaper* for the first time. While,
for practical considerations, Primary
Information's publication doesn't replicate
the original's format and material, the issues
are presented in their entirety, giving light
to the boundary-pushing publication that
Hujar, Lawrence, and Ullrick smartly edited.
The content of ***Newspaper* (Primary
Information, 2023; 416 pages, $40)**, edited
by Marcelo Gabriel Yáñez, is kaleidoscopic.
The book forces the reader to consider
connections between and create meaning
across multiple visual registers. Photographs,
drawings, collages, imagery from high
and low culture—all chaotically coexist
within the pages. The effect is befuddling,
cerebral, and provocative. Reproduced
in Primary Information's volume, the
content of *Newspaper* can at times feel
dense and indecipherable.

However, once primed to imagine
the work within its earlier form and context,
one can sense the underlying dynamism
between the riotous arrangement of imagery,
the casual and disposable form of the
original tabloid, and the larger ecosystem
of artist publications and queer periodicals
of the late 1960s and early '70s. In his
preface to a detailed timeline of *Newspaper*'s
history included in the back of the book,
Yáñez clearly states his intentions:
"to make the periodical accessible as a
document. My hope is that by doing so,
further information and scholarship about
Steve Lawrence and *Newspaper* will arise."
—Noa Lin

Giulia Parlato

Giulia Parlato is drawn to false accounts and
fictional retellings, to the tension between
museums and cultural objects—particularly
how each endows the other with historical
meaning. The Italian photographer
conceived of her debut photobook,
***Diachronicles* (Witty Books, 2023; 120
pages, €35)**, while researching forgeries
and counterfeits at the Warburg Institute in
London, and she argues that this meaning is
first and foremost a construct, unstable and
often the result of numerous interventions.
Photographs play a split role in this equation,
sometimes as displayed object and other
times as document. For Parlato, they also
offer a clever form of investigation and play
as she appropriates the visual language of
archaeological excavations, forensics,
dioramas, and museum archives and displays
to stage her own constructions, which are
somewhere between evidence and fiction.
Parlato's photographs—which she made
between her London studio, Sicily, and
several European museums—appear stark
and direct, almost instructional. A gap in
the painted ceiling of an eighteenth-century
palace in Palermo reveals innards of wood,
stone, and rubber piping. Gloved hands
confer archaeological meaning to an object
concealed in tarp, seemingly exhumed from
a dig. "Indeed, it is almost as if the more
straightforward the imagery seems, the less

Giulia Parlato, *Gap*, 2020,
from *Diachronicles* (Witty
Books, 2023)
Courtesy Palazzo Butera,
Collezione Francesca e
Massimo Valsecchi

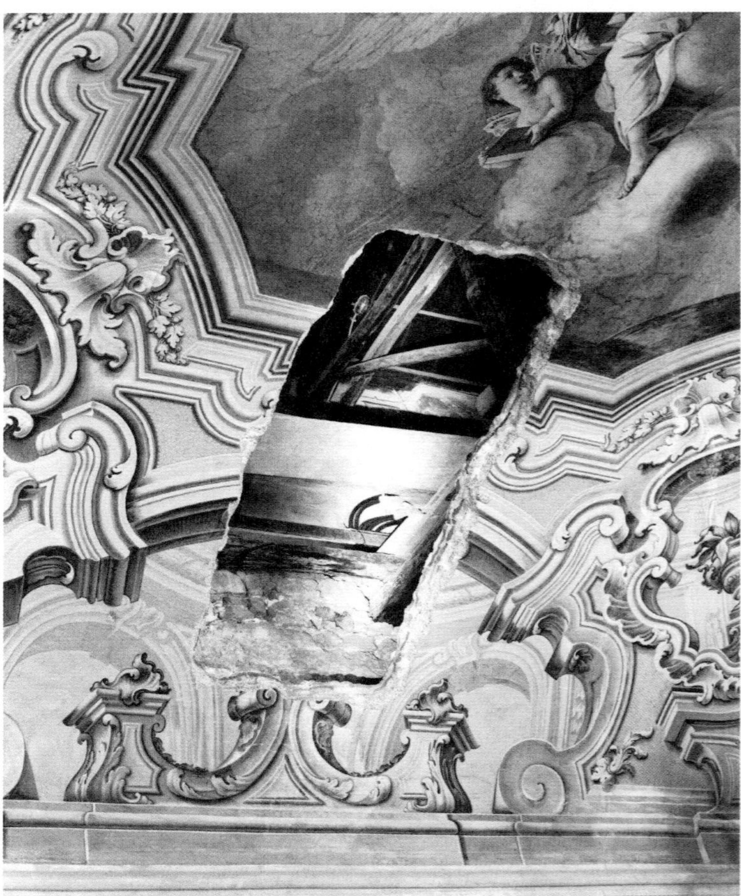

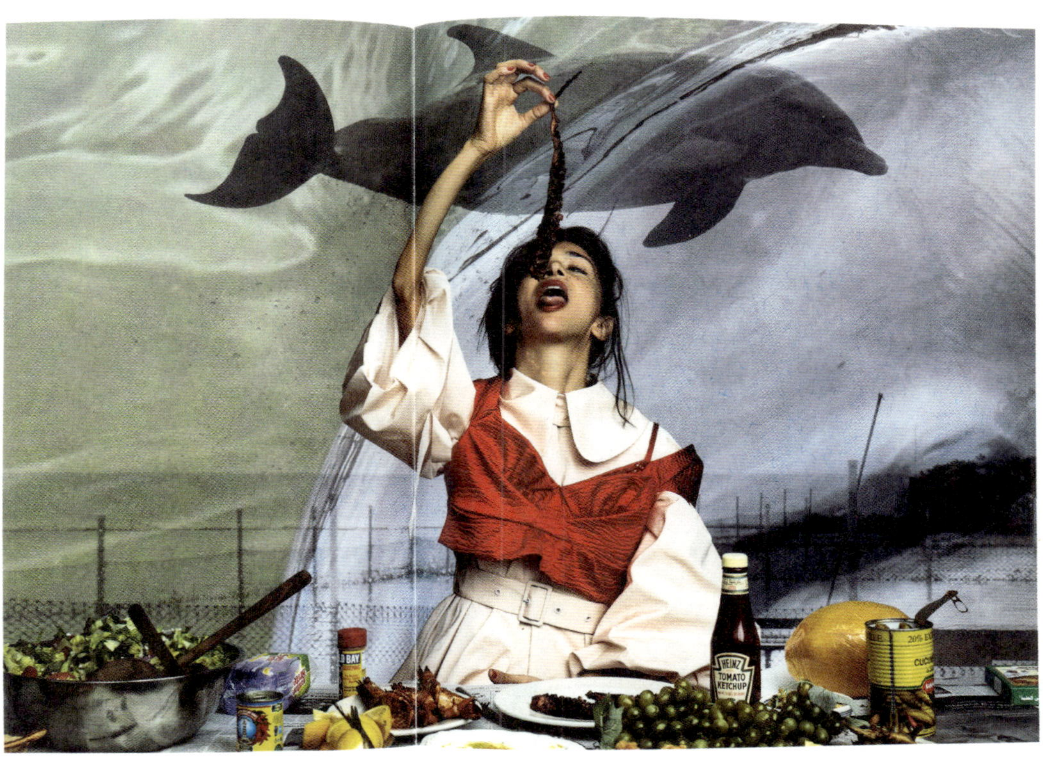

Page 133 and this page:
Spreads from Roe
Ethridge, *American
Polychronic* (MACK, 2022)

straightforward it really is," writes David Campany in his introduction. A curious reader might equally wonder whether the lack of context, and the book's rather austere layout, limits its overall effect. One must invariably work backward and reconstruct the story; must look, and look again. By developing fictional histories from fragments and fakes, *Diachronicles* is both about what is said and what is withheld, positioning the photographer as both chronicler and unreliable narrator. —**Varun Nayar**

Roe Ethridge

A refrigerator, a black eye, a tennis player, a highway. Chloë Sevigny, Willem Dafoe, Weebleville, and then—wait, an ad? For Hermès? Oh, this is a Roe Ethridge book! Ethridge being the American photographer who has unlocked that little velvet rope between art and commerce to delirious and delightful effect, who has compiled four hundred "and something" images into a massive book, **American Polychronic** (**MACK, 2022; 480 pages, $70**), "some of which were for art exhibitions and some which were made for magazines and advertising," as he notes in an addendum. "A healthy portion are both and a lesser portion neither." So, anything goes, from a babe in a bikini to Telfar Clemens naked on a sofa to a screenshot of a conversation about a twenty-year-old Lexus. It all feels like a decadent European magazine (there's even a French-fold dust jacket protecting

the paperback covers), the kind you buy when you're hungover and dreaming of a life in fashion. You certainly wouldn't throw *American Polychronic* in the recycling bin, but is it a masterpiece for the bookshelf? Maybe! Jamieson Webster compares Ethridge's photography to psychoanalysis— "symptom and repression are attacked through evoking an assemblage of fantasy, memory, and reality that shakes the frame"—in an essay printed in small type at the end of our photographer's elliptical journey through his archive, from 1999 to 2022. (At first glance, the text appears quite literally like an afterthought.) Still, you didn't come to *American Polychronic*, a production of staggering charm and shrewd editing, a monument to one of the most successful image makers of our era, to learn something new about fugue states or "hysterical flowers." You came for the Chanel tennis balls, the beach umbrellas, the winsome smiles, the paper towels. You came for Anna, Karl, Hans Ulrich, Thanksgiving, laughter, tears, birds, sunsets, and "pure beauty" (as one chic cannabis brand would have it), beauty so pure and sweet you might need to take an aspirin and turn on Cat Power's *Moon Pix*. —**Brendan Embser**

Endnote
Patty Chang

In her fearless performances and videos, Patty Chang has often pushed herself to the limit, provoking questions about food, gender, sex work, and the environment. A new project finds Chang collaborating with scientists who study porpoises, creating a database that might foretell the future in the era of climate change—and show the way toward healing.

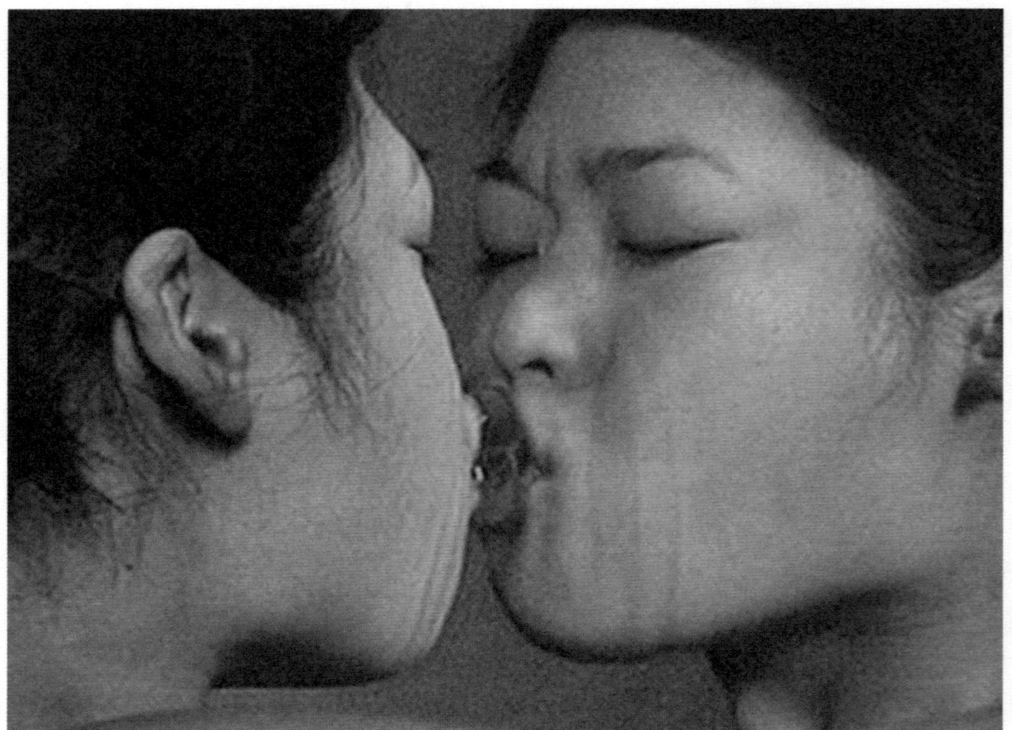

Patty Chang, Still from *Fountain*, 1999. SD video, 5 minutes, 30 seconds
Courtesy the artist

You presented your video essay *We Are All Mothers* (2022) for the first time in Beijing last year. Where did the idea come from?
We Are All Mothers is a video essay that details my thoughts on the project *Learning Endings*, which is a collaboration with the feminist ecological scholar Astrida Neimanis and her sister, Aleksija Neimanis, who is a wildlife pathologist. We came together to think about necropsy. Necropsy is like autopsy, but for animals. The scientist cuts open the dead animal in order to find out why it died, and also to try to get information to help the species or the animals in the future.

The vulnerability of the body is a recurring theme in your performances. How did you develop such a bold style and approach, especially in your work from the 1990s?
It was about necessity and immediacy—not having resources but wanting to make things and express things.

For *Mothers*, what was the protocol for working with the animals?
Science is full of protocols, which is another way to name ritual. I asked Aleksija if she would be willing to include an additional ritual before she began her necropsy, and that ritual was to take a

moment before she started—to be alone with the animal, and then to take a picture to record that moment for people other than herself, because it is a private moment.

With climate change and extinctions, there's a lot of endings. When scientists began studying the species they study, they may not have imagined that instead they would be recording the decline or even extinction of that species, and that may bring with it sadness or grief or other states that aren't reflected in objective scientific study.

As you archive the images with memory cards, you could say the piece is about both remembering and forgetting.
I use the images in the touch archive in a memory game, and the bigger it gets, the harder it is to play. Because you can't remember every single individual animal, where it is on the larger grid of the board of all the other animals. The same is true in the oceans, where we can't see the lives of marine mammals or know where they are or what their lives are like, except when they emerge onto the surface, and this is usually in death. There's some point where our brains cannot contain everything.

What have you learned about photography versus live performance?

We started this project during COVID, and we all live in different time zones. I sent Aleksija a camera so that she could do this ritual, take pictures, and share them with us. The event of photography became a kind of a relational event, or a collaborative process.

And did the porpoises teach you something, too?
Alexis Pauline Gumbs writes in her book *Undrowned: Black Feminist Lessons from Marine Mammals* (2020) that she identifies as mammal, but also identifies with and learns from Africans who were "transubstantiated into property," and that she also loves marine mammals. I love identifying at many levels of community simultaneously. How all these marine mammals started on land, but when the land became too dangerous for them, over generations, they moved into the water. I was at a whale museum in Baja, and they said, you know, the future marine mammals are, like, your sea lions and elephant seals, because they're half land, half water.

What if that happens again, where land becomes inhospitable and people have to turn to the sea? Maybe we'll just all become mermaids.
Right! We are the future marine mammals.